MW01289729

Smeltertown Shenanigans

History, Stories, Confessions of Growing Up in Hurley, New Mexico, 1950-1970

Jerry Boswell

Los Weasels Publishing Company

Silver City, New Mexico

DEDICATION

This book is dedicated to my family and friends who shared many experiences with me over the years. It is also dedicated to the many people in Hurley who took time out of their lives to provide mentorship for the local kids during our formative years. It was the parents, Little League coaches, Cub Scout den mothers, teachers, church youth group leaders, and even local police officers who did their best to steer my friends and I along the path to success and happiness.

With that being said, I should also acknowledge a few of my older childhood friends who spent much of their valuable time mentoring me in the opposite direction. (I must confess that I mentored a few younger kids to the "dark side" as well.) It could certainly be argued that without the devious influence of a few recalcitrant adolescents in and around Hurley, most of the stories in this book would have been more tame and mundane. Perhaps it is this inherent tension and interplay between socially acceptable behavior and foolishness that set the stage for kids to create mischief as they navigate their way toward adulthood.

Therefore, to all of those influential bad boys and girls, I would like to say, "Thank you for the laughs and good times. Thank you for much of the material I used for this book." I would like to express my profound admiration for those young souls who were bold enough to put that thumb tack in the teacher's chair, crass enough to fart in church, and sneaky enough to tie that kid's shoe laces together while he was asleep in class. Without you, there would be no Smeltertown Shenanigans.

CONTENTS

PREFACE

I hope you will enjoy reading some southwest mining town history in addition to nearly 20 years of memoirs and stories about my life as I grew up in Hurley, New Mexico. The objective of this book is to offer a perspective of what the town of Hurley was like in the 1950's and 1960's through the eyes of a boy growing up there during that time. You will get to know a little about some of the fine people that lived there and how politics, racial relationships, and the local history helped to shape their attitudes, ethos, and behaviors.

Like many small towns during that era, Hurley was a village where everyone knew everyone, where kids played in the streets and took shortcuts through their neighbor's yards, and where you could hop the fence and ask your neighbor for a cup of sugar. While Hurley certainly was a friendly place, the size of the town made it somewhat difficult for locals to live with a high degree of autonomy or privacy. As a general rule, residents had to maintain a low profile if they wanted to avoid getting sucked into the local gossip circles and rumor mills.

Most of the historical information presented in this book is from my memory or the memories of many of my good friends and family who lived in Hurley during the 1950's and 1960's. I'll be the first to admit that my recollection of events and people from over 50 years ago is not perfect, but my intent is to make descriptions, interpretations, and portrayals that are as accurate and truthful as possible. In order to validate my recollections even further, I spent a significant amount of time over the last few years researching Hurley historical data from various sources in the Grant County area.

Since PART I of Smeltertown Shenanigans focuses on Hurley history, most of the names mentioned in that section of the book are the actual names of real people. However, in PART II I tell numerous stories and express opinions that are told within the historical framework of Hurley from the early 1950's until around 1970. Therefore, I chose to use fictitious names for most of my characters and, in some cases, I even invented characters. While most of my stories in Part II are true, others are only partially true or totally fictitious. As a general rule, I only used real names in those stories if the character is deceased or I felt there was no potential for incrimination or hard feelings. Fictitious names were also used in many stories in order to protect the guilty parties involved.

The stories that have three stars below the title (***) are typically fictitious and provided me with an opportunity to create interesting characters and dialogue. I exercised a degree of artistic license and measured embellishment as I wrote these particular stories in order to give them more dimension and color. They are included in the book because they offer the reader a broader perspective into the life and times of Hurley, New Mexico, as I was growing up there, and furthermore; they were just plain fun to write.

i

I suspect that many readers may become offended by the content of some of my stories or my use of vulgarity throughout the book. My feeling is that, just as it would be inappropriate to change or sugarcoat historical events and facts about the town of Hurley during this era, it would be patronizing of me to change my writing style, opinions, and perspectives in order to broaden the appeal of this book to a larger reading audience. In other words, it is what it is. It was quite common back in those days for kids to use vulgar language when adults weren't around and I can assure you that, after a career in the public schools, things haven't changed much in the last 50 years.

Lastly, we must not forget that every person who lived in Hurley has his or her own story, and theirs is as valid and true as any story about Hurley, particularly mine. While I went to great lengths to paint an accurate picture of the community and the people there during the 1950's and 1960's, some area residents will undoubtedly see things differently than me. Therefore, it is my hope that this book will encourage others to come forward and share their stories and personal accounts of Hurley, New Mexico, so that future generations will have a broad perspective of what things were really like during that period of time.

PART I

HURLEY HISTORY AND BACKGROUND INFORMATION

CHAPTER ONE: HURLEY: A COMPANY TOWN

"Welcome to the plains of southwest New Mexico."

Hurley was a small smelter town in southwestern New Mexico with a population of approximately 1,850 people and was situated on a plateau well over a mile high in elevation. To the north and east of Hurley were rugged mountains and foothills, to the south were open plains and Chihuahuan desert, and to the west were rolling hills and plains where herds of antelope could be seen roaming near the outskirts of town.

Like most mining towns of its day, Hurley was laid out in a very orderly way. It was a rectangular town with a grid of streets running east to west and north to south, and had railroad tracks that separated the south side of town from the north side of town. The railroad tracks were quite symbolic back then because the residents on the south side were predominantly English speaking northern Europeans, whereas the residents on the north side were mostly Spanish speaking people of Mexican descent.

This ethnic segregation was no accident. The town of Hurley was built and owned, up until the mid 1950's, by copper companies who intentionally kept the town divided by ethnicity. The Hispanics typically held lower paying, less skilled positions with the company and their chances of being promoted to management level positions were, in many cases, less than for the Anglo employees. There was a higher level of poverty on the north side of town and the homes there were generally more run down and shabby than the homes on the south side of town. Many of the streets in North Hurley weren't paved or lined with curbs and sidewalks like some of the south side streets.

The streets of Hurley that were north of the railroad tracks were referred to as North Hurley. They were considered to be part of Hurley proper. The settlements along the old Highway 180 heading toward Bayard were also considered to be part of North Hurley but each little cluster of houses along the way had specific names. Quatro Milpas was about a mile from North Hurley and Mimmsville was up the road in the area of the Pénjamo Night Club and the A and B Grocery Store. As you continued farther north near "dead-man's curve", there was another settlement called Chinatown.

Just north of E Street in North Hurley were three elementary school buildings where the Hispanic children attended school until they were abandoned in 1955 when the Cobre Schools first became integrated. Nearby was a large concrete slab or platform where kids played basketball and roller-skated. The local kids called it "la plataforma".

Directly north of the old schools was the Hurley Golf Course, which had a small clubhouse and an 18-hole course (there were actually only nine holes, but golfers would play the back nine by teeing off from different tee boxes). The smelter and smoke stacks for Kennecott Copper Corporation were located in the southeast corner of North Hurley, and the parking lot and main gate entrance into the smelter complex were located nearby. On the west side of town at the end of A Street was the American Legion Hall and a large water reservoir referred to as "el tanque". El tanque was built up from ground level and had a chain link fence surrounding it. It supplied water to the mining operation and the water wasn't safe for swimming or drinking.

There also was an old swimming pool located near the railroad tracks in North Hurley but it was never open and functional during my childhood. My father told me once that Lois Bates, mother of my childhood friend Tommy "Sido" Bates, nearly drowned at that pool in the 1940's. Apparently, the lifeguards weren't paying much attention as she floundered in the water, so a young man named Tenny Blackman eventually dove into the pool and saved her.

There were no commercial buildings in the town site of North Hurley but along the old highway, heading north toward Bayard, there were two or three small neighborhood tiendas that sold basic food items to the area residents. There were also three or four bars scattered along the way. Around 1955 and 1956 the old highway to Bayard was replaced with Highway 180, which rerouted traffic away from Hurley and these small settlements. Over the next 10 years many of the businesses were boarded up and gradually fell into a state of disrepair and ruin. Some of the North Hurley businesses, such as the Chino Buffet, The Pénjamo Night Club, and Frank Baca's A and B Grocery Store managed to hold on a little longer but eventually succumbed to the lack of traffic and business volume.

Once the new Highway 180 project between Hurley and Silver City was completed, it was only a matter of time before the economic independence and prosperity of Hurley proper would gradually deteriorate as well. Before the new highway was completed it would take about 45 minutes for Hurley residents to get to Silver City. The same trip on the new, four-lane highway took about 20 minutes. Hurley residents could now comfortably drive to Silver City to shop and pay less for almost everything money could buy. When the large franchise stores like K-Mart, Safeway and Furrs opened in Silver City, businesses in Hurley had trouble competing with them. It also became more plausible for Kennecott employees and their families to move from Hurley to Silver City or Bayard and commute to their jobs in Hurley.

South Hurley was the commercial hub of the area and also had the business offices of Kennecott Copper Corporation, Chino Mines Division. On the eastern end of South Hurley, along Chino Blvd., was the concentrator/milling operation of the company. There was a warehouse at the end of Pattie Street and a small office building at the end of Elguea Street. Next to the office building was a reservoir, referred to as "the spray pond", that provided water and steam for the turbines at the power plant just north of there.

Located at the east end of Romero Street was the main gate to the mill operations. Employees who entered the plant here worked at the secondary crusher, the ball mills, the power plant, the warehouse, and the primary crusher. The primary crusher was where the railroad train would bring raw ore from the Chino open-pit mine in Santa Rita to begin the process of turning it into copper. The smelter operation and smokestacks were north of the primary crusher.

Right outside of the main gate on Romero Street were a couple of two story red brick office buildings. One of the brick buildings was the Time Office, where the payroll time cards for plant employees were processed. (I knew this because my father worked in the Time Office.) These buildings were among the first structures built in Hurley.

To the north of the old Time Office were a one-story red brick office building that housed engineers, an assay office, a private residence, and then finally a doctor's office near the curve where Chino Blvd. intersected Cortez Ave. Later on, in about 1958, a large office complex called the Comptroller's Office was built at the east end of Anza Street which housed various administrative departments such as accounting, purchasing, payroll, and the key punch/computer operations.

Photo 1-1: The Doctor's Office served Hurley residents and Kennecott employees for many years. Photo courtesy of New Mexico State University Library, Archives and Special Collections.

Photo 1-2: The Comptroller's Office building housed the accounting, purchasing, payroll, and machine accounting (computer dept.) for Kennecott. It also housed the main switchboard for all telephone calls. The voice of Kennecott for many years was a switchboard operator named Joyce Brewer. Photo courtesy of New Mexico State University Library, Archives and Special Collections.

The railroad tracks from Santa Rita entered Hurley from the west and ran eastward behind the two red brick Hurley Stores buildings on the north side of

Cortez Avenue. At Chino Blvd. they curved south behind the doctor's office and ended at the primary crusher. There was a chain link fence that spanned the entire length of the tracks and separated the north side of town from the south side.

Located between the two Hurley Store buildings was a concrete underground pedestrian tunnel that crossed under the tracks. It was the only walkway that connected North and South Hurley and was referred to as "the underpass". A short distance north of the underpass was a large cottonwood tree referred to as the "Álamo". It provided lots of shade and was a popular place for the kids that lived in North Hurley because they would stop there to roughhouse and wrestle on their way home from school.

At the east end of Santa Rita Street was an employee dormitory, which housed employees without families. There also was a large, two-story dormitory/bunk house a half a block east of the Chino Club that housed workers. The two-story dormitory was torn down in around 1955. I remember seeing it when I was a little kid as I walked to the Chino Club.

Photo 1-3: This was the employee dormitory located at the east end of Santa Rita Street on Chino Blvd. This picture was taken long before I was born, but the dormitory looked like this when I was growing up in Hurley. Photo courtesy of New Mexico State University Library, Archives and Special Collections.

West of the two-story dormitory/bunk house was a one-story building called Mulligan Hall. It was located east of the Chino Club near the Big Ditch and people would gather there on occasion for social events like square dancing. Mulligan Hall was probably torn down in the late 1940's or early 1950's. The lot where the bunk house and Mulligan Hall once stood remained permanently vacant during my years in Hurley.

The downtown commercial area of Hurley was located on Cortez Avenue. One of the businesses located on the south side of Cortez Avenue and across the street from the Hurley Stores was the Copper Café. It was situated on the corner of Cortez Ave. and Chino Blvd. At the west end of that block was a two-story building that housed the town barbershop, a beauty shop located behind the barbershop, the post office, and the Chino Sweet Shop. The Hurley Masonic Lodge occupied the second floor of the building. My father was a member of this lodge for over 50 years and was buried wearing his Masonic apron.

On the next block of Cortez Ave. to the west was the old movie theatre called "The Tejo". It was torn down around 1956 and was managed at one time by a lady named Sadie Bryant. I remember seeing a funny Ma and Pa Kettle movie there when I was very young.

5

OCT. 1953 Studio S.A.TEX.

Photo 1-4: Shown here is a picture of a young buckaroo named Howie Miller. The photo was taken at his residence at 14 Carrasco Street in 1953. Note the two-story dormitory/bunk house behind him. It was located east of the Chino Club. Photo courtesy of Howie and Kathy Miller.

This same block also had the Town Hall and jail, the Hurley Bar, the Hurley Garage, and the American Laundry. Further to the west were two red brick buildings that housed teachers and were eventually turned into offices for Kennecott Copper Corp. To the west of these buildings was the Catholic Church. There also was an old wooden building between the Hurley Bar and Hurley Garage called "The Casino", which was torn down in the early 1960's. It was a recreational facility for Hispanics that had a snack bar, poker tables, shuffleboard, and pool tables. It was also used for events such as parties and wedding receptions.

Tucked away behind the Hurley Bar near the railroad tracks was a small building called the Hurley Builder's Supply. I think this building, at one time, was the real estate office for the company of John W. Galbreath, who purchased the town of Hurley from Kennecott Copper Corp. in 1955. Later it became the Hurley Builder's Supply and sold a small inventory of building materials. Private residences occupied the remaining lots on Cortez Avenue.

Photo 1-5: Shown here is a monthly calendar of some of the movies that were featured at the Tejo Theatre. There is no date shown on the calendar, but many of the featured movies were made in 1939. Photo courtesy of Terry Humble.

Incidentally, John W. Galbreath was a wealthy entrepreneur from back east who made part of his fortune by purchasing company owned mining towns in the west and reselling the properties to private residents and businesses. He was not related to any family in the Grant County area.

Photo 1-6: Pictured is the Hurley Town Hall in the foreground. In the background to the left is the small building that probably was the real estate office for John W. Galbreath. It was later used as a store that sold building materials. Note the smelter smoke floating above the Town Hall. Photo courtesy of New Mexico State University Library, Archives and Special Collections.

At the west end of Cortez Ave. was the train depot. The railroad company that hauled the ore from the Santa Rita open pit mine to Hurley was the Atchison Topeka and Santa Fe Railroad and their main offices were at the Hurley depot. Directly behind the depot were north/south bound railroad tracks that ran northward to Bayard and Santa Rita and southbound to Deming.

A few houses were situated south of the depot along the nearby railroad tracks. They provided housing for some of the railroad employees that worked in the Hurley railroad yard. The homes were generally smaller than the Hurley homes, and there was at least one railroad boxcar that had been converted into a residence. I remember several kids who lived in those houses that attended the Hurley Schools as I was growing up.

The south side of town also had the Chino Club, which was an "Anglo only" recreational facility. Surrounding the Chino Club were a public swimming pool and some tennis courts. Across the big ditch from the Chino Club was a large firehouse and fire station located on Santa Rita Street. Near the west end of Carrasco Street were three elementary school buildings, the old Hurley High School facility, and the Hurley Community Church. The church was multidenominational and was attended by Anglos. A second gas station (Enco) opened at the west end of Carrasco Street in the early 1960's and was owned and operated by a man named Ted Carr.

All of Hurley's sports fields were located at the south end of South Hurley. The little league baseball field and an adult baseball stadium were at the southeast corner of town below Nevada Street. At the southwest corner of town was the Hurley High School football stadium. It was called Chino Stadium and was decommissioned in 1956, shortly after the schools were taken over by the Cobre Consolidated School District. Kennecott, who owned the schools until 1955, donated the lights and some of the bleachers from Chino Stadium to

Cobre High School. The remaining bleachers, the black cinder track, and football field were torn down not long after the 1963-64 school year and eventually cleared the way for a housing development in the late 1960's called the DITTROW Addition. DITTROW was an acronym for several people, three of which were city officials named Dave Diaz, Harold Trapp, and Willard O. Willis.

Photo 1-7: The Hurley Fire Dept. housed the fire truck shown here at the fire station across the street from the Chino Club. Photo courtesy of New Mexico State University Library, Archives and Special Collections.

East of the football stadium, near the big ditch that ran through the center of town, was a small cemetery that had a handful of gravesites. Many of these graves belonged to people who died during the flu epidemic of 1918. There was also a Catholic Cemetery located southwest of Hurley on the west side of Highway 180.

A couple of other structures worth mentioning were the Hurley Gates. They were located on the west end of Cortez Avenue. They consisted of two separate brick structures situated on opposite sides of the street, and each structure had two ornate street lamps mounted on top. My friend Guy Ozment told me that he saw men with machine guns stationed at the Hurley Gates in February of 1942 in response to the bombing of Pearl Harbor. The gates helped to fortify the town and the mining operation during World War II.

Photo 1-8: The Hurley Gates were located at the west end of Cortez Avenue. Photo courtesy of Joe Wade and Terry Humble.

CHAPTER TWO: THE TOWN, THE PEOPLE, AND FOND MEMORIES

"Let's take a closer look at some businesses, people, and places in this thriving little town."

Cortez Avenue was the main street of Hurley and most of the town's commerce happened there. Several private residences were situated on the street as well. Cortez Avenue was considered the "downtown" of Hurley.

The Sweet Shop was a nice place to go for kids as well as adults. It had a restaurant and a soda fountain in the back of the shop and a counter in the front that sold candy, tobacco, magazines, comic books and periodicals, and a few other odds and ends. I remember buying Reese's Peanut Butter Cups, Paydays, Almond Hershey's, Peanut Patties, Bazooka Bubble Gum, Cracker Jacks, and weird tube-shaped hollow cylinders made of wax that had colored liquid inside. You had to bite off the end of the tube to drink the liquid.

When I went to the Sweet Shop, I spent most of my money on baseball trading cards. I had cards of all of the New York Yankee greats of the day, including Mickey Mantle, Roger Maris, Whitey Ford, Elston Howard, Moose Scowron, and Bobby Richardson. My brother had a great card collection of the Chicago White Sox that included his favorite players Nellie Fox and Louie Aparicio. To my dismay, while I was away at college, my father cleaned out my bedroom and threw away all of my baseball cards.

By the time I was in sixth grade I frequently went to the Sweet Shop to buy the latest issue of Mad magazine, which was the greatest magazine ever published. (Actually, it was the greatest magazine ever published until I discovered Playboy magazine). Kids also enjoyed going there after school or on weekends to play the jukebox and get good milk shakes and hamburgers. My mother was a good friend with Luisa Ball, who ran the business. She used to go there occasionally to drink coffee and catch up on the local gossip.

The Copper Café opened around 1956 and was located on the corner of Cortez Ave. and Chino Blvd., directly across the street from the smoke stack. The first owners were two sisters named Verna Johnson and Liz Herring. They ran the company mess halls in Santa Rita and Hurley prior to opening the Copper Café. It was a nice restaurant that had a large counter with swivel seats, several booths and tables spread out over the large floor space, a good sized kitchen, and a banquet room in the rear for private parties and banquets. I used to enjoy going there to eat hamburgers and drink strawberry milk shakes when I was young, and it was a very popular lunch destination for Kennecott office workers. In the evenings I would see people there from Silver City or Bayard who drove to Hurley for an "evening out".

Photo 2-1: The Chino Sweetshop was the social hub of downtown Hurley. The Hurley Masonic Lodge was located on the second floor of the building. This photo was probably taken shortly before 1950, but the building hadn't changed as I was growing up in Hurley. Photo courtesy of New Mexico State University Library, Archives and Special Collections.

Next to the Sweet Shop were the U.S. Post Office, the town barbershop, and a beauty salon. A lady named Fannie Stearman was the Postmistress in the 1950's and Dub Archibald took over for her in the early to mid 1960's. The barbershop next door was owned by an older, grey/white haired man named Harold Trapp. He became the second Mayor of Hurley after Dave Byington, and allegedly learned to cut hair when he was in prison for bootlegging during prohibition. His wife Emma was a short lady who spent lots of time in the shop visiting with Harold and the customers. I got my first few haircuts from Harold Trapp but by the time my parents actually cared about how I looked, they started taking me to Silver City for haircuts. I think Mr. Trapp only knew how to cut hair one way...short. I faintly remember a beauty salon located directly behind the barbershop but I don't know who owned or operated it.

The Hurley Garage was a Chevron gas station with a full service automotive repair shop. As soon as you pulled up to the gas pump, someone would come out of the office to put gas in your car, clean your windshield, and check your oil. The two kinds of gasoline available were regular and ethyl. Ethyl was higher octane. You could also get kerosene for appliances such as heaters and camping cook stoves.

The Hurley Garage was a successful small-town, family run business. Owner Eddie Hickman and his right-hand man, Ray Sigman, worked the gas pumps and were the main men up front. They always wore classic railroad engineer caps made of cloth with small lines imprinted in the fabric. Mrs. Hickman worked in the office and sold everything from deer hunting licenses to radiator hoses. Back in the shop there was a good mechanic named Monte Montes who worked for the Hurley Garage for years and lived in a little trailer behind the garage.

The garage was always one of my favorite places to go because they sponsored my little league baseball team and gave us free sodas when we won. I also liked going there because I was a friend of the Hickman family, who owned the business. Eddie and Helen Hickman had a son, Ronnie, and a daughter my age named Cheryl. When I was in junior high school I used to go there and hang out with Ronnie while he worked on cars.

Beginning in the early 1960's the Hickman family was plagued by a little bad luck. Eddie sustained a serious injury when he somehow got caught up in a moving airplane propeller down at the Grant County Airport. Then, in around 1971 there was a fire inside the garage. Ronny Hickman sustained some burns from the fire and his pants were burned off up to his knees. Fortunately, the fire wasn't catastrophic and it wasn't long before the garage reopened.

Finally, Eddie Hickman died and the business was eventually sold to a man named Jack Loomis in around 1973.

The American Laundry was located next to the Hurley Garage and was owned by a man named Randall Gose. A thin, older man named Henry Wallis was the deliveryman for the laundry. He would pick up and deliver clothes all over town in the laundry service van. Everyone in Hurley knew him and liked him because he was so friendly to all of the customers. Later on, Henry retired from the laundry and became a Hurley policeman for a while. I always had a hard time visualizing Henry making an arrest because he was old, slight of build, and didn't have a mean bone in his body.

Another laundry employee who became a good friend over the years was a man named Jerry Harter. Jerry was a "Mr. Fix-it" kind of guy who enjoyed tinkering with motors and machines. Whenever I had mechanical problems with my Honda 90 motorcycle I would drive it to the shop area in the back of the laundry building and he would always help me do repairs. Then, when I was in high school, my friends and I would go to the Harter's home and spend a lot of time goofing around and visiting. He had three daughters that were popular and loved to laugh and joke around with my friends and me.

Directly west of the American Laundry were two red brick buildings that were used to house teachers for the Hurley Schools. Not long after Kennecott sold the town to John W. Galbreath, the teachers moved out and the buildings were converted into offices for the upper level management of Kennecott Copper Corp.

Photo 2-2: Until the mid 1950's, these two buildings housed teachers for the local schools. They were later converted into offices for Kennecott. Photo courtesy of New Mexico State University Library, Archives and Special Collections.

The Hurley Bar was always an interesting place to go when I was a kid. Lou and Sally Wakefield owned the bar for most of my childhood until they sold it to Ernie and Suki Venegas in the mid 1960's. Lou and Sally's son, Troy, was my friend and sometimes he and I would go to the bar at night to get a soda and some bar snacks, such as dried shrimp, jerky, potato chips, or beer nuts. Troy's parents were always friendly and generous whenever we dropped by.

Late one night, as one of the bartenders was driving home from the bar, she drove her car into the big ditch at the Aztec Street bridge. She smashed through the pipe guardrails on the bridge and drove the car right into the ditch. I don't think she was injured in the accident but it was certainly the talk of the town for a few days. There was a very high probability that alcohol may have been involved in the accident.

After the Venegas' bought the Hurley Bar, they built an addition onto the west side of the building and opened up a barbershop and a package liquor drive-up window. When I was in high school, I got to know them fairly well because I used to go there to get my haircuts from Ernie. Occasionally, on the evenings that Ernie and Sukie were not working in the bar, I would go to the drive-up window and use my fake I.D. to buy beer for my friends and me.

Kennecott Copper Corp. owned the Santa Rita Store Company in Hurley before it was sold to John W. Galbreath in 1955. It was a company store and customers used ticket booklets called boletas to purchase groceries and dry goods. On December 1, 1959 a man named Frank Lea purchased the Santa Rita Store Company from John W. Galbreath and changed the name to The Hurley Stores.

Frank Lea was a stocky man with a shiny, baldhead, wore glasses, and almost always wore a white shirt and a tie. He would come up to me and joke around whenever I came into the store. I usually responded to his teasing by making some joke about his baldhead or calling him a silly name.

Of all of the private businesses in Hurley, the Hurley Stores was the busiest and had the most employees. The red brick building to the west was the grocery store and the one on the east was the dry goods department. There was also a wooden warehouse storage building attached to the east side of the dry goods building that served as the original store. It was built in around 1911.

In the very back of the dry goods store was a business office with a couple of cashier's windows. In addition to accepting cash or checks for merchandise, the Hurley Stores did a lot of business on credit. Customers would set up accounts and the store would bill them at the end of the month. Probably the worst arguments my parents ever had while I was growing up were over the grocery bills there. The stores would also cash paychecks on payday, so it was common to see people waiting in long lines after work.

The Hurley Stores gave out S and H Green Stamps with purchases, and on a certain day of the week people would flock there to cash in on "Double Stamp Day". I remember sitting in our kitchen with my mother as we licked stamps and pasted them into a stack of empty booklets. Silver City had a Green Stamp redemption center on the corner of College Avenue and Arizona Street and we would trade our booklets for merchandise like waffle irons, coffee pots, dishes and glassware, and assorted home furnishings.

Photo 2-3: The red brick Hurley Stores building on the left was the grocery store and the one on the right was the dry goods store. Between these two buildings was the pedestrian underpass to North Hurley. Photo courtesy of New Mexico State University Library, Archives and Special Collections.

Another customer service that was offered by The Hurley Stores was taking phone orders for groceries. Most of the time my mother preferred to order by phone rather than shop in the store. Not long after she would place her order, a store delivery van would pull into our back yard loaded with brown paper bags full of groceries. The white van was usually driven by a couple of young men named Guy Ozment and Felipe Gomez. They would carry the groceries into our home and set them on the kitchen table for us.

A few people who worked at the stores became friends with my family over the years. Felipe Gomez sometimes worked at the checkout counter in the grocery store and Henny Massey and Alice Carreon rotated around in the dry goods store next door. A few other employees that I remember were Mel Rivera and Pete Trujillo in the meat department, and a man named Ruben Ramos sometimes worked upstairs where they sold toys and sporting goods. Several other employees worked in both stores over the years but I can't recall who they were.

In addition to the grocery store, the dry goods department sold just about anything imaginable. It was said that you could buy everything you need from birth to death at the Hurley Stores. They sold liquor, beer, guns, ammo, knives, fishing gear, model car and airplane kits, baseball gloves, bats, footballs and basketballs, games, cosmetics, shoes and clothing for men, women and children, jewelry and watches, hair tonic and cosmetics, school supplies, work clothing, suits, trench coats, swim suits, small appliances like toasters, cowboy hats, transistor radios, and even 45 and 33 vinyl LPs for your record player. They made a killing selling fad items to kids, like U.S. Keds canvass tennis shoes, Red Goose Shoes (as advertised on TV cartoon shows, complete with a golden egg inside one of the shoes with a toy prize inside), black, pointed toe Beatle Boots in the early 1960's, and even Hoola Hoops. They even had a hardware section where you could buy hand tools and assorted hardware items. There was also a gas pump located in front of the dry goods store where customers could drive their car up and fill the tank.

The Hurley Stores employed a few kids as well as adults. Some kids worked as carryout boys on the grocery side and other kids were given jobs distributing sale flyers. On Thursdays they would come in to pick up the flyers and deliver them door-to-door in Hurley, Bayard, Central, and Santa Rita.

There was an older Hispanic man named Hilario Mariscal who would always stand right outside the entrance to the grocery store. He wore a suit, usually blue in color, and sometimes wore a pork pie hat. He drove an old Plymouth, probably about a 1949 model, and would stand stoically in front of the store on most days, rain or shine, for hours and hours. He rarely spoke to anyone, presumably because he may have suffered from some sort of mental illness. A few people in Hurley used to call him "Blue Jay". We would tease him on occasion just to make him mad or get him to change the expression on his face. Once in a while Hilario would follow a kid carrying a sack of groceries and try to reach in and grab a grocery item out of their bag.

Every Christmas season the Town of Hurley would put up decorations on Cortez Avenue. Lights were strung across the street in the downtown area near the Hurley Stores and poles were adorned and hung with seasonal signage and decorations. The Hurley Stores would put a sled with Santa on the roof of the porch above the entrance to the dry goods store building. The downtown decorations were especially colorful during the infrequent winter snowstorms that occurred.

A few days before Christmas, Santa would come to visit Hurley. Children would wait in long lines in front of the old warehouse at the Hurley Stores to get a chance to sit on Santa Claus' lap and tell him what they wanted for Christmas. Santa would sit on the loading dock in front of the old warehouse as kids took turns going up to visit with him. Once they were done, Santa would give them a brown paper bag filled with candy, nuts and fruit.

One year I sat on Santa's lap and he asked me what I wanted for Christmas. I must have figured that I had nothing to lose, so I told him that I wanted every toy I could possibly imagine. I was quite disappointed on Christmas day when I opened my gifts and received only a couple of toys and various articles of clothing. I felt like I had been double-crossed and my faith in Santa Claus diminished very quickly.

In the mid 1950's the town always set up a nativity scene at the east end of Cortez Avenue near the curve. It was a large installation that was probably built on the bed of a large trailer. The scene had figurines that were about two to three feet tall situated in a manger setting. The stage was covered in straw and the display had an arc cover overhead that was shaped like a concave parabola. A few years later the nativity scene was moved to the west end of Cortez Avenue near the Hurley gates.

Other Places In and Around Town

The Chino Club was the social center for kids when I was growing up. The building and surrounding premises were like a country club, with facilities such as a ballroom/library with a nice hardwood dance floor, a billiards/pool room, a ping pong room, pinball machines, a bowling alley, a "men's only" room for dominos and cards, two tennis courts and a basketball court, and, of course, the Hurley Swimming Pool. There was also a concession stand that sold cold soft drinks, candy bars, jerky, nuts, ice cream, cigarettes, cigars, chewing tobacco, rolling papers and even pipe tobacco.

Photo 2-4: The Chino Club is shown here. Notice the concrete pillars in front of the building. I used to stand on the pillars next to the stairs when I was four years old and cuss-out adults as they entered the Chino Club.

17

On a typical Hurley evening, older men would be in the domino/card room smoking pipes and cigars while kids played pool, ping pong, or just listened to the jukebox in the ballroom. The Chino Club made it clear to the kids to never make too much noise or bother the men in the domino room. Whenever the men would come or go, they were aloof and rarely spoke to the kids as they walked by.

Over the years there were a handful of people who worked in the concession stand. Their job was basically twofold. They not only ran the concession stand but they also kept an eye on all of the kids and made sure they didn't tear anything up, cause trouble, or get into fights. They also made sure that the bowling alley was open on the nights that there was league bowling.

The lady who worked the concession stand the most over the years was Carrie Dodson, although Marian Bassett worked there regularly when Mrs. Dodson took her days off. Carrie was an older lady who was sometimes grumpy with the kids, but over time I became good friends with her and tried not to make her life too miserable.

I spent most of my Chino Club time in the ping-pong room. We had some great games playing singles and doubles, and Sido Bates was always the reigning ping-pong champ of the Chino Club. He taught me how to play when I was in elementary school and I eventually got good enough to play toe to toe with him. After Sido left for the Army, I became the heir apparent in the ping-pong room.

Sido taught me to hold the paddle with my thumb and index finger behind the paddle, which was great for forehand shots but became a liability for backhand shots, especially against good opponents. I eventually taught my good friend Carney Foy how to play ping-pong using this same grip and by the time he was in college he got good enough to kick my ass on a regular basis.

A bowling league met twice a week in the bowling alley located in the basement of the Club. There were four lanes and a small gallery where spectators could sit and watch the games. The league usually started around 7:00 p.m. and would finish around 10:00 or 10:30 p.m. The pin setting machines were manual and kids were hired each night to set pins for the bowlers. I spent many nights setting pins with other boys and I think we were paid 35 cents per game for three games per night. It was hard work and by the end of the night the pinsetters were soaking wet from sweat. Once in a while we were short handed and one pinsetter would set pins for two lanes simultaneously, which usually left us totally exhausted. If we did a good job and didn't mess up anybody's game, we usually picked up a little extra money in tips.

In the early 1960's the Chino Club had some large dances in the ballroom. The band that I remember seeing there the most was a local country band called The Rhythm Wranglers. The Chino Club also hosted ice cream socials during the summers, which were held outdoors on the tennis courts. Once in a while there were outdoor dances on the tennis courts and I remember seeing a Chicano band called The Royal Tones play there. Their drummer was a young kid that I knew from school named Georgie Marrufo. The band would set up in the corner of the tennis courts and I used to stand behind Georgie on the outside of the chain link fence and watch him play. Georgie's uncle, Al Marrufo, was the bandleader and they had a good group of musicians in the band.

I spent more time at the Chino Club than I did at home. At least my parents always knew where I was in the evenings. They also knew that if they wanted me out of the house, all they had to do was give me a little money and send me to the Club.

When I was in the fifth grade my older sister eloped to Palomas to marry my new brother-in-law. Apparently, my parents had a problem with the legitimacy of the marriage license from Mexico so they insisted that another wedding be held in Hurley at the home of the Justice of the Peace. Mr. John Birdwell was the JP at the time and he was an older man who lived on Santa Rita Street across from the elementary school.

I wanted to attend the wedding, but for some reason my parents decided that the wedding ceremony would run a little smoother if I wasn't there. At first I was disappointed that I couldn't attend, but on the night of the ceremony my mother bribed me by giving me a 50-cent piece and said, "Go to the Chino Club tonight and have yourself a good time."

Once I walked into the Club it didn't take me long to forget about the wedding. By the time the wedding was over I had stuffed my face with as many sodas and candy bars as I could buy. Considering the fact that sodas cost about a dime apiece and candy bars were probably a nickel each at the time, my blood sugar level was probably off the charts.

The school bus from Cobre High School would drop us off in front of the Chino Club after school and once in a while there would be a fight as soon as the bus was gone. One afternoon in front of the Club there was a fight between Red Necker, who weighed nearly 200 lbs., and Raul Varela, who weighed about 240 lbs. They were both varsity wrestlers at the time and the majority of their fight took place in the dirt next to the steps at the front entrance. Up to that point in my life, I had never seen two larger humans trying to beat each other's brains out. By the time they were done they were bloody, dirty, and totally exhausted.

Another time, there was a dispute between two high school boys who were a few years older than me at the time. Rather than fighting over their problem, the boys and the two factions that supported them decided to hold what they referred to as a "kangaroo court" proceeding in the ballroom of the Club. One kid acted as a judge and several others were the jury. Each boy had to get up in front of the group and answer several questions. Witnesses were also called upon to testify. Eventually one boy, probably the least popular one, was deemed the guilty party. I don't think that the court verdict meant much other than providing the innocent kid with an opportunity to say something like, "See. I told you I was right." Probably everyone that was involved in the "kangaroo court" had watched "Perry Mason" on TV a few too many times.

Every once in a while someone would break into the Chino Club and rob the place. I don't think they ever stole too much other than candy, sodas, cigarettes, and a little bit of money. One afternoon I was walking down the sidewalk in front of the club a couple of hours before it opened when, all of a sudden, the front doors flew open. Out trotted a kid named Mac Morten with an armload of goodies from the concession stand. I'm pretty sure he never got caught, since I didn't tell anyone about it and I don't think anyone else ever saw him breaking into or leaving the building.

I always considered the Chino Club to be a special place where a young man could go to spend a little quiet time alone in pursuit of self-reflection and inner peace. Of all of the places in the Club to seek solitude, perhaps my favorite was the men's restroom. There were a couple of urinals and two toilet stalls next to each other, and scribbled onto those ageless stall walls were tidbits of graffiti that represented many generations of the most profound wisdom and superb intellectual prowess known throughout the entire town of Hurley. For the entire duration of my childhood there was one particular short poem that always brought a smile to my face whenever I sat in that old toilet stall. I still carry these golden words with me to this day. The poem read, "Here I sit all broken hearted, tried to shit and only farted."

During the summer months the Hurley Swimming Pool was where most of the kids went to hang out for the afternoon. The pool would open from 2:00 p.m. until 6:00 p.m., seven days a week, all summer long. In the mornings there would be swimming lessons for younger children and once a week there would be adult swimming from 7:00 p.m. until 9:00 p.m. On the north end of the swimming pool complex was a baby pool and an intermediate pool for young children. At the south end was the main pool, which was three feet deep at one end and over nine feet deep at the other end. The baby pool area had a shaded bench where young mothers or guardians could sit and monitor their toddlers. The main pool had a long bench located under a grove of shade trees where spectators and friends could sit and cool off from the summer heat.

When my friends and I weren't actually swimming, we were either lying on our towels on the hot concrete near the diving board or we would walk over to the Chino Club to buy a cool treat from the concession stand. A back door to the concession stand was located up a flight of stairs on the second floor of the Club. Snacks were served to kids as they stood on a small porch outside the door. It cost 25 cents to swim for the afternoon, and if you had another 5 or 10 cents you could buy a soda, an ice cream cone, or a candy bar.

The pool was a great place for junior high and high school aged boys to socialize with girls. Back in the early 1960's my friends and I were extremely fortunate and forever grateful for two absolutely amazing inventions that transformed our generation and set into motion a new era of American culture. Of course, the two inventions I'm referring to were the transistor radio and the bikini, not necessarily in that order. I remember lying on my towel next to the pool with a couple of good friends, day after hot summer day, as we listened to KGRT radio out of Las Cruces and watched tanned young girls parade around the pool in their bikinis. In the course of a mere summer, we went from pulling pigtails and being romantically oblivious to actually concocting elaborate schemes to get the attention of these beautiful creatures.

One scheme that worked amazingly well was to persuade girls to sneak into the pool with us late at night. Once we were in the water, one of the boys would snatch a hairbrush, a shoe, or some other object from one of the girls and we would play a game of "keep away". The girls would grab us or jump on us to try to recover the stolen object but we would always manage to throw it to one of our buddies a few feet away. The game was a perfectly polite and clean way to get our hands all over each other without worrying about some adult screaming at us, taking our allowance away, or getting grounded for a couple of weeks. When we were done with our late night swim, there was always one lucky guy who would pair up with a girl that he had a "crush" on. Then there were one or two other "slower moving" guys in the group that would get up enough nerve to ask one of the girls out on a date a few days later.

Every summer the Hurley Pool hosted a swim meet for kids from all over the county. Kids from Silver City came to Hurley to compete in various swimming races and diving competitions, but there were always a few Hurley kids who were ready for the challenge. Virginia Smith, who lived up the street from me, always did well in the diving competition and Larry Benavidez and Kathy Willis usually won some of their swim races. Troy Wakefield, Gene Valles, and Marcel Kirkmans were also strong swimmers who usually did very well. I competed a couple of times in the meet, but I finished the races in the middle of the pack.

One afternoon in the boy's showers, a male lifeguard happened to be walking through the room and noticed a young teenage kid changing his clothes. The kid had just taken off his underwear and was putting on his swimsuit when the lifeguard noticed that the kid had soiled underwear. He asked the kid, "Do you smoke cigarettes?" to which the kid replied, "No".

Then the lifeguard asked him, "Then why do you have nicotine stains in your underwear?"

The kid didn't like to be teased, and this remark made him visibly upset. On the verge of crying, he went into the basket room/office and called his dad on the telephone to tell him that the lifeguard, who was several years older, was picking on him.

About 10 minutes later the boy's father showed up in a fit of rage and called the lifeguard out to fight him next to the pool behind the Chino Club. The father was a fairly large man and had a reputation for being hot headed and quick to fight. The lifeguard was in his early 20's and was a skilled fist fighter.

When the lifeguard came out to the grass area where the father was standing, he was bare footed and wearing only his red swim trunks. After a few words, the father took the first swing and then the lifeguard systematically beat him down to his hands and knees with his superior boxing skills. I remember the man looking up at the lifeguard with his face all bloodied and saying something like, "Well, you're a better man than I am."

Unfortunately, all of the kids at the pool witnessed the fight and by the end of the afternoon everyone in Hurley knew what had happened.

Kitty Duvall became one of the lifeguards at the pool when we were in high school, replacing her sister who had moved away to finish college. She was dating my good friend Tubby Porkman at the time, and he and I regularly went up to the swimming pool in the afternoons to visit her.

One afternoon, Kitty proudly drove her dad's beautiful, brand new yellow and white two-toned V-8 1965 Chevy pick-up to work. When Kitty mentioned during our visit that her dad had just purchased the new truck, Tubby and I immediately walked out to the street to check it out while Kitty tended to her lifeguard duties. It was indeed a beautiful truck and we spent several minutes walking around and admiring how shiny and clean the body and fenders were. We then crawled inside and sat behind the steering wheel and were very impressed with the comfort of the big bench seat and the modern design of the interior. Next, we slid out of the cab and looked at the nice, unscratched truck bed with real wood on the floor of the bed, and finally we walked around to the front of the truck and opened up the hood. The big V-8 engine was spotless, and everything under the hood was in "mint condition".

As we were standing there looking under the hood, I inadvertently mentioned to Tubby that a friend of mine had recently shown me how to hotwire a car. I pointed out that this truck would be very easy for someone to steal because the starter was in a very accessible location. I said to Tubby, "It's a piece of cake. All you have to do is get a screwdriver and bridge the two wire contacts on the starter and you're off."

I didn't think anything more about what I had just told Tubby, but a few seconds later I glanced at him and he had a huge smile on his face. He quickly looked back at me and said, "Well, what are we waiting for? Let's go for a ride."

At first I thought he was joking and I briefly chuckled at his remark. Then, I looked at him again and realized he was dead serious. We started laughing so hard we could barely stand up. The next thing I knew I was lying on my back, underneath the truck with a screwdriver in my hand while Tubby sat behind the wheel ready to give it some gas. After a couple of tries we started the truck and I climbed in on the passenger side and shut the door.

This was a nice truck. I mean a really nice truck. It ran unbelievably smooth and it had a great radio. We dialed in some tunes, leaned back and got comfortable, and put the new truck through its paces on the streets of Hurley. As Tubby drove the truck he became enthralled with every button, switch, and knob on the dashboard. Meanwhile, I was slumped down in the passenger seat with my feet on the dashboard and my elbow sticking out the window and thoroughly enjoying the ride. The new truck was truly a dreamboat. It was everything we had imagined and more.

Finally, after about 15 minutes of pleasure cruising, Tubby wheeled the truck back to the Hurley Swimming Pool with the radio blaring and the engine revving. Tubby carefully returned it to the same parking spot and we shut off the engine and jumped out of the truck. Still giddy from laughter, we went back into the pool area to visit Kitty at the lifeguard stand. Fortunately for us, she had been preoccupied and didn't have a clue about our little joy ride.

Later that evening there was a phone call at the Porkman household. It was for Tubby, and on the other end of the line was Kitty. Once she got Tubby on the phone she began her rant. "You idiots. Now I'm in deep trouble. My father thinks I let you knuckleheads drive his new truck all around town this afternoon.

He was reading the newspaper in the living room and when he looked out the window he saw his new truck drive by. He also got phone calls from several people around town who saw you cruising around and he is really pissed off."

I don't know exactly where the conversation went from there, but I think Tubby eventually married Kitty so he could get her father off of his back for pulling off this stunt.

The following summer I was at the swimming pool with my good friend Toby Parker. We were standing out in front of the entrance talking to a girl who was working in the basket-check room as a cashier. While we were chatting with her, Toby and I noticed there were about 20 bicycles parked in front of the swimming pool that belonged to younger kids who were swimming for the afternoon.

Before long we became bored and decided to do something fun and creative with these bicycles. For a laugh, we methodically took the bikes and stacked them into a huge pile, making sure to tangle the pedals and handle bars of each bike into the spokes of the other bikes lying underneath it. By the time we were done with our sculpture piece, we had a pile of bicycles about five feet tall lying on the sidewalk in front of the swimming pool entrance.

Later that afternoon, as the kids checked in their baskets and left the pool, they walked out to the sidewalk to find one huge, tangled-up and gnarled mass of bicycle. Just as we had hoped, the first kid to claim his bicycle made an attempt to extricate it from the middle of the pile. He yanked, lifted, kicked and cussed, but his bicycle wouldn't budge. As other kids spilled out onto the sidewalk and attempted to pull their bikes from the mass of rubber and metal, they soon realized that the only way to free their bicycle would be to systematically remove one bike at a time from the pile, beginning at the top. It must have been 30 minutes before the last kid rode off on his bike, but Toby and I observed the entire fiasco with tears running down our cheeks from laughter.

Another time, well after midnight when the summer nights were beautiful, warm, and long, Toby and I walked through some back alleys to the Hurley swimming pool with the sole intention of wreaking havoc. We quietly hopped over the chain link fence surrounding the pool complex and walked around to the east side of the large pool. There were two lifeguard stands that stood about 10 feet tall and were positioned only a few feet away from the pool. Each stand was made of wooden 4"x4" posts and must have weighed about 250 lbs. They had steps leading up to the chair where the lifeguard sat and had a nice roof overhead to provide shade.

Along the chain link fence behind the lifeguard stands hung nets and vacuum pipes that were used for cleaning the pool. Donut-shaped life preservers also hung every few feet in case of emergency. Toby and I assessed the situation for a minute and then we quickly grabbed everything off of the fence and threw it into the pool. Not satisfied, we then muscled the heavy lifeguard stands to the edge of the pool and pushed them into the water. When we were done, we hopped the fence and ran up the alley as fast as we could.

The next afternoon we came to the pool a few minutes before it opened, just to see what was going on. To our delight, there were about 4 people in the water trying to fish the heavy lifeguard stands out of the water and reposition them so that they could open the pool for the day. Lyncho Jaramillo, who was one of the town policemen, was standing nearby to take note of the vandalism. As we approached the pool to bathe in the glory of our mayhem, Lyncho walked up to me and queried, "Jerry boy, you don't happen to know who did this, do you?"

Lyncho was a nice man, and he knew from years of police experience there was a good chance I had something to do with any act of vandalism that ever happened around town. He also knew that if I didn't do it, I would probably know who did do it.

I calmly raised my eyebrows, slowly shook my head from side to side, and innocently responded, "No, Lyncho, I sure don't know anything about it."

Then, Lyncho, sensing I might be willing to do some detective work for him, asked me, "Well, if you happen to hear anything, would you let me know?"

I looked back at him and replied in an earnest and sincere tone of voice, "I sure will, Lyncho."

Then we turned away and snickered as we walked over to the shaded observation area on the other side of the pool.

The heyday of the Hurley baseball stadium was over by the time I was old enough to go there and play baseball with my friends in the late 1950's. Prior to that, the mining operation sponsored a semi professional baseball team who played in a league with teams from around the area. The company built the Hurley stadium for the home team and the ball players were given jobs at the plant. They were allowed to leave their jobs early so that they could practice or attend games. I think the company sponsored ball teams came to an end when World War II broke out in 1941. By the time I was in elementary school, I knew several of the men who played in the league and some of their kids became my good friends.

The stadium was made of wood and was about three stories tall. It had a coat of old, faded green paint and was built in three connected sections. One wing ran out toward first base, another wing ran along the third base line, and the center section connected with the wings behind home plate. Baseball fans were protected from the sun and rain by a large tin roof and a solid wooden wall that connected the highest bleacher row to the roof. In the front open area of the stadium was a heavy gauged wire screen that provided protection from foul balls. Underneath the bleachers was a locked storage room and several support beams and rafters that ran every which way, some being very high off the ground.

Two wooden outhouses were situated to the west of the stadium near the edge of a bosque that we referred to as "the jungle". We used to go to the jungle after school and on weekends to play "Hide and Go Seek", "Army", and "Cowboys and Indians" because there were so many great places to hide. Several narrow trails ran through the jungle in every direction. The jungle was not only a good place to play, but it was also a place where kids would go to smoke cigarettes or fight because it was so overgrown with vegetation and out of view from adults at the nearby ballpark.

One morning several of the neighborhood boys and I went to the jungle to play Army with our BB guns. At one point during the pitched battle that ensued, Butch Steyskal and I sought cover in one of the corrugated tin outhouses, where we held off an onslaught of hostile BB gun fire. While we were holed up inside we could hear waves of BBs pelting the outside of the outhouse. During the brief and infrequent moments of calmness we would poke our heads and guns out the door and take pot shots at our enemies situated in the surrounding jungle. The battle finally ended when someone shot Butch in the forehead right between his eyes. We called a truce once we realized that shooting each other with BB guns might not be such a good idea after all. Afterwards we laughed and showed each other the red spots on our bodies where we had been hit. A couple of kids had so many red spots on their bodies that it looked like they had just come down with a case of chicken pox.

By the early 1960's the dirt baseball field and the stadium complex were no longer actively maintained and gradually fell into a state of disrepair. I remember seeing a couple of Cobre High School baseball games and an occasional adult fast-pitch hardball game there, but that was about the extent of its use. Because the stadium was fairly remote, it also was a common meeting place or "clubhouse" for kids. When we were young we would run around on the bleachers or hang out at odd times during the day or evening. Some kids would even go there to smoke cigarettes they had stolen from their parents.

Once in a while, when the stadium was empty and things were quiet, you could hear the wind howling eerily through the bleachers and rafters. I remember playing in those bleachers on several occasions and being overcome by a haunting and unsettling feeling. It was as if I was being watched by a devious person who was lurking somewhere in the stadium, waiting for an opportunity to perpetrate a perverse act on anyone who was there alone.

The south side of the stadium, which was out of view from Hurley, was where people would park at night and have parties. There were always broken beer bottles, used condoms, cigarette butts, and the stench of urine that lingered there from the night before. The baseball stadium was yet another key spot in and around Hurley where scores of babies were conceived and many extramarital affairs took place.

Once, when I was about 11 or 12 years old, Tubby Porkman and I were down at the old stadium fooling around behind the bleachers. Out of curiosity and boredom we climbed up to one of the horizontal wooden beams, which was about 20 feet above the ground. Once we were up on the beam, Tubby crawled out to the middle of it so that he could hang from it by his hands. I soon crawled out to keep him company as he was hanging beneath me, and for some reason I began cracking jokes. Tubby started laughing at my jokes and, the more he laughed, the more jokes and funny stories I told. Finally, after several minutes Tubby's hands began to fatigue. Just when I thought he was about to let go of the beam, he miraculously pulled himself back up to avoid falling. We continued laughing for several minutes before we climbed back down to the ground. I remember sitting up on that beam overlooking Hurley to the north and having the feeling of what it would be like to be a pigeon perched on a power line.

I don't know much about the Hurley Catholic Church because I never attended services there, but I do remember their membership was always much larger that the Hurley Community Church and the congregation was primarily Hispanic. The one thing I do remember about the Catholic Church, however, is that everyone in town always knew when there was a wedding because the wedding party would drive through town in a huge procession while honking their horns. The cars in the procession were decorated with several strands of fluffy flowers spaced a few inches apart on top of the car and stretched from bumper to bumper.

The flowers were made from Kleenex tissue. To make a flower, the tissue was first folded back and forth into a long narrow strip. Next, a knot was tied in the middle of the tissue with a long string. The flowers were spaced a few inches apart on the string and ran the length of the car. Once the folded tissues were in place, the ends of the tissue were roughed up and spread out by hand to make the flowers.

Photo 2-5: **The Hurley Catholic Church was located on Cortez Ave. The smokestack was not far away. Photo courtesy of New Mexico State University Library, Archives and Special Collections.**

When I was in first grade I began attending Sunday school at the Hurley Community Church. At six years of age my primary incentive for attending Sunday school was to receive a little metal "perfect attendance" pin that was worn on the breast pocket of your dress shirt. For every subsequent year of perfect attendance, another pin was awarded that would attach to the previous year's pin, and after three years of attending Sunday school you were given a free Bible with a hand knit place marker in the shape of a cross. By the time I finished fourth grade I had cashed in on every freebee the Sunday school program had to offer and I was ready and motivated to keep the loot rolling in for years to come.

My perfect attendance scheme came to an abrupt end one Sunday morning just as I was getting ready to leave for Sunday school. I was standing in my front yard, all dressed up in my Sunday school clothes, when Butch Steyskal happened to be riding his bike up the street. He was one of my best friends and we rode bicycles everywhere together. He rode up to my front gate on his bicycle and asked me, "Hey, Jerry, do you want to go ride bicycles with me?"

With a hint of disappointment in my voice, I replied, "I can't. I have to go to Sunday school in a few minutes."

Sensing my conundrum, Butch countered, "Well, what would you rather do, go to Sunday school or go ride bikes?"

Without thinking twice I instinctively responded, "I would rather go ride bikes."

By now it was quite obvious to Butch that Sunday school wasn't high up on my list of fun things to do. With a confident look on his face, he threw up his hands and responded, "Well then, what are you waiting for? Let's go."

So, I went into my house, changed clothes, and went bike riding with Butch instead of going to Sunday school. As it turned out, I never went back to Sunday school again after that day. I had been enlightened. Thanks to Butch, I suddenly began doing things that were important to me rather than being manipulated by rewards or the need to please other people. In hindsight, I sometimes think that I never should have been exposed to Butch's profound wisdom at such an early age. Ever since that fateful day I was constantly butting heads with teachers, authority figures, or anyone in general who sponsored activities that were rife with rules which impeded my sense of freedom and fun.

The Sunday school teachers during my four-year tenure at the Hurley Community Church were Sissy Duvall and Billie Womack. Rev. Alfred S. Kline was the pastor in the mid 1950's and I faintly remember him having a daughter named Phoebe, I believe, who was a few years older than me. Rev. Berkley succeeded Rev. Kline as the next full-time pastor in the early 1960's. He and his wife had a daughter and two sons, one of which was in my grade at school.

Rev. Berkley was well liked in the community because he was a fairly young, well educated, and intelligent man. He also had a nice wife and got along with the youth at the church. His daughter Penny was a year older than me and was a cute blond girl that caught the attention of many of the boys at school. His two sons, Jeff and Neil, were pretty nice guys as far as I was concerned but, as it turned out, both of them were small town purveyors of mischief who fit in well with some of the guys in my friendship circle.

Jeff was older than me and became good friends with Sido Bates, and his younger brother Neil hung around with a variety of kids, including me on occasion. Jeff and Sido used to get into trouble around town once in a while and,

27

whenever Neil and I got together, we were usually up to no good as well. In fact, the only time I ever broke into someone's house during my childhood was with Neil. As I remember, Neil took me to a house just up the street from where he lived and we crawled through a window and went inside. He had been in the house a couple of times before and knew when the owner was gone and which windows were always left unlatched. Once we were inside, Neil took about 25 cents in small change off of a dresser but I was too chicken to take anything.

Photo 2-6: The Hurley Community Church is where I began my religious training. The folks there tried their best to keep me in line, but my love for mischief got the better of me. Photo courtesy of New Mexico State University Library, Archives and Special Collections.

The experience of breaking into someone's home made me feel like a cheap thief and my conscience bothered me all evening long; that is, until we went to the Chino Club and treated ourselves to Pepsi's and candy bars with the stolen money. It's funny how something as simple as a soda pop and a snack can make a kid forget about their recent criminal behavior.

The next Pastor after Rev. Berkley was a guy named Don Roberts. He was a goofy sort of guy, and the kids (well, a couple of us anyway) liked to make fun of him. Tubby and I called him "Daddy Don" and always made monkey noises when he was talking.

One night, when our youth group was at Camp Thunderbird, several of us young lads in the Pilgrim Fellowship youth group managed to get Daddy Don very upset at bedtime. At about 10:30 p.m., Rev. Roberts declared "lights out" in the boy's bunkhouse and everyone was supposed to get quiet so that we could go to sleep. A few minutes after the lights went out, a kid named Robby Hartman began making "rivet" noises like a frog. At first, a couple of boys tried to hold back their laughter but couldn't. Then more boys began laughing and, before long the entire bunkhouse was cracking up.

Initially, Daddy Don said, "OK boys, let's just knock it off and get to sleep."

But after about 10 more minutes of relentless "riveting" and laughter, Daddy Don finally jumped up out of bed, turned on the light, and yelled, "God damn it! Shut the hell up!"

Then, the following night we got Daddy Don mad at us again because we put steel wool inside of some kid's bedroll as a prank. As we were getting ready for bed, the kid crawled into his bedroll and immediately sprang back out as if an army of ants were crawling on his skin. To make matters even worse, the kid's bedroll was ruined because the steel wool became imbedded in the fibers of the material and was impossible to remove. It seemed like the madder Rev. Roberts became, the more difficult it was to hold back our laughter.

The church's Pilgrim Fellowship (PF) group met on Sunday nights in the Recreation Hall next to the Hurley Community Church. Tubby and I liked to attend PF because there were always a few cute girls who came. We spent more time clowning around to get their attention than we did following directions from the pastor. The PF group would do activities like go on hay rides at Cameron Creek, go door to door and collect for UNICEF, have picnics and outings, sing Christmas carols at night in front of elderly peoples homes, play games, and attend a one week summer camp at Camp Thunderbird with kids from other towns.

Photo 2-7: The Rec Hall was located directly west of the Hurley Community Church. Our Pilgrim Fellowship (PF) youth group met here on Sunday evenings. The community also held events here such as awards banquets for Cub Scouts and Boy Scouts. Photo courtesy of New Mexico State University Library, Archives and Special Collections.

In spite of our mischief and horseplay at PF, Tubby and I used to spend a lot of time discussing philosophy and religion with each other. We were proud of the fact that, for the most part, we took our debates to a higher intellectual level than most of our witless peers. Over a period of time we became quite adept at defending our perspectives while shooting holes in ideas that were contrary to our own.

One evening at PF when we were in eighth or ninth grade, we got into a discussion/argument with a girl about religion. We asked her, "Does God know everything?" and her rote response was, "Well, of course he does."

Then we asked her, "Does he know if you are going to go to Heaven or Hell?" and she replied, "Well of course he does."

Then we dropped the bomb on her by asking, "Well if He already knows if we are going to Heaven or Hell, then what in the Hell are we doing piddling around here on earth for? Why don't we just head straight for our final destination instead of wasting a human lifetime?"

We totally buffaloed the poor girl, so she went to the Pastor for guidance and support for her side of the argument. A few minutes later she returned with the pastor and he indignantly informed us that, "Even though God knows whether you are going to Heaven or Hell, He wants the choice to be yours," or some such bullshit.

We knew right then and there that their religious doctrine was arbitrary because the Pastor had to fish around for a reply that made any sense. After that discussion, we didn't believe much of anything they said since none of their answers were based on logic.

Another favorite question we loved to ask other kids was, "Who created the universe?" and they would confidently reply, "Why, God created everything."

Then we would ask, "Well who created God?"

At that point in the discussion, the wires in their little brains would begin to smolder and short-circuit, and the dormant religious fairy tales that were peacefully stored away in the depths of their feeble memory banks would awaken and erupt into a free flowing fountain of saliva and spittle, and any thread of spoken logic or common sense in their reply to our query would abruptly sink like a rock to the bottom of a cold and dark river, never to surface again for the remainder of the conversation.

Camp Thunderbird became a special place for many of my friends and me as we were growing up. Located near the upper Mimbres River on the road to Lake Roberts, it was where our Pilgrim Fellowship youth group always went for a weeklong summer camp. I attended summer camps there from seventh grade through tenth grade with kids from the Santa Rita Community Church, the Hurley Community Church, and churches from Albuquerque and El Paso. Our camps were multidenominational in their approach to religious teachings, and the solitude of the trees and mountains created a strong spiritual connection that was impossible to ignore. Rev. Harold Johnson from Santa Rita was very active in promoting the summer camps for kids and I always felt as though he personified Camp Thunderbird and its many natural gifts more than any other person. He was somehow able to use the natural beauty of our world as a bridge that enabled us to cross over and touch something greater than what we could sense in our human state of consciousness.

I never bought into the Christian perspective of spirituality while I was there but I must admit that my visits to Camp Thunderbird helped me formulate my own sense of spirituality and define my relationship with nature and the universe. It was also a perfect place to go for a "coming of age" experience, and we were all very fortunate to have this opportunity at such an important time in our lives. In fact, the first time I ever held hands with a girl was when we went out on a late evening group hike on a mesa across the road from Camp Thunderbird.

Although the daily camp itinerary was fairly regimented, a few of us found ways to create a little mischief in spite of it. During a typical day, the camp directors would wake us up around sunrise to attend an outdoor group session that always included a prayer or two, religious discussions, and an outline of what we were to do for the remainder of the day. Then, we would have breakfast and go on about our daily activities, which included things like arts and crafts workshops and hikes. In the evenings after dinner we would have some free time before attending social events. At the end of the evening it was off to bed and "lights out". Or, so it was for most of the kids there.

Directly outside of the main lodge building was a fairly large metal bell that sat on top of a utility pole that was probably 20 feet high. The ringing of the bell signaled it was time for everyone to come together for meetings, meals, or events. One of the camp counselors would repeatedly pull the long rope that hung from the bell to make it ring.

One night, near the end of our week at camp, a small group of us snuck out of our dorm room in the early morning hours and got a large pitcher from the kitchen and filled it with water. Then, one of the kids in our group climbed up to the top of the bell pole and turned the bell upside down. A couple of other kids climbed part way up the pole to form an assembly line. We then passed the pitcher of water up to the boy at the top of the pole. He carefully filled the upside down bell with water from the pitcher and then everyone climbed back down the pole. The most dangerous part of our operation was making sure we didn't accidentally ring the bell as we manipulated it. Finally, we returned the pitcher to the kitchen and quietly snuck back to the boy's bunkhouse and went back to bed.

A couple of hours later, right on schedule, one of the adults went out to ring the "wake up" bell. The minute we heard the first ring we jumped up to see if our prank from the night before had worked. It was a wonderful sight to behold. One of the camp directors was standing there looking up at the bell as water splashed off of his head and ran down his shirt.

Another evening we snuck out of a social event at the lodge and executed what we referred to as a B.R.A.D., more commonly known as a "bra raid after dark". Phase one of our operation was to clandestinely sneak into the girls' bunkhouse and steal a bra off of some girl's bed. Once the bra was safely hidden in the bushes, we quickly returned to the social event so that our brief absence would go undetected.

On the north slope of the lodge's roof was a painting of a large thunderbird, and on the ground below was a fire circle where we held our early morning meetings. The thunderbird was visible from the fire circle. For phase two of our operation, we snuck out of the bunkhouse in the middle of the night and climbed up onto the roof of the lodge. We carefully draped the bra across the chest of the thunderbird and then climbed down and went back to bed.

The following morning when we gathered around the fire circle, we patiently waited to see how long it would take before anyone noticed our creative rooftop masterpiece. One of the pastors began the day by leading the group in our usual morning prayer. As the kids gradually began to notice the well-endowed thunderbird overlooking the fire circle, snickering and muffled laughter began to set in. Before long the entire group of nearly 40 kids were nudging each other and the Pastor was having a difficult time settling everyone down. When the camp counselors and directors finally looked up to see what all the commotion was about, the entire camp broke out into a good laugh.

On the south side of Nevada Street and west of the big ditch was the old Hurley Cemetery. Many of the graves didn't have marble headstones and the cemetery was overgrown with weeds and tall grass from lack of maintenance. Strangely, I never knew one person from Hurley that ever mentioned having relatives or friends buried there.

It was rumored that sometimes late at night there was a creature that emerged from the cemetery known as "The Dog-Faced Man". Once in a while, a story would float around town about someone who was walking home alone at night and would suddenly panic because he was following them. It was interesting to note that stories about the Dog-Faced Man usually originated from kids who were a few years older than me and they tended to surface when ghost stories were being told on a dark summer night while sitting out on someone's front lawn or perhaps when gathered around a camp fire in the nearby woods.

On one such summer eve, some friends and I decided to evoke the legend of the Dog Face Man as a way to scare some young teenage girls and get them to snuggle up close to us for protection. We came up with a brilliant plan as we were sitting in the bleachers watching a men's fast pitch softball doubleheader down at the Hurley Little League baseball field. The late game was almost over and there were still several groups of kids hanging around the baseball park.

After a bit of spirited discussion and brainstorming, our idea was to convince a group of cute girls to walk down to the old graveyard with us to see if we could conjure up the Dog-Faced Man. My task was to slip away ahead of the group and run down to the graveyard before everyone arrived. Once I was there I would lie down in the weeds near the graves and, whenever the group entered the graveyard, I would jump up and make animal noises and scare the hell out of everyone. The girls would then cling on to the boys for protection and my friends would become their heroes. Once everyone was safe and sound, the heroes would be showered with hugs and kisses from the girls.

As soon as I got the signal that the girls were on board with our plan, I made my move. I gave a lame excuse for needing to go home for the evening and left the ballpark. Once I was out of sight I took off running until I reached the graveyard. I arrived there several minutes ahead of my friends and sought out a cozy spot to lie down and hide in the tall, dry grass. I walked around for a bit and soon found a level area next to a grave in the center of the graveyard. I then dropped to my hands and knees and cleared out a smooth area so that I could lie on my stomach. The spot was perfect for our prank. I was well hidden and could jump up and chase everyone out of the graveyard and into the street when the time was right.

As I was lying there in the quiet of the warm, dark night, all alone in anticipation my friends' arrival, something strange happened. I began to sense a lonely and empty feeling as I contemplated the lives and deaths of the people buried around me. I thought about the sadness of one's death and the vacuum they left behind, which really amounted to nothing more than a single and pathetic gift to the people that loved them for so many years. I thought about the suffering and pain that accompanied the dying process and how difficult it must have been for friends and family to witness it firsthand. Finally, an eerie and frightening thought occurred to me. Serendipitously, it could be me who gets murdered by the Dog Faced Man and my friends would come and find me lying here, dead. Then I grinned and thought to myself, "This is going to be really fun."

Everything fell into place just as we had planned. My friends finally showed up and slowly approached the graveyard with the girls snuggled up close to them. I could hear them giggling cautiously and talking in low voices as I laid there in anticipation, nestled among the graves and the dead and the tall weeds.

Suddenly, a few feet away from where I was lying, I noticed something moving between the weeds and among the graves. Panic shot up my spine as I slowly raised my head and turned to take a look. I was instantly dismayed by what I saw. Rumple, my dog, had followed me to the graveyard and was on the verge of foiling our entire scheme. As my friends were getting closer, all I could do was lie still and hope that Rumple stayed out of sight until the gag was over. I knew if I moved or attempted to call him, our entire plan would be exposed.

The group slowly entered the graveyard and the girls were now walking arm-in-arm with the boys as a mood of apprehension and fear slowly fell upon them. Inch by inch, step by step, they walked further out among the graves and closer to where I was lying. As they approached me, I began to cautiously move into position to spring up from the ground and launch "The Dog Faced Man" into action. I placed the palms of my hands flat against the ground to push myself up when suddenly I heard a low pitched, guttural growl that gradually grew to a crescendo in volume and intensity. From behind the tall weeds, Rumple stopped the approaching group dead in their tracks. I knew it was now time to make my move.

It couldn't have worked out any better. In a state of terror, the girls immediately started screaming and turned to run for their lives. In response, I quickly jumped up and chased everyone out of the graveyard and into the street until they finally ran under the streetlight on Nevada Street. Once everyone turned around to look back toward the graveyard, they were relieved to find that it was just me who was chasing them, with Rumple following close behind. Everyone got a good laugh, and we certainly accomplished our goal of getting the girls' attention for the night.

Miscellaneous Services in Hurley

I remember in the 1950's there were a couple of delivery businesses that brought goods into Hurley. If you wanted milk, cream, or half and half, a man named Pasqual Jimenez would deliver fresh bottles to your door from the T and M Dairy in Hanover. Pasqual was a short, stocky man who was always very friendly, and sometimes his son Mike accompanied him when he made his deliveries. The dairy finally went out of business sometime in the early 1960's, I believe.

One other delivery service I faintly remember in the early 1950's was a coal delivery service. At that time there were several families in Hurley who were still using coal instead of natural gas to heat their house, and a truck would come down the alley and deliver coal to their back yard. The coal was hauled to Hurley by train and was delivered to the Santa Rita Store Company, where it was unloaded down a chute that led to the basement of the warehouse. The train also brought kerosene and deposited it in underground tanks between the store and the railroad tracks.

The only truck that ever came door to door to pick anything up was the garbage truck. Before I was old enough to go to school I used to routinely run out to our fence by the alley and watch the garbage man jump off of the back of the truck and dump our full metal garbage can into the back. The truck driver was Mrs. Lopez and she was always very friendly to me when she came to pick up the garbage. One time she gave me an old bamboo birdcage that someone had thrown away. As a young boy I always thought it would be fun to be a garbage man. These lucky guys got to cruise all over town while hanging off the back of a garbage truck and whistle at women as they drove by.

During the 1950's, the streetlights in Hurley didn't turn on automatically, nor was there a master switch that turned all of the lights on at once. At dusk, a man from the power company would drive a truck around town and stop directly under each streetlight to turn it on. He would grab a long pole out of the back of his truck and reach all the way up to the streetlight to flick a switch that was mounted on the side of the pole. Then, he would get back into his truck and drive to the next street light. A gentleman named Mr. Youngs was usually the streetlight switchman who drove around in his red Community Public Service (CPS) truck.

Telephone service in Hurley in the mid 1950's was a party line system, which meant most families had to share their phone line with another household. When you picked up the receiver of your phone, you had to listen for a second to make sure you weren't interrupting a neighbor's conversation before you dialed the desired number. If someone was talking, it was a matter of common courtesy that you hung up the receiver and waited a few minutes before you attempted your call again.

The system generally worked well, although it wasn't unusual for people to eavesdrop on phone conversations. And, if you were unlucky enough to share a line with a household that had teenagers, it could be hours before the line was free for you to use. If someone had to wait a long time for the party line to get free, they would occasionally "butt in" to the neighbor's conversation and say something a little nasty, like, "Excuse me, but I need to make an important phone call and you have been hogging the line for the last hour. Could you please hang up so that I can use the phone?"

If the person on the other end of the party line didn't like your tone of voice, they would reply by saying something like, "Mind your own business," or, "Why don't you keep your nose to yourself."

Needless to say, it was a great day in Hurley when party lines were finally replaced with private telephone lines.

When I was very young I remember going with my father to North Hurley to buy tamales from a Hispanic family. The home was located near the golf course and we would pull up into the dirt driveway behind their house and honk the horn on our 1949 Chevy coupe. There were always chickens running around the yard squawking whenever we arrived. A kid from inside the house would come out to our car and take our order and would return a few minutes later with our tamales.

My older brother inherited a Silver City Daily Press paper route from his friend Derry Blackman in the summer of 1961. I had just finished my 5th grade year in school and my brother asked me to be his helper. We delivered 155 Daily Press newspapers six evenings a week and would go from door to door and collect money from every house each week. We carried a small, hardbound booklet with punch cards for each customer and we would use a paper punch to punch out a particular date when they paid.

The weekly cost of the Silver City Daily Press was 30 cents, but eventually the price went up to 35 cents. I remember lots of customers complaining about the price increase. After the summer of 1963 my brother left for college and I took over the paper route until I left for college in August of 1968. For a couple of summers I also delivered the El Paso Times at 5:00 a.m., seven days a week in addition to my Silver City Daily Press route in the evenings. The El Paso Times route had about 110 customers, so I was a very busy kid.

I delivered the newspapers on my bicycle until I saved up enough money to buy a Honda 90 motorcycle in the fall of 1965. Every evening I started delivering the papers around 5:00 p.m. and it took me about 35 minutes if I had a helper. It took me a little over an hour when I delivered the route by myself. On winter evenings when it snowed, I had to deliver the route on foot and I would sometimes get home between 8:00 and 8:30 p.m.

The boundaries to my route extended from the south side of Romero Street to Nevada Street. A classmate of mine named Lorenzo Pino delivered the Daily Press from the North side of Romero Street up to Anza Street. Lorenzo was a frugal kid and I would occasionally run into him at the Hurley Post Office when he was purchasing U.S. Savings Bonds with his paper route money.

There was a family named the Sneeds who worked for the Daily Press in Silver City. Their job was to deliver the newspaper bundles from Silver City to each paperboy's home on the eastern side of Grant County. Once they delivered our bundle, my mother and I would roll up each newspaper and put a rubber band around it before I put them into my canvas delivery bag. The rolled up newspapers were easy to throw into yards as I rode my bicycle up and down the street. Every Saturday morning either Mr. or Mrs. Sneed would come to our home to take the money I had collected for the week's worth of newspapers. Any money left over above what I gave them was my profit. I usually earned about $17 per week, which financed lots of beer and spending money, and later paid for most of my freshman year of college as well.

The Sneeds had a son named Joe who was about four or five years older than me. Occasionally, he would deliver the newspapers to me when his parents were unavailable. He was a clean-cut teenaged kid who was always polite to my family and seemed like a really nice guy. One day, in around 1965, I went out to our front gate to get my bundle of newspapers but the courier was someone I hadn't seen before. As I took the bundle of papers from the new courier I asked him where the Sneeds were and he responded, "Mr. and Mrs. Sneed have been murdered."

Shocked, I took the bundle inside and opened it up and pulled out a newspaper. Sure enough, the headline article was about the murder. Mr. and Mrs. Sneed had been found shot to death in their home in Silver City.

A few days later their son Joe delivered the bundle of papers to our front gate. I hadn't seen him for a long time because he had graduated from high school a couple of years earlier and was living out of state. When I took the bundle from him I told him how sorry I was to hear about his parents, and he made a brief reply, like, "Thanks," and got back in his car and left. That was the last time I ever saw him.

A couple of weeks later, as I was reading the newspaper before I started on my delivery route, the headlines stated that Joe Sneed was being held in connection with the death of his parents. He had been living in California and the police discovered a receipt that indicated he had purchased something in route to Silver City on the night his parents were murdered. He allegedly drove from California to Silver City, murdered his parents, and drove back to California. Months later I remember reading about his trial as it progressed, and he was eventually convicted of murder and sent to the State Penitentiary in Santa Fe.

I delivered newspapers in Hurley for seven years. It was always time consuming and required lots of work. Sometimes I had to collect money from customers who were drunk, rude, or accused me of cheating them. Other times people would invite me in for dinner or just chat for several minutes. I always had to be on the lookout for dogs, and once in a while I had to run and jump over a fence to avoid getting bitten.

Periodically a dog would come out and chase me on my motorcycle as I drove by their house. Before long I learned that I could turn my motorcycle around and chase the aggressive dog back into their yard. I found it amusing that dogs were always brave when I was riding away from them, but they were cowardly when I turned around to chase them.

One summer before my senior in high school, I knocked on someone's door to collect for the newspaper and a young mother came to the door wearing only her bra and panties. She was an attractive lady and was friendly, but I was young and naïve and a little embarrassed. I stood on her porch and sheepishly looked down and away from her while she paid me. In hindsight, that was one experience I wish I could redo all over again. If I knew then what I know now, things may have turned out a little differently.

The last street on my delivery route was Nevada Street, and one of the last customers I delivered newspapers to was the home of Mr. Tubby Porkman. Many times Tubby would be sitting in his bedroom plucking away on his electric guitar as I rode by. If I heard him playing, I would ride my motorcycle up to his bedroom window and we would visit for a while. He always played a special little guitar ditty when I showed up because he knew that it made me laugh. He would slide his finger down the neck a couple of times and finally hit a few funny notes to greet me.

Once in a while when we were bored, Tubby and I would climb up onto the roof of his house with his binoculars and look southward toward the Grant County Airport. When Tubby eventually joined the Army and was deployed to Viet Nam, I continued to stop and visit with his mother to catch up on how he was doing.

There were two types of public transportation that served Hurley. The Whitfield Bus Lines from Las Cruces sent a bus to Hurley and the surrounding area in the later 1950's and 1960's. The bus would come to town shortly after noon during the weekdays and take passengers to Silver City, Deming, Las Cruces, and El Paso.

There also was a Frontier Airlines terminal located at the airport south of town. A turbo-prop passenger airplane would shuttle passengers between Hurley and Albuquerque daily and the flight usually took about 45 minutes. My dad often took my brother and I to the airport to watch the airplanes take off and land, and I remember thinking how fun it would be to fly in an airplane someday.

When I was in first grade I became good friends with a kid in my class named Timmy Gardner. He lived down at the Grant County Airport and his dad worked for Frontier Airlines at the time. One Saturday Timmy called me and invited me to come down to the airport and spend the afternoon with him. I was very excited to get a chance to go visit my new friend and spend some time around the airport, so my dad agreed to take me there and drop me off for a few hours.

Timmy and I had a grand time playing around at the airport complex and at his house, which was next to the Frontier Airlines lobby area. We walked around and looked at the airplanes that were parked out on the runway and we watched a couple of airplanes come in for a landing. Then we walked over to the airport radio control terminal where Tuck Grimes and his family lived, and after that we went inside of a hanger to see the parked airplanes. Timmy then took me to see where they refueled private airplanes, and we even watched Timmy's father sell Frontier Airlines tickets and receive luggage from passengers.

Photo 2-8: The Frontier Airlines airplane that came to Hurley was a twin-engine turbo-prop plane that flew back and forth to Albuquerque. Photo courtesy of New Mexico State University Library, Archives and Special Collections.

On the west side of the Frontier Airlines lobby building was a white wooden box about two feet wide by three feet high that had a door on it. It was mounted on a stand and it stood a few feet off the ground. Neither Timmy nor I knew what was inside of this white box but it wasn't long before our curiosity got the best of us.

We reached up and unlatched the door and opened it to take a look inside. Little did we know that we were looking at a field weather station with instruments that provided weather data for the Frontier Airlines terminal. Timmy's dad gathered weather information several times a day and radioed the data to incoming and outgoing aircraft.

The first thing we noticed were gauges and needles on the various instruments, so we reached into the box to touch and play around with them. Before long, we were grabbing the fragile and sensitive needles with our nubby little fingers and twisting them around to see if we could bend or break them. Within a couple of minutes we had either destroyed or damaged nearly every instrument in the white box and rendered the weather station virtually useless. We laughed and laughed as we finally closed the door to the box, and then quickly ran away so that no one would see us fooling around in the area.

Before my afternoon visit with Timmy was done, his dad ventured out to the weather station to routinely gather the weather information he needed. When he opened the door, he immediately noticed that all of the weather gauges had been damaged, and it didn't take him long to figure out who the culprits were. He immediately came looking for Timmy and me and scolded us for trashing the weather station. It wasn't long before my afternoon visit with Timmy was cut short. Timmy and I remained good friends throughout our school days, but I don't remember ever being invited out to the airport again after that incident.

A few weeks after I spent the afternoon at the Grant County Airport with Timmy, a freak storm swept through the complex. In mid-October of 1957 during the early morning hours, a tornado demolished six airplanes and damaged two others. A private hanger was also destroyed and the U.S. Forest Service building nearby was swept 50 feet into the air before it landed on the site of the demolished hanger. Incredibly, the only damage to the Forest Service building was a broken roof beam. Cast iron skillets that had been hanging on the inside wall of the building were still in place after it crashed to the ground. Total damages from the storm were estimated at between $75,000 and $100,000.

The funnel cloud traveled eastward across the airfield, crossed over the tailings south of Hurley, and continued into the mountains south and east of town. Many people were worried that the tornado might hit the Hurley town site but, fortunately, it moved eastward. My older sister said she was released from school later that morning because of the weather threat.

The Mining Operation

The milling and smelting operations of Kennecott Copper Corporation were located to the east of the Hurley town site and employed nearly 1,300 people in the mid to late 1960's. The mine was the economic heartbeat of Hurley and Grant County. If the Chino mine was in full production and copper prices on the global market were high, life was good.

The copper-rich ore was loaded onto train cars at the open pit in Santa Rita and transported to Hurley for milling and smelting. Once the ore arrived in Hurley, its first destination was the primary crusher. The train would back the loaded ore cars into the crusher building where they were rotated upside down and emptied. The heavy boulders of raw ore would fall into large chutes where they were crushed into smaller rocks.

The crushed rock chunks from the primary crusher were then taken by conveyor belt to the secondary crusher and crushed into rocks that were about two inches in diameter. The two-inch aggregate was then taken by conveyor belt to the ball mills, which were large barrel shaped cylinders that crushed the rocks into a powder. Next, the powder was sent to flotation tanks that separated the copper from the remaining ore by adding water and chemicals. From the flotation tanks, the copper rich muck was sent to large cylinders that would dry it back into a powder form and the waste muck was sent to the tailings south of town. Finally, the dry cake powder was sent on to the smelter to be melted down into copper. The molten waste material from the smelter was called "slag" and was transported to the slag dump north of the smelter via a smaller slag train.

Photo 2-9: The Santa Fe train engine is shown backing the loaded ore cars into the primary crusher, one by one. Also notice the plant safety and security building in the foreground. The main employee entrance into the plant was through the three doors on the right side of this building. Judging from the cars in the parking lot, this picture must have been taken sometime after 1961. The parking lot was located at the east end of Romero Street. Photo courtesy of Terry Humble.

Photo 2-10: A train car is being turned upside down in the primary crusher. The ore would empty into a chute below the car, where it would be crushed into smaller rocks. Photo courtesy of New Mexico State University Library, Archives and Special Collections.

Whitewater Creek was a small creek that started near the Santa Rita open pit and ran along the eastern edge of Bayard and eventually east of Hurley. The water in the creek was contaminated by the Chino Mine and had a high concentration of copper in it. There were a few smalltime entrepreneurs who used to collect hundreds of pounds of cans and set up small leaching operations along Whitewater Creek. First, they would lay the cans on the ground and run over them in their car or truck until all of the cans were flattened. They would then place the cans in the creek and leave them there for a few weeks until the copper-tainted water would leave deposits of copper on the cans. When the cans were ready, they would gather them up from the creek and sell them to Kennecott for a small profit.

A large power plant building used natural gas to heat water in order to power the steam turbines. These turbines generated electricity and provided power to run much of the operation. The power plant also had a loud whistle that ran on pressurized steam and could be heard for miles away.

The whistle blew several times per day to signal shift changes for employees. It went off at 6:30 a.m. to wake people up and 7:30 a.m. and 4:30 p.m. everyday to signal the shift changes. It also blew at 9:30 p.m. to signal the town curfew (kids under the age of 15 or 16 were supposed to be off the streets by then). If a fire broke out somewhere in town or in the plant, the whistle would blow a coded series of long and short toots, which indicated the general location of the fire. On New Year's Eve there was always some joker working the graveyard shift in the power plant that would blow the whistle with a variety of toots to usher in the New Year.

It was amusing to watch the dogs in Hurley react to the whistle. They would usually howl when the whistle blew on schedule, but when there was a fire and the whistle pitches changed for an extended period of time, Hurley would break out into a state of canine pandemonium. Every dog in town would sit on his haunches with his head straight up in the air and howl until the whistle finally stopped.

There were lots of different noises coming from the plant throughout the day and night. Everyone got used to it and after a while you didn't even notice it unless there was something out of the ordinary. I remember many summer nights sitting out in someone's yard listening to the train engine as it maneuvered ore cars, one by one, into the primary crusher to be uncoupled, turned upside down, and emptied. Then you could hear the banging of metal-against-metal as the cars were being coupled together, or the slamming of huge falling rocks as they fell into the crusher chute. Sometimes loud hisses could be heard, like massive amounts of compressed air or steam being released. And then there was the loud drone of giant electric motors as they turned heavy pieces of equipment. If the wind direction was just right, odors from various parts of the plant would subtly waft into the evening air over town.

On warm evenings I would occasionally see Oscar Bates, who was a foreman in the Power Plant, walking to work for the graveyard shift. He always wore a khaki long sleeve work shirt, khaki pants with hard toed boots, and carried his lunch bucket in one hand. He wore safety glasses and had his white hardhat firmly planted on his head, which indicated that he was a foreman.

Many times his wife Lois would walk him to the main gate of the plant and bid him farewell for the evening.

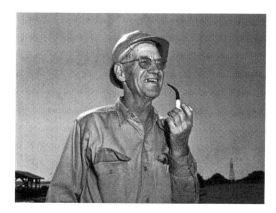

Photo 2-11: Oscar Bates and family lived a few doors away from my family. I probably spent more time during my childhood at the Bates' home than I did my own. Photo courtesy of New Mexico State University Library, Archives and Special Collections.

Every summer around July 4th the plant closed for a "vacation shutdown" that lasted a couple of weeks. Kennecott would begin their maintenance program by doing things like rebuilding the brick furnaces in the smelter and replacing the metal liners that were bolted inside of the ball mills. Many employees used this downtime to take family vacations. Little League baseball season always ended before the shutdown so that families could leave town without interrupting the baseball schedule.

Kennecott was a company that took a very active role in the community. The company was good about hiring college-aged kids during the summers to help put them through school. I worked for two summers in the comptroller's office and one summer as a laborer in the mill to help pay for my college expenses.

The company also held a summer picnic for employees and hosted an annual open house for several years in the mid 1950's. During the open house and at various awards ceremonies, the company gave away things like plastic key chains with small particles of copper encased inside, ceramic ashtrays with the Kennecott logo on them, little miniature ingots of copper, solid copper ash trays, or even nice cigarette lighters with the company logo on the side.

Company employees enjoyed good retirement and health care benefits during the 1950's and 1960's. The unions were strong and wages were generally very good, especially compared to wages in other businesses around Grant County.

The prosperity, however, didn't come without its share of problems. There were instances where the negotiated job descriptions between management and the unions were so rigid that employees were not able to do simple tasks because it wasn't in their job description. For example, a plumber couldn't pound a nail because that task was only in the job description of the carpenters. So, the carpenter would stand around and kill time watching the plumber work until the plumber needed the nail to be pounded. Once the carpenter pounded the nail, they would continue to stand around doing nothing until they were needed again.

The company was also plagued with theft at all levels of plant operations. Little things like work gloves and hand tools were easy to carry out in a lunch bucket at the end of the shift. There were also stories of employees driving truckloads of equipment out of the plant in broad daylight.

Employee work ethic was another problem plaguing the company. The plant was fairly large and had lots of hiding places where employees could go to avoid doing any work. I remember people jokingly refer to their job at Kennecott as "working down at the Lazy K".

Throughout the 1950's and most of the 1960's there was only one smokestack in Hurley until a second larger stack was built in 1967. The smaller, older stack was 500 feet tall and the newer stack was 625 feet in height. Day by day, as Hurley residents observed the construction of the new stack, workers could be seen walking around on scaffolds several hundred feet above the ground. I remember being very impressed at the nerve these employees had to be able to work in that environment. The completion of the new stack was considered a milestone because it was it an engineering feat as well as a major landmark for pilots, travelers, and hikers.

Photo 2-12: Until 1967 there was only one smokestack in Hurley. Photo courtesy of New Mexico State University Library, Archives and Special Collections.

Several years after the second stack was in operation, I was discussing the project with my father. He mentioned to me that his friend, Larry Elliot, worked on the stack project as an electrician. Larry, who was a great guy but had a serious drinking problem, eventually lost his family and several jobs due to his alcoholism. I asked my dad if Larry was drinking when he worked on the stack and he said, "Yeah, he would work up on the stack during the day and then get really drunk in the evenings. I'm sure that there were many days when Larry went to work while he was still half-in-the-bag from the night before."

For many residents of Hurley, the smokestacks were used informally as a unit of measurement. For example, I was hiking with a friend one day in the Gila National Forest and he asked me, "How tall do you think that mountain up ahead is?"

I thought about it for a minute and then replied, "Oh, probably about one and a half smokestacks."

Photo 2-13: The second smokestack was built in 1967 and was 625 feet high. The smokestacks were landmarks for motorists traveling north on Highway 180 from Deming, and for many residents in Silver City. Photo courtesy of New Mexico State University Library, Archives and Special Collections.

The tailings were located south and east of Hurley below the ballparks. They were vast, mountainous tiers of white-yellowish sand that was a waste by-product of the milling process. This low-grade sand was mixed with water and piped to the tailings in the form of slurry. The large wooden pipes had openings at intervals along the way and would spill the slurry onto the surface below. Once the slurry dried into a sandy powder, bulldozers would spread it out to form a terraced landscape several layers high. On the north end of the tailings was a large lake called Lake One that served as a reservoir for the plant operations. There was also a small office building about a mile south of the Hurley little league baseball field that served as a headquarters for the company employees who worked at the tailings.

This office building near the tailings was of special importance to the kids from Hurley because the men who worked there did not want us trespassing on the tailings. If we ever did get caught hiking around there, these men would take us back to the Security office and call our parents and/or threaten to arrest us for trespassing.

That threat obviously never stopped us from sneaking down there to play anyway. We rarely got caught because we had a few rules of survival. Rule number one was to always stay away from service roads to avoid being seen. Rule number two was to hit the dirt if we heard a company truck pass nearby. Rule number three was to say that we were alone if we ever got caught. We figured it would be better if only one of the kids in our group got in trouble instead of the entire group.

Photo 2-14: Wooden pipelines carried the slurry of waste material from the mill to the tailings. The material dried into a white colored powder and formed the large dunes south of Hurley. Photo courtesy of New Mexico State University Library, Archives and Special Collections.

When the coast was clear it was fun to hike on top of the tailings because the landscape was so stark that it seemed like we were walking on the moon. Sometimes we would play Army there when we had a group of kids together. When we got to the edge of one of the tiers, it was fun to roll down to the next tier in the soft sand. We didn't realize it at the time, but the tailings sand had residual, low levels of assorted chemicals and toxins left over from the milling process that could have potentially caused health issues. In fact, one time I came home from rolling down the tiers and I developed an itchy rash on my body.

During the winter snowstorms, it wasn't unusual for kids to find an old car hood and turn it into a sled by simply inverting it. We would attach it to the rear bumper of a car with a long rope and pull it up and down the streets and roads around Hurley. During the snowy Christmas break of my senior year in high school, some friends and I decided to pull a car hood on the road that went around the tailings. After everyone had a turn riding on the car hood, we stopped at the base of the tailings to take a break. While we were standing around talking, someone came up with the bright idea of dragging the car hood several tiers up the tailings and sledding down to the bottom. We figured the slope at the edge of each tier was about 40 degrees and the sled run was about 40 feet to the next tier. Each tier leveled out briefly before it dropped off sharply to the next one.

After some discussion, we took turns dragging the car hood to the top of the third tier. Once we got there and looked down from above, we realized the tiers were much steeper and scarier than we had anticipated from below. Initially no one was eager to volunteer to fly down the hill on the old car hood, but after a little teasing and arm-twisting, Toby Parker stepped up and volunteered to make the run.

Photo 2-15: The tailings were terraced and had long steep slopes that made for a scary sled ride in the snow. Photo courtesy of New Mexico State University Library, Archives and Special Collections.

We placed the hood near the edge of the tier and Toby hopped on. A couple of us got behind the hood and pushed him over the edge and watched him accelerate toward the next tier. Within a couple of seconds it became obvious this was going to be the ride of a lifetime. When he hit the level area at the bottom of the first tier he was unable to stop or slow down before he launched out over the edge of the second tier. From there, he became airborne and never touched the ground again until he slammed into the snow 40 feet below.

Looking down from above, we were amazed at how long he was in the air. It was as if he was in slow motion; the car hood gradually separated from Toby as he quietly accelerated toward the ground. Then, all of a sudden, the ride ended abruptly with a huge "Kawhaaaam". We were laughing so hard that the tears were freezing on our cheeks.

Toby was stunned from the impact of the fall and immediately got up and sprinted about 50 yards back to the car. He jumped inside and closed and locked the doors and didn't come back out again. Later on as we were driving away, Toby admitted that he was going so fast and fell so far that it scared the living hell out of him. Toby was the best stuntman I have ever known, but this was the first time I ever saw him visibly shaken.

Fun Places Near Hurley

The main reason for hiking across the tailings south of town was because it was the shortest route to our favorite hiking destination. Giant's Bathtub was a swimming hole about a mile and a half east of the tailings and south of Little Geronimo Mountain. It took most of the day to get there and back from Hurley, so we made sack lunches, filled up our canteens, and left town fairly early in the morning. It was the only place near Hurley to go skinny-dipping in the heat of the summer. The Hispanic kids that hiked there referred to Giant's Bathtub as "Las Pilas".

Giants Bathtub was a swimming hole made from large slabs of rock that were situated below a waterfall. It was fed by an arroyo that was dry for most of the year but magically trapped an abundance of water during the rainy months. The main feature that made Giant's Bathtub a great hiking destination was the waterfall and tall rocks that surrounded the pool. The pool was about five or six feet deep when it was full and kids used to climb up on the rocks and jump into the water. There also was a nice large, flat rock with lots of sun exposure where you could lie down to dry off, get a tan, or eat a sack lunch with friends. The swimming hole was very remote and somewhat difficult to find, and rarely was anyone else there.

Once in a while an afternoon windstorm would develop while we were walking across the tailings from Giant's Bathtub. The wind blew so hard at times we had to tie a handkerchief over our faces in order to breathe and keep sand out of our mouths and noses. Sometimes we had to seek out a place to hole up until the wind subsided. Unfortunately, the tailings were so vast and flat that it was difficult to find cover. We usually came home with tailings sand lodged everywhere and would have to take a shower and change clothes to get rid of the grit.

About three miles west of Hurley is a drainage called Cameron Creek. Kennecott Copper Corp. had a lime quarry near there and they maintained a good road from North Hurley to the quarry. North of the quarry was a rough dirt road that eventually dropped into Cameron Creek. A small grove of cottonwood trees near where the road crossed the creek provided shade for a popular picnic spot. There were always empty beer bottles, broken glass, and used condoms at the grove, but otherwise a perfect place for parties and gatherings. We spent many evenings drinking there when I was in high school because it was safe and we rarely saw traffic out that way. If you continued up the road from the cottonwood grove you would eventually head north past Craun's Pond and connect with what is now Race Track Road in Arenas Valley.

When I was younger we would hike or ride our bicycles out to Cameron Creek and spend the day walking around looking for Native American artifacts or old mine shafts. Sometimes we ate our lunches in the shade trees at Craun's Pond or maybe we would hike down Cameron Creek to look for fossils and explore a cave that was there. There was also an old homestead ruin upstream from the cotton wood grove that was supposedly the family home of a man from

Hurley named Spike Kelly.

When we were about nine or ten years old, my neighbor Jimmy Robbins had an August birthday party under the cottonwood grove at Cameron Creek. The first thing all of the boys at the party did was go down into the dry creek bed to play because it was about 10 feet below ground level and had several interesting vertical dirt embankments on either side which formed a small box canyon. As the creek wound its way upstream to the north, we would hide in the nooks and crannies of the dirt walls and chase each other around in the sandy creek bed.

When it was time for the kids to have the birthday lunch, an adult came to the top of the embankment and yelled down to us. One by one, we all found our way up out of the creek through small openings in the embankment and returned to the shade of the cottonwood grove to enjoy our hot dogs and hamburgers.

We hadn't been up out of the creek for more than a minute when we began to hear a faint rumbling noise off in the distance. After a few seconds the noise and vibration became more intense and it sounded like it was coming from the creek. Out of curiosity, several of us ran over to the edge of the embankment to peek into the creek to see what was going on. As we were looking upstream toward the source of the rumbling crescendo, a huge wall of water raced around a bend and came roaring past us. It was a flash flood that was about four feet tall with water the color of mud. I stood there watching as it swept by, thinking to myself, "If we had remained down in the creek two minutes longer we would have all been swept downstream."

On Sunday mornings my father would occasionally take my brother, cousin James, and me cruising out to Cameron Creek or the Ridge Road in our '49 Chevy two-door coupe. He would let us take turns driving the car and sometimes we would pull over to practice target shooting with his 22-caliber rifle. My mother packed lunches, snacks, and eight ounce bottles of Coca Cola for us boys while my dad drank beer. Our Sunday morning outings were probably the best bonding experiences I had with the males of the family during my childhood. They also were the only reprieves my mother had from us during the week and I'm sure she enjoyed having the house to herself.

Learning to drive our car was one of my greatest thrills while growing up. When I was young I would sit on my dad's lap and steer the car while he shifted, accelerated, and braked. When I got older and my legs were long enough to reach the floorboard I would drive while my father sat in the passenger seat. We usually drove along the Ridge Road or the Whitewater Road until we reached Highway 90. From there, my father would drive into Silver City and back to Hurley.

Somewhere along the way we would stop and set up beer cans or bottles to be used as targets for our 22-caliber rifle. It wasn't unusual for us to use up a box or two of ammo while target shooting from various distances away. Sometimes we leaned over the hood of the car and sometimes we shot while kneeling, sitting, or standing. My dad would give us tips like, "Don't flinch," or "Squeeze the trigger as if you were squeezing a lemon."

My dad told us an interesting story about how he came to own his 22 rifle.

At the beginning of World War II when my dad was stationed at Ft. Bliss, some soldier was shipping out to the war, was hard up for money, and sold him a pawn ticket to the rifle for $15. The next day he went to the pawn shop in downtown El Paso and claimed the rifle. It was always his favorite rifle because he liked the peep sight that was mounted on it.

One unusual memory I have of our Sunday outings is the way my dad used to flick his empty beer cans out the driver's side window as he drove down the road. He held the top of the can with his fingertips and used a backhand flicking motion to toss it out. Later on when I was in high school, I employed the exact same flicking motion to throw my own beer cans. (Up until the late 1960's it was common for people in the Grant County area to litter, but the environmental movement gained traction when I was in college and littering soon became taboo). Interestingly, this also became the same technique I used to toss a rolled up newspaper onto a customer's front porch or lawn when I was a paperboy. I eventually adapted and further perfected the technique when I learned how to throw a Frisbee.

By the time I was in high school, the Ridge Road, Whitewater Road, and Cameron Creek were our "drinking grounds" of choice and we spent many evenings "cruising and boozing" there. We usually cruised with a carload of guys and a couple of cases of beer in an ice chest and would creep down the roads, going about 10 miles an hour. We would stop frequently for bathroom breaks or just to get out of the car and lean against the hood and drink beer. Sometimes, if we had a football, Frisbee, or a baseball with us, we would play catch until the sun went down. If we ran out of beer while it was still early in the evening, we would drive back to the Hurley Bar or the Pénjamo and restock our ice chest and set out for some other destination.

PART II: STORIES, CONFESSIONS, AND OPINIONS

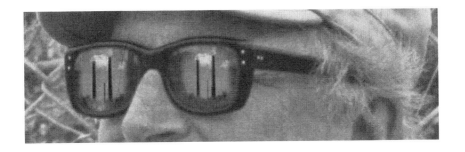

CHAPTER THREE: HURLEY POLITICAL AND SOCIAL ETHOS

"Hmmm. So you think they were weird back then, huh?"

Up until 1955, Kennecott Copper Corp. owned the town of Hurley. The company maintained all of the houses, the schools, the businesses, the streets, sewer pipes, and the utility infrastructure. When I was about four or five years old we had a bedroom added onto our house and the carpenters who did the work were Kennecott employees. Kennecott also made the decisions on what to fix up and what to tear down, what streets were paved, which employees lived in the nicer homes, and what the town ordinances were. If the company didn't want you to live in Hurley they could ask you to leave town.

The railroad tracks that ran through Hurley created a social barrier of separation between the Hispanics and the Anglos, but on the south side of town there was yet another level of social stratification. A person's position in the company would, in many cases, determine who your friends were, how much prestige you had around town, or the size of your house. Skilled craftsmen and blue-collar workers lived in the smaller, lap-board siding homes, while the engineers, foremen, and middle management employees lived in larger homes, usually referred to as "bungalows". The upper management personnel lived in the largest and nicest homes in town.

On Dec. 1, 1955 Kennecott sold the town of Hurley to John W. Galbreath, who in turn sold the homes to individuals. Hurley was now a municipality. Once these houses went on the open market, people could buy whatever home they could afford, although many people ended up buying the home they were living in at the time. A city government with elected officials was formed and people were hired on for municipal positions such as maintenance workers, clerks, and police officers. Some Hispanics bought houses on the south side of town and a few Gringos bought houses on the north side of the tracks, thus beginning an era of neighborhood integration.

The first city council convened sometime after Hurley became a municipality. The first Mayor of Hurley was a company carpenter named Dave Byington, and there were four members serving on the city council. I knew councilman Allard Bartlett better than the others because he was my little league coach and he and his wife did a lot of things for the community and for the kids of Hurley. His two sons, Bryan and Bub, were good friends of mine and we had some great times playing team sports with the kids in our neighborhood.

Photo 3-1: This is a photo of the first Hurley Town Council in 1956. From left to right are Chris Pena, Richard Elvira, possibly an unknown attorney holding the notebook, Mayor Dave Byington standing on the right, Allard Bartlett, and Shorty Smith. Photo courtesy of Bub Bartlett.

A few years later, I remember seeing Mayor Harold Trapp and his wife Emma drive slowly around town frequently in their black 1955 Buick. They gazed out the window of their car as they observed how people kept their yards, checked up on town infrastructure, and even admired everyone's Christmas lighting during the holidays. My friends and I found it amusing the way that Mr. and Mrs. Trapp appeared to lord over their new municipality and loyal subjects, all from behind the wheel of their car. If they happened to drive down the same street where we were playing a game of touch football, the kids on both teams would fall to their knees and bow down in a mock display of allegiance as the Mayor and First Lady drove by.

Every three years the contract between the unions and the company had to be renegotiated by June 30th. On several occasions the two sides could not find common ground and the unions would go on strike until the contract was settled. If the strike lasted for more than a month or two, many families had to leave town and search for work elsewhere. It was fairly common for kids in my class to be gone when school started in August and then enroll later in the school year when their father returned to his job in Hurley.

During the strikes, the union would set up a picket line at the main gate entrance on Romero Street to keep employees from entering the plant to go to work. Once in a while Hurley residents would hear about "scabs" that tried to cross the picket line and were presumably roughed up by the union picketers. One strong union supporter named Ray Brindley used to drive around town in his old white Jeep whenever a strike was under way. He always had large signs propped up in the back of the jeep that read "SCAB PATROL".

It was peculiar and interesting to note that during the strikes, no matter how long they lasted, the Hurley Bar parking lot was always full of cars from morning until night. I was continually amazed at how people who were unemployed could afford to hang out at the bar and drink for several hours a day. Whenever the strikes lasted for several months, many families couldn't buy groceries or school clothes for their children and were forced to go into debt. Some families would run up their charge account at the Hurley Stores in hopes the strike would soon be settled and they could pay off their debt before it got out of control.

From the mid 1950's to mid 1960's Hurley seemed to reflect many of the values of America in general. Families were trying to keep up with the times by purchasing their first television set, while kids were encouraged to join Cub Scouts, Brownies, Boy and Girl Scouts, Rainbow Girls, or DeMolay. Just about everyone in town knew each other, which made it difficult for us kids to get away with mischief. Maybe that's one reason why I enjoyed raising a little hell around town…it was a challenge to keep from getting caught.

In the mid 1950's, several families in town dug huge holes in their yard to build bomb shelters that would keep their families safe from Russian atomic bombs and nuclear missiles. Schools and radio stations had test runs and drills to prepare the public in the event we were bombed or overrun by those pesky communists. There was strong anti-union sentiment among many conservative people in town because they believed that unions were just another form of communism.

At Cobre High School, boys wore flat top haircuts and had a varsity athletic program. Girls had to wear dresses to school and had no varsity athletic program. Kids were supposed to say "yes sir" and "yes ma'am" to adults, and they were discouraged from questioning authority. Corporal punishment was the strong right hand of the public school justice system, and when the school was done beating your skinny little butt, you got spanked again when you got home. The courts prosecuted criminals fairly and justly and people were hired based on their job experience, education, and character, unless they knew somebody or had a lot of money. All in all, it was the heyday of America, and consumerism and economic expansion were the driving forces behind it.

Up until the early 1950's in Hurley, the mines were influential in perpetuating discrimination against Hispanics. The layout of the town of Hurley and the segregated schools created a barrier of separation between the Anglos and Hispanics, while the conditions inside the plant reinforced racial discrimination on the job. Fortunately, things began to change by the time I entered school in 1956. There were several factors that contributed to this change.

The Empire Zinc Strike in 1953 should be given a tremendous amount of credit for ushering in a new era of racial tolerance and opportunity in Grant County. The unions that represented mine workers were instrumental in the fight for fairness and equality in the workplace throughout my entire childhood. They helped to jumpstart the civil rights movement that would sweep the country a few years later.

Another factor that made a huge impact on the community was when Kennecott sold the town of Hurley to John W. Galbreath in 1955. Kennecott could no longer control where everyone lived and the residents of Hurley were free to buy whatever house they could afford. Over time the areas of North Hurley and South Hurley became more integrated and the railroad tracks that separated them became less of a barrier.

The one factor that arguably affected the kids in my age group the most was the integration of the Hurley elementary schools in 1955. Beginning with my first year in school I made friends with many Hispanic children and took an early interest in our cultural differences. For example, I remember sitting out on the steps of Mrs. Holly's first grade classroom one morning during recess as I talked with a Hispanic boy that had become my friend. I was trying to get him to teach me Spanish. I would ask him how to say certain words in Spanish and he did his best to translate for me.

Organized sports like Little League baseball and school athletic programs also provided kids of all ethnicities an opportunity to become friends based on a common interest. By the time I graduated from high school, many of my classmates felt the experiences and opportunities of our generation were instrumental in helping to dismantle the strong historic barriers of social prejudice that existed in Hurley prior to the school integration process.

Although there were many people in Grant County who began to embrace cultural diversity, racial prejudice in various forms remained alive and well. For example, many Anglo kids would have to sneak out to go on dates with Hispanic kids. If their secret was discovered, their parents would be furious or they would be ostracized or belittled by their friends. One of my friends up the street had an older sister who was berated because she ended up marrying a Hispanic guy. Another interesting situation arose when a girl from a prominent family in Hurley dated a Hispanic boy from Cobre High School who was one of the best athletes in the state at the time. It was amusing to observe how carefully the Anglos chose their words when there was discussion about this particular couple. The gossip circles probably would have ripped them to shreds if they had been average kids from average families.

The kids in Hurley loved winter snowstorms because the schools would close for the day and we would be free to go play in the snow. One winter activity that Hurley kids looked forward to was what we called "The Annual Mexican/Gringo Snowball Fight" that took place between the Hurley Store buildings at the underpass. By midmorning, a group of Hispanic kids from the north side of the tracks would slowly emerge from the underpass, snowballs in hand, and cautiously spread out into the parking lot where the Gringos would be waiting for them. Things were always exciting and tense at first because we never knew how many kids from the north side of town would show up. Our goal was to hold our own in the parking lot and ultimately drive the Chicanos back into the underpass and chase them back to the north side of town. If the Gringos were seriously outnumbered, we would have to either take a butt kicking in the parking lot or retreat back across Cortez Avenue. I remember the snowball fights were always fun, with no one ever getting injured or getting into a fight. The next day at school we would get a good laugh with our Hispanic schoolmates as we talked about the highlights from the day before.

When I was a senior in high school in 1968, a Hispanic friend and I were in Hurley one afternoon and decided to go to the Chino Club to get a soda. We entered the Club and went to the concession stand counter and ordered our drinks. The lady behind the counter brought us the sodas and then subtly called me aside. When I went over to speak with her she pointed to my friend and said in a low voice, "He's not supposed to be in here."

Surprised, I asked her, "Why not?" and she responded, "Because he's a Mexican."

I couldn't believe what I had just heard. I was truly shocked. I turned and walked over to my friend and said, "C'mon, let's get out of here."

How sad. I had spent my entire life going to the Chino Club to play pool, ping pong, listen to the juke box, bowl, and hang out with my friends, but when I walked out the door with my friend that spring day of 1968, I never returned again. At the time I didn't realize it, but this incident turned out to be one of the defining moments in my life in terms of how I was personally affected by the remnants of institutional racism that somehow managed to slip through the cracks of the civil rights movement.

One Sunday morning in around 1971 I was sitting in my living room on Elguea Street reading the Sunday El Paso Times. As I was reading, I happened to glance out the window and noticed a group of people walking up the street. As they got closer I realized there must have been about 15 people, all younger men, and all wearing brown berets. They appeared to be marching in unison as a form of protest, but I don't recall whether they were shouting or carrying any signs. I had heard of a militant Hispanic group that called themselves the Brown Berets, but I can't say for sure if these guys were the real Brown Berets or not. Anyway, I was really surprised to see them marching up Elguea Street in Hurley, New Mexico. I don't remember hearing or reading any stories about whether they caused any trouble, but I know for sure they got everyone's attention. They were obviously from out of town and were marching, presumably, to make people aware of Hispanic rights. I can only speculate, but they may have chosen Hurley because of its history of segregation and unfair labor practices at the mines.

In the mid 1950's and early 1960's, there were a few young men and older boys in the area that enjoyed "souping-up" cars and driving everywhere at high rates of speed. My first exposure to this culture came when my older sister started dating boys. One afternoon a couple of teenaged boys from Silver City came to Hurley to take my sister for a ride in their 1953 Ford. The car had flames painted behind the front wheel wells and it was loud and fast. The boys were probably typical Grant County "hot-rodder" types who loved to work on their cars and enjoyed racing other cars on the streets or highways. I thought that they were cool guys and one day they even took me for a ride in their hot-rod.

Many of the "hot-rodders" around town were sort of cowboy or country folks who wore western yoke shirts with snaps instead of buttons. Some had their hair slicked back on the sides and some had flat top haircuts. Some smoked cigarettes and rolled the pack up into the sleeve of their tee shirt. A lot of the hot-rodders used to hang out at the T and H Drive-In across the street from the Silver City Women's Club, which was a great place to show off their cars and find challengers to race. Two stretches of highway that were popular for racing were the highway between Silver City and Cliff, and the highway between Hurley and Deming.

When my older sister was in high school she dated a guy named Don Clifton who always had cool cars. He used to pick her up for dates in a nice looking two tone 1954 Ford that had the spare tire mounted above the rear fender and had fender skirts covering the rear wheels. Later on he drove a green 1957 Pontiac CJ2 that had three two-barrel carburetors that came stock from the factory. The Pontiac ran pretty fast, but after a few years he bought a new 1966 Mustang. The Mustang was also really cool, but he got rid of it to buy a beautiful 1964 Thunderbird, which in my opinion was the best car he ever owned. He let me borrow it one night to take a girl to the prom at Cobre High School, and I was in "hog-heaven".

Don also had a 1953 Ford that didn't look like much of a car because the paint job was faded and ugly, but it was a "sleeper". It had a 427 cubic inch motor stuffed underneath the hood that was powerful enough to snap the back of your head against the car seat when he shifted gears. This car could smoke the tires in three gears and accelerated like a jet.

Unfortunately, the popular trend of "hot-rodding" around the county wasn't without its casualties. I remember a few stories about teenage car wrecks in the mid to late 1950's that were the talk of the town. Perhaps the most tragic accident of all involved a young man from the area named Phillip Spruill, who had just bought a new 1957 Oldsmobile Rocket 88. Phillip was well known among my sister's friends as well as the "hot-rodder" crowd in Grant County.

It was early May of 1957 when Phillip and three of his friends set out on a high speed drive from the T and H Drive-In. The 1957 Oldsmobile had a powerful V-8 engine that could run at speeds in excess of 120 miles per hour and the boys were eager to see what the car could do on the roads in the area. There was some debate as to the exact route they drove that fateful day, but most people agree their intended route was from Silver City to Lordsburg, then on to Deming, and back to Silver City.

The story was they rolled into Deming from Lordsburg and headed north toward Hurley on Highway 180, which was a narrow two-lane highway at the time. They sped along Highway 180, passed the turn-off to the Grant County Airport, and powered their way up the hill and around a sweeping curve near the old pumping station settlement just south of Hurley called Apache Tejo. When they were about a quarter of a mile north of Apache Tejo, they lost control and the car flipped over, killing everyone inside. One boy died at the scene, two others died not long after the accident, and another died about two weeks later. I think every teenager in Grant County knew at least one person in that accident.

When I attended Cobre High School from 1965-68 the Viet Nam war was in full swing. As a sophomore I started to make friends with a few older classmates, and many of them went into the military service after graduation. At the time, the military was drafting the non-college-bound 18-year-old boys right out of high school. They were given a "1-A" draft rating, which meant they were prime candidates to be drafted into the Army to serve a two-year hitch. Boys that attended college were given a "4-F" deferment and weren't eligible to be drafted unless they quit college or flunked out. After high school, most boys didn't have the luxury of finding work or traveling or living at home and hanging around with friends. They either served in the military or stayed in school.

Boys that were drafted didn't get to choose their career field. The Army trained them and put them wherever they were needed. If you decided to join the Army for a three-year hitch you got to choose a career field, but they still shipped you to wherever they needed you. Your only other option for military service was to join another branch of the service before you got drafted. For those who were drafted into the Army or joined the Marines, there was a very high probability that you would end up in a combat role. All in all, it didn't take long to figure out that no matter which branch of the service you joined, your odds of going to Viet Nam were pretty high.

American involvement in the Viet Nam war happened less than 20 years after World War II and many of our parents had served in that war. Since World War II was still a part of so many people's lives, many adults in our community felt that it was important for high school graduates to "answer the call of duty" and "serve your country". They felt that joining the military was the patriotic thing to do in time of war. Questioning the purpose of the war or the draft was not really an option for high school graduates at the time.

As young soldiers began returning from their tour of duty in Viet Nam, they would come home and reconnect with their friends and loved ones. But, as more and more veterans returned, it became clear that this generation of veterans had a different attitude about the Viet Nam war than their parents. Most of my vet friends were telling me things like, "Go to college so that you won't get drafted," or, "This war is totally fucked up," or, "If you don't do everything you can to stay out of the military and Viet Nam, you're a dumb ass."

These conflicting messages from our peers and adults in the community created an interesting dilemma for many of us high school seniors who were getting ready to graduate. To complicate the issue even further, we could see from the news on TV that college students around the country were beginning to question authority and speak out against the war. Who were we supposed to believe? Our parents? The media? The Army recruiter? Our friends? College kids that we didn't even know?

One afternoon shortly after I graduated from high school, I was visiting my friend Tammy Williams, who lived in North Hurley. Kids were always coming and going from their home because the Williams daughters had lots of friends. During my visit, one of our friends who had just returned from Viet Nam happened to drop by. He had graduated from Cobre High School about three years before Tammy and me and had also grown up in Hurley. In fact, I had known him and his family all of my life.

He sat down with us at the kitchen table and asked, "Is anyone interested in seeing some photos from Viet Nam?"

None of us had ever seen war pictures of Viet Nam before, so he laid a fairly large stack of photos on the kitchen table that were taken from a Polaroid Instamatic Camera. (The "Instamatic" camera was popular because the film had some chemical on it that miraculously developed the color photos within a minute after they were taken...no need to send the negatives off to get developed). As we began to thumb through the photos, we were shocked to see photo after photo of U.S. soldiers standing on top of piles of human bodies while holding up decapitated Viet Cong soldiers' heads by the hair, one in each hand, as if they were showing off sport hunting trophies to their beer-drinking buddies. I had never witnessed such overt, yet casual carnage in my entire life. After viewing these photos, I realized that Viet Nam was probably not the safest place to spend a year of one's life.

Grant County has a rich and colorful history steeped in drinking culture and "borrachohood". By the time I was in high school it was purported that Grant County had the second highest rate of alcohol consumption per capita in the entire United States. The only county in the U.S. that drank more than we did was some anonymous county near the Pittsburgh steel mills. Naturally, we believed the mining and ranching industries in our area, as well as the Grant County frontier mentality and proximity to the Mexican border, were the primary reasons so many people drank copious amounts of booze on a daily basis.

I can say with absolute certainty there was no shortage of bars in Grant County during the 1950's and 1960's, especially on the eastern side of the county. If you were to go bar hopping from Hurley to Bayard and then on to other towns, the number of bars you could stop at was absolutely staggering (no pun intended). There were several bars, such as the Pénjamo, the Brown Derby, and the Casa Blanca, that had large dance floors and stages for live music, and when they hosted Mexican wedding dances they were totally packed with hundreds of people. On several occasions, when I drove by the Casa Blanca I saw dozens of cars that had to park along the highway to Mimbres because the parking lot was totally full.

Even though it was illegal to sell package liquor on Sundays back then, there were certain bars that would clandestinely sell booze "to go". Everyone knew who they were and all you had to do was pull up to the package liquor window and push the electric doorbell button. Within seconds an employee would come to the window and slide it open and poke their head out to take a look around the parking lot. If the coast was clear, they would ask you, "What do you want?"

Bar owners made a lot of money from Sunday liquor sales because they were taking a huge risk. They also knew that the customers were probably hard up for booze and were eager and willing to pay a high price. To no one's surprise, liquor prices nearly doubled. And, as long as they were selling booze illegally, they really didn't care whether the customer was a minor.

High school kids usually had to buy beer using fake I.D.s. I was given a New Mexico driver's license and Social Security card from my friend Sido Bates the night before he left for Viet Nam. He told me, "Have a great time with these cards because I may never be back."

Sido's I.D. was like having a free pass to the beer cooler of every bar in the county. I was rarely turned away from a package liquor window or a bar, and thanks to the I.D.s I was able to fuel countless dozens of parties and "pedas" as a minor. In fact, I eventually became such a regular customer at the Pénjamo Bar in North Hurley that the guy at the drive-up window gave me a free half pint of Jim Beam as a Christmas present for two years in a row.

There is an urban legend (OK, a Hurley legend) about a man who used to live up the street from me that would set a couple of cans of Schlitz on his fences when he mowed his lawn. Whenever he pushed the mower over to the east side of his yard he would stop and take a drink from one of the beers, and when he mowed to the west side he would take a drink from the other one. His lawn never looked that great, but he never complained about mowing it.

The Eastside Barhoppers
***

Just to give you an accurate understanding of how things were back then, I would like to take you on an imaginary drinking adventure that represents a collage of true stories and events. These forays into the world of binge drinking are referred to in Spanish as "la peda".

For fun, I would like to insert you into the story so that you can experience the adventure firsthand. It will be you who walks into an air-conditioned bar on a hot summer afternoon and encounters that cool blast of stale beer and urine as soon as you open the door. It will be you that puts your quarter on the pool table and uses the crooked, beer-sticky pool stick, and it will be you that does your very best to drive your car to the next bar without running it off into a canyon or smashing into a tree somewhere along the way.

Oh, and by the way, every bar in this story really existed.

To begin this story, let's say that it was a very hot summer day in Hurley and you happened to be a restless and somewhat bored young man. You and a friend decide to drive around and hit a bar or two until you find something to do, such as meet women, get into a fight over a pool game, or find someone to argue with about religion or politics.

Now, to get things started you would obviously head up to the Hurley Bar and belly up for an ice cold beer because that is the nearest bar. If nothing was going on there, and there was a good chance that nothing was, you would buy a six-pack for the road and head up Cortez Avenue towards the highway. By the time you get to the west end of Cortez Ave., you and your friend already have your first beers polished off and are opening number two of the remaining six pack. (Proper "Hurley Beer Drinking Etiquette" dictates that whenever the driver takes the last drink of their beer, the passenger should have another cold one opened while eagerly taking their empty in exchange for the full one. If the driver experiences any lag-time between beers, the passenger is not doing his/her job.)

Once you are out of town and on the open road, your friend grabs the empties by the top of the can and flips them, one by one, out the window of the car and onto the side of the road. Life was good back then because you could litter without dealing with social pressure from your friends. And, if a cop pulled you over and you had an open beer in your lap, they usually wouldn't say anything unless you were obviously drunk. Sometimes, if they thought you were too drunk to drive and they happened to know you, they would make you drive home and follow you to make sure you got home safely. This was just another way that our local police helped create a sense of community that appears to be lacking in small towns today.

All right, back to the drinking tour. Your first stop outside of Hurley is The Chino Buffet on the old North Hurley road about a mile north of Hurley. You drain a beer or two there and then head up the road about a half a mile and stop at the Pénjamo Night Club for another quick beer. Then you continue your drinking tour another quarter of a mile north to the Three Aces Bar adjacent to Baca's A and B Food Store. If nothing was going on there you would hop back in the car and cruise another quarter of a mile north to "Chinatown" and pull into the Copper Inn owed by a gentleman named Gaspar Fernandez. (By the way, Chinatown was so named because of a family who lived in the settlement that apparently had Oriental facial features.)

Since there was nothing going on at the Copper Inn, you continue heading north on the old highway. Once you get to Bayard you would probably head to the Triangle Bar and then on to the Lincoln Bar or the nearby Sportsman Bar. After a couple of shots of tequila, you jump back into the car and drive east, down the hill toward the old downtown, and stop at the El Charro Bar across from Mi Ranchito Tortilla Factory. You go in for a beer or two there, shoot a game of pool with an older Hispanic man, and pick up another six-pack as you hop back into the car and weave your way toward Santa Rita. About a mile north of Bayard, near Vanadium, you would surely stop for a shot of tequila at the Question Mark Bar, conveniently located right on the edge of the highway.

Now you are back in the car and you work your way another couple of miles toward Santa Rita and stop at Bell's Bar. (One historical incident worth mentioning is that the Bell's Bar abruptly closed down in the mid 1960's because the bar tender and another person were murdered there. The crime was never solved.)

After stopping to urinate down in the creek across the highway from Bell's

Bar, you fall down while climbing back up to the road and your hand lands in a cholla cactus. When you finally get back to the car, you spend about 10 minutes picking hair-like spines out of your hand while your friend laughs at you from the passenger side of the front seat. Finally, you start the car and slowly cruise toward Fierro.

Heading up the canyon to the north, you turn right and cross the bridge that was made famous as the filming site for the banned movie "Salt of the Earth" in 1953, and pull up to the Country Club Bar. You have two beers here because you are intrigued by the stories of an older Hispanic couple named Louie and Chavela, who were the only people in the bar at the time. After listening to some great history of the area, you continue up the canyon to the El Patio Bar. Along the way, it dawns on you that it was probably more than mere coincidence these bars were perched along the road that led to the entrance gate of the UV Mine site.

It is starting to get dark now, and you are getting pretty drunk. Fortunately for you and your friend, you are a safe drunk driver. You have had years of practice and have never wrecked your car. In fact, your friends prefer that you drive when everyone in the car is drunk.

If you could just find your way back out of the canyon to the intersection at Hanover, you now had a choice to go either east or west. If you went west and drove up the hill beyond Hanover you could stop at the Beehive Bar right on the curve. From there you could drop down into Central and drink at the Smoke House and the Brown Derby. From Central, you could loop back toward Hurley, although you would have to watch out for cops on the road.

Since you are a responsible drunk driver, you choose to head out toward the Mimbres because there was less traffic. As you weave your way past the now-extinct town of Santa Rita you realize that the steering wheel of your car is gravitating toward the Manhattan Bar, which was located right below the old Santa Rita Ballpark.

After another beer or two, your friend helps carry you out of the Manhattan so you can puke in the parking lot as you lean against the open driver's side door of your car. Your eyes begin to tear up as the stomach acids in your vomit come out of your nose and mouth at the same time, but when it's over you feel somewhat relieved and are ready to pop open another warm beer. You wipe the puke off of your face with your forearm and slowly look over to tell your friend that you are now ready to continue bar hopping just up the road to the Casa Blanca Bar.

A few hundred feet from the Manhattan Bar you notice a little clearing on the side of the road with a small shade tree. Many generations of drunk drivers before you have pulled over to park and drink here. You pull in and let your motor cool down while you and your friend lean against the front quarter panel of your car and finish off the last of the six-pack sitting on top of the hood. A little more urinating, a little more puking, and then it's off to the Casa Blanca.

After a beer or two at the Casa Blanca and a drunken conversation with two older Hispanic men about how the "culos" at Kennecott are trying to fuck over the union, you realize it is now time to head up the road another half mile or so to the High Spot Bar to pick up another six pack for the road. By this time, you are far enough out of town that the bartender at the High Spot will sell you anything you want, even if you can't stand up. You lay $1.35 on the counter, the bartender puts your six-pack into a brown paper bag, and you stumble out the front door as you clench the beer tightly under your arm. Once you get to the car, you wisely decide to let your friend take over the wheel for the long trek out to the bars on the Mimbres because you are now seeing double and can barely walk.

The first stop along the Mimbres River is the Bear Canyon Dam Bar below the lake. You don't stay here for long because you and your friend are so drunk that the bartender refuses to serve you and kicks you out of the bar. You mumble to the bartender, "Fuck you. We don't want any of your fucking beer anyway," and stagger out the door.

You fall down in the dirt near the front entrance to the bar and crawl back into your car and, after your friend eventually figures out where to stick the ignition key, he starts the car and pulls out of the parking lot and heads south on the wrong side of the road. He miraculously navigates the car down the curvy road to San Lorenzo to see whether the bar on Galaz Street is still open. It isn't, so he drives another mile down to the Black Range Store on the Black Range highway in hopes of picking up another six-pack to go. They are also closed because the owners Blackie and Terry Oliver are on vacation.

You are now out in the middle of nowhere and, after some drunken deliberation, you decide that the nearest bar is the Copper Rose, which is three miles south in the settlement of San Juan. You cruise down the highway going about 25 miles per hour and when you get to the Copper Rose your friend turns into the dirt parking lot just off of the highway. He misjudges when to stop and runs into a barbed wire fence next to the bar, bending a metal fence post and scratching up the front bumper and grill on the car. You both spill some of your beer as your heads abruptly jerk forward toward the windshield, but you have a good laugh and then get out of the car and help each other into the bar. You stay there long enough to drink a beer but decide to leave because a couple of Mexican cowboys sitting at the end of the bar are staring at you and are dying to come over and kick your asses.

While the "vaqueros" are in the bathroom, you and your friend manage to slide out the front door and get the hell out of the bar before they come back out. Your friend backs the car into the road, throws the shifter into drive, and punches the accelerator with his right foot. Your heads snap back over the car seat as the car lunges forward. You run along the dirt shoulder of the road for about 100 yards and kick up lots of dust in your wake, but eventually your friend navigates the car back onto the center stripe of the road.

It's starting to get late so you decide to make one last stop down the road at the Union Bar near Faywood. By the time your friend finally pulls up to the parking lot of the bar, he is "blind" drunk and you are leaning against the passenger side door of the car, passed out. He tries to wake you up to go inside with him, to no avail, so he spends the next two minutes searching for the handle to open the car door. Finally he finds it, gets out of the car, and holds himself up against the open car door. As he walks toward the bar, he stabilizes himself by running his right hand along the hood of the car. He somehow weaves his way to the front door, figures out how to open it, and enters. At first there is no one in the bar, but after a couple of minutes an old man appears in a doorway leading to his living quarters in the back of the building. He slowly limps behind the long bar and stops to ask your friend what he wants.

Your drunken amigo mumbles for several minutes until the old man finally understands what he was trying to say. Before long, your friend stumbles out the front door with a half-pint of Jim Beam in one hand. As he returns to the car he can barely stand up, but he is certain about one thing: he needs to avoid traffic and steer clear of cops. No problem. He backs the car onto the highway and heads south towards the City of Rocks.

After dozing off behind the wheel of the car and waking up in the wrong lane at least three times along the way, he enters the City of Rocks State Park and finds his way to a picnic area on the east side of the park. He pulls up next to a concrete picnic table and parks the car. He then opens the door and wrestles himself out of the car and unscrews the lid to the bottle of Jim Beam. The last thing he remembers that night is drinking two swigs of whiskey before things start spinning around in his head. He is suddenly overcome with nausea and within two minutes he is passed out, face down, on the picnic table.

A few hours later, the hot morning sun awakens you and your friend. You both have splitting headaches and are nauseous and dehydrated from the night before. You have dried puke in your hair, your friend is missing his shirt, and your breath smells like a buffalo took a shit down your throat. There is nothing to drink or eat except for warm beer and a nearly full half-pint bottle of Jim Beam. Your car smells like stale beer and vomit and has empty beer cans scattered on the floorboard. The only logical thing to do at this point in your leisurely outing is take a swig of Jim Beam, get back on the highway, and head towards Hurley.

CHAPTER FOUR: SCHOOL DAYS, AND FRIENDS ALONG THE WAY 1956-68

"Awww, c'mon. I wasn't THAT bad."

Hurley Elementary School Years

The principal of the Hurley Schools in the mid 1950's until the early 1960's was a man named William T. Fallis. His office was in the Hurley High School building and he presided over the elementary and junior high school grades. It seems like the only time I ever saw him was when I got into trouble and was sent to his office to get a paddling. I never knew much about him personally but I do remember his paddlings didn't hurt that much. A few of the kids at school used to refer to him as "Mr. Fatass".

There were three large wooden school buildings that housed the elementary school children in Hurley. The elementary school and playground were located on the north side of Carrasco Street and occupied the entire block. The westernmost building, which was directly east of the Hurley Community Church, housed first and second graders. There was no kindergarten back then. The building in the middle housed the third graders and the eastern-most building had the fourth grade classrooms. Fifth graders went to a separate building northwest of the old Hurley High School, across the street from the Hurley Community Church's recreation hall. The sixth grade classrooms were upstairs on the second floor of the old high school.

Students were "tracked" in the later elementary school grades based on their academic performance. The high achieving students were placed in one class (a.k.a. the smart class) and the low achieving students were placed in the other class (a.k.a. the dumb class). Every school year the two teachers at each grade level would alternate teaching the high achieving class or the low achieving class. Interestingly, the high achievers were made up of Anglo students and some Hispanics that spoke good English. The low achieving class was made up almost entirely of Hispanic students and a handful of Anglo students who made bad grades. The school made absolutely no effort to deal with the language barrier of Hispanic students other than to place them in the low achieving class.

Cobre Consolidated Schools took over the Hurley Schools from Kennecott in the fall of 1955 and that was when the full integration of students began. I started first grade a year later. The three North Hurley school buildings that were located on E Street were eventually torn down in the early 1960's.

Photo 4-1: Pictured are the three Hurley Elementary School buildings, probably before 1950. The building in the foreground housed the classrooms for first and second grade. The middle building held the third graders, and the distant building had fourth grade classrooms. Photo courtesy of Terry Humble.

Hispanic students were forbidden to speak Spanish while at school. If they were caught they would get into trouble with the teachers. One day some of my classmates and I were playing a game of football on the playground during recess. At the end of recess the opposing team was declared the winner. As we were lining up outside the door to the school to go back to class, one of the Hispanic kids on the winning team made a teasing remark to some of the boys on our team for having lost the game. This made us mad so we decided to get even with him. For revenge we walked over to the playground teacher and told her that we had heard the Hispanic kid speaking Spanish on the playground. We knew he would get into trouble with the teacher and we would get the last laugh.

The elementary schools were old wooden frame buildings with lapboard siding like most of the houses in Hurley. There were large windows and high ceilings in all of the classrooms and the entire school building had hardwood floors. Classrooms were heated with radiant floor heaters that circulated hot water made by boilers. I also remember seeing a large black and white framed picture of George Washington hanging in one of the elementary school hallways.

The dirt playground was fairly large with a baseball backstop in the northwest corner and a sandbox in the northeast corner. There was a nice metal slide, some teeter totters, a set of swings, a merry-go-round, a tetherball pole, and on the east side of the playground there was a piece of equipment called a giant stride.

Most of the kids lived for the morning and afternoon recesses. When I was in first grade I enjoyed jumping rope and playing jacks with the girls because I was really good at jacks and rarely lost to anyone. I was also good at jumping rope on the long rope that had kids turning it at each end. My favorite jump rope rhymes were "Teddy Bear, Teddy Bear, Turn Around" and "Mabel, Mabel, Set the Table". The boys would also bring marbles and wooden tops to school and have great games all around the buildings and on the sidewalks. The games would usually go without incident until someone won and got to keep another kid's prize marble or top, which occasionally led to big arguments and sometimes a fight. Everyone wanted to win but nobody wanted to lose, especially when we played "for keeps".

The teacher would collect our "milk money" every morning before the lesson began, and at mid-morning we always had a milk break. As I remember, the price for an eight-ounce carton of milk was two or three cents. In the first grade they brought in snacks for the kids during the milk break. The snack was usually a quarter of a white bread sandwich with a slice of processed cheese and mayonnaise inside. Apparently, even back then the school knew children learned better when they weren't hungry.

Students were forbidden to chew gum in class. I think teachers became annoyed when students would blow bubbles or "click" the gum between their teeth during class. And, for some reason, the chewing gum always ended up getting plastered under desks or stuck on the bottom of someone's shoe.

It was popular for students to bring treats to school to share with their friends. After hunting season kids would bring bags of homemade venison or elk jerky. In the late fall, piñon nuts were very popular and sometimes kids would bring some that were roasted and salted. Of course, piñon nuts were a problem because kids would spit the shells onto the floor or throw them inside the desks where they were seated.

Another popular treat that was fairly common were toothpicks soaked in cinnamon oil. The cinnamon oil tasted great, but it could sting your lips because it was very strong. And, in the early fall some kids would even bring chopped sections of sugar cane. We would split the cane open with our teeth and chew on it as we sucked the sweet juice from the center.

Later on in the higher elementary grades we used to have classic games of baseball and football during recess. In order to make full teams, the Anglo and Hispanic boys would always play together. Sometimes there would be a little bullying, but all in all we got along and had lots of fun.

It seems like once we began playing team sports, the pecking order among the boys started to form. Certain kids would always want to be the quarterback or the first batter, and they usually got their way as long as none of the other kids were big or tough enough to kick their ass. Once in a while, after several minutes of arguing and political maneuvering, a different kid might get a chance to be quarterback as long as he didn't screw up or always threw passes to guys who were the most popular. The big kids and the popular kids usually got to choose teams and were always the first kids to get chosen for a team, even if they weren't very good at that particular sport.

It didn't take long, even as first graders, to figure out how to create mischief on the playground. It seemed like everything we did that was really fun ended up getting us into trouble. I remember sliding down the slide "head first" and flying off the end and landing "belly first" on the ground. The teachers didn't like that. Then we would get two guys on one end of the teeter-totter and only one guy on the other end. When the one guy was up and the two guys were down, the two guys would sabotage the one guy by bailing off of the teeter totter, causing him to come crashing straight down. Well, the teachers didn't like that. Then we would swing as high as we possibly could in the swings (almost horizontal with the top pole) and bail out, falling eight or 10 feet onto the hard-packed sand below. The teachers didn't like that either. Or we would get lots of guys to turn the merry-go-round really fast and then bail off and go scuffing end-over-end across the dirt playground. As you can imagine, the teachers didn't like that.

Then there was my favorite piece of equipment on the whole playground, the giant stride. This thing was a tall vertical pole with a cap at the top that spun around on ball bearings. Attached to this cap were several long chains with handles built into the lower end so that kids could hold on from below. The contraption worked sort of like a May Pole. We would all run around the pole in the same direction and once we got going fast enough we could lift our feet and legs off the ground and be airborne from the centrifugal force. The faster we went, the higher we would fly around the pole. Once we were flying high enough we would let go of the handle and get flung several feet away. You can probably imagine what the teachers thought about that. They just didn't understand that recess was a complete failure to us boys if we didn't return to class dirty, bloody, and with torn clothes.

I managed to keep my nose fairly clean for most of the first grade year until I finally violated my first big school rule. The town kids who lived within a few blocks of the school would usually walk home for lunch and return at 1:00 p.m., while the kids who lived out of town, like ranch kids, would stay and eat their lunches at school. Teachers were very adamant about the town students returning from lunch on time and not being tardy.

One day I returned to school a couple of minutes before the tardy bell rang. As I approached the school grounds from the street, I turned around and noticed that my dog Rumple had followed me to school. My heart sank when I saw him standing there. Now I was in big trouble because I had inadvertently violated a school rule: "No Dogs Allowed At School". I was in a strange predicament. I had to decide whether I wanted to get yelled at for having my dog at school or get yelled at for taking him home and returning to school late. Since the tardy bell was about to ring, I had to concoct a quick plan.

Miraculously, an incredible scheme popped into my head that solved all of my problems. It was brilliant and simple. All I had to do was ditch the afternoon class and go hide out with my dog until school was over. Then I would go home and pretend that nothing ever happened. So, Rumple and I spent the afternoon underneath one of the bridges at the Big Ditch. Problem solved. (Incidentally, I've always been proud of the fact that I started ditching school in the first grade.)

Another time during my first grade school year, I was walking home from school and I noticed a short piece of 2x4 lumber lying next to the street. I bent over to pick it up and take a look at it, and at about the same time a utility truck from the gas company happened to be cruising up the street nearby.

With the block of wood firmly in my hand as the truck drove by, something strange and inexplicable suddenly happened. From somewhere deep in the center of the earth, an evil demonic monster jumped up directly behind me. The monster was much bigger than I was and it was impossible for me to run away or resist its powers. Before I knew it, my right arm became possessed by the demon and I was rendered helpless and unable to control my hand or any part of my arm. As I stood there, my arm suddenly raised the block of wood near the side of my head and launched it at the gas truck as it passed by.

In a one-in-a-million throw, the wood block hit the left front wheel between the tire and the hubcap and was flung very quickly in an upward trajectory, hitting the driver's elbow that was resting on the door panel of the truck. The driver reacted to the sharp pain in his arm by jerking his head and upper body away from the window.

He immediately stopped the truck in the middle of the street and jumped out. As he opened the door, he began to yell at me and said, "What the hell do you think you are doing? You're going to be in big trouble when I tell your parents about this."

When I heard him say that, I turned and ran away as fast as I could. I ran for several blocks and didn't stop until I got to the jungle by the ballpark south of town. I followed one of the trails into the jungle and hid among the trees for a few hours until it started to get dark.

By nightfall I was getting hungry and decided to go home and deal with my parents, take my punishment, and get this incident over with. I figured there was an outside chance my parents might declare a little mercy on me if I came clean and admitted guilt right away instead of denying what I had done.

As soon as I walked in the front door of my house I immediately told my parents, "I'm sorry."

My parents looked at each other in confusion and replied, "Sorry for what?"

I was caught off guard at first, but I quickly realized that they didn't know what I was talking about. I now had to come up with a quick reply or they would become suspicious. After gathering my wits, I answered, "Sorry for coming home late from school."

This brief interaction turned out to be an important lesson that served me well, even to this day. I learned that, if you think you might be in trouble, you should always play dumb and never admit guilt unless you know for certain they know you did something wrong. Several years later I received further affirmation of this valuable lesson when a fellow Hurley street hoodlum shared this profound advice with me. He said, "If you are being accused of something, you should always lie, deny, admit nothing, and demand proof."

When I heard that, I knew that I was on the right track.

My claim to fame in the second grade was that two other boys and I were considered candidates for skipping second grade and going to third grade. Apparently our teacher, Mrs. Henry, thought we were excellent readers and were academically advanced enough to be in third grade. She used to let us go out into the hallway and read alone while the rest of the class did their lessons in the classroom. I don't know what happened but, as it turned out, none of us got to move on to third grade after all.

Third grade was a fairly boring year, but when we got to fourth grade with Miss Quatier, things really started to change. One activity that I enjoyed in her class was learning the multiplication table. The teacher placed tag board cards (about 4"x6" in size) into the chalk caddy and leaned them against the bottom of the blackboard. Each card had single digit numbers that were multiplied by other numbers, i.e. 4x6, 7x3, and so on. The teacher would time us to see how long it took to speed through the multiplication table. The exercise was competitive and you were considered pretty hot shit if you had a fast time.

The one thing I remember most about fourth grade was the realization that girls were in the beginning stages of breast development. The boys would hang out at recess and discuss which girls actually were in the beginning stages of endowment and which ones were stuffing Kleenex into their trainer bras. It wasn't long before some of the boys began to get these weird, terrifying notes during class that said bizarre things like, "Suzie has a crush on you".

Another fond memory of fourth grade was when I brought a sack lunch to school one day so I could eat in the lunchroom with some friends. I happened to be sitting across the table from some girl that had just taken a banana out of her lunch box and was peeling it. Just as she was ready to take the first bite, a young lad named Jimmy Joe Moreno snatched it out of her hand and ate it. I thought that this was incredibly funny, but apparently the teacher nearby didn't think so. She yanked Jimmy Joe out of the lunchroom and immediately paddled him. By the way, I am fairly certain that Jimmy Joe was the reigning "paddle champion" of Hurley Schools by the time he finished seventh grade. That poor kid was sent off to the principal's office for a butt beating every time he turned around. He wasn't a mean young man per se, but always liked to goof off and stir things up in the classroom. Over the years I found Jimmy Joe to be quite entertaining.

I actually liked school up to this point, but by the end of fourth grade I was beginning to get bored and was developing an attitude. I didn't like being controlled and told what to do all day long. My grades started to slip a bit and by fifth grade things began to get even worse. I was also beginning to lose confidence in my academic abilities. As my grades dropped lower and the teachers began to dog me for not turning in my homework, my interest in school spiraled downward. In hindsight, I'm certain that puberty had a lot to do with my attitude, and I didn't have the self-discipline to get my daily assignments done. Another difficult issue for me was the other kids began to grow much faster than me and I became one of the class runts.

One of my fondest fifth grade memories was when Timmy Gardner, my elementary school best buddy, and I got stuck in a jacket and couldn't get out of it. His right arm was in the right sleeve and my left arm was in the left sleeve and our other arms were wrapped over each other's shoulder. When we came in from recess the teacher had to help us out of our predicament. The class was laughing harder than we were as the teacher pulled and tugged on the sleeves and tried to pry us apart.

By sixth grade I became the class clown. I owned the class. I had everyone in tears from laughter every day and the teacher was becoming increasingly displeased and annoyed with my disruptive behavior. Meanwhile, my grades were getting worse and I realized I was having a difficult time reading the chalkboard. I eventually had to get glasses. And, like many kids that age, I was developing self-esteem problems. Not only had I become a runt with glasses, but this puberty thing was becoming a perplexing issue for me as well.

In the beginning of sixth grade I was interested in drumming so I signed up for the school band. The band director told me that they needed a cornet player instead of a drummer so I reluctantly started playing the cornet. Since I didn't own a cornet, I had to use the one that the school provided. Every day at the end of class I would return it to the shelf in the band room where I found it. One day I went to the band room a little early and noticed another kid from the previous class playing the same cornet that I had been playing. I became so repulsed at the thought of having to share the same cornet mouthpiece with the other kid that I quit the school band the following day.

It seems like we always had something going after school when I was in elementary school. I used to enjoy going to Cub Scout meetings because we always had cookies and punch and did fun activities and games. One of my favorite games was when the Den Mother would read the first part of a sentence and we would complete the sentence with silly phrases or words that were printed on cards that were drawn out of a hat. Later on we learned how to make kites and would take them to the school yard after school and fly them until the kite would get tangled in the power lines above the nearby street. We also made simple telephones by stretching a string between two tin cans and talking into the can at one end. Another time we made stilts and would chase each other around the yard until we either fell on our butts or the stilts would break.

Once in a while we took an occasional Cub Scout field trip. One time they took our Den to the T and M Dairy in Hanover for a field trip. We walked through the dairy and saw how they milked the cows and made milk and milk products. At the end of the tour they gave all of us a frozen treat, like an ice cream bar or a Popsicle. Another time they took us to John and Alice King's house on Aztec Street in Hurley to view his vast Native American artifact collection. John King's collection was better than any collection I had ever seen and he eventually donated it to the Mimbres Museum in Deming.

Deer hunting season was in full swing around Thanksgiving and lots of kids would be absent from school so they could go hunting with their families. Hunters returning from the hills would proudly drive down the streets of Hurley with a dead buck draped over the front quarter panel of their car or lying in the bed of their pick-up truck. When they got home they would hang the deer in their garage to skin it and let it cure for a few days. If someone killed a large buck they would have the head mounted and hang it on their living room wall. The dogs in town loved deer season too because they would scavenge around the neighborhood and drag a femur bone or a deer hide home to chew on for a few days.

Most of the time I would go home after school and watch television. By the time I was in fourth grade, my favorite show of all time was The Three

Stooges. I would go to school the next day mimicking and acting out all of the funny things that Curley did the evening before. The teachers must have hated the Three Stooges because class was constantly disrupted as we reenacted their foolishness. My favorite line from the Three Stooges was when someone asked Curley, "Does the deer have a little doe?" and Curley responded, "Yea, two bucks." Then they slapped Curley around for being a wise guy.

The Hoover Maneuver
***

For a brief time when I was in elementary school I had an older friend named Bobby Porter. Bobby's family was always nice to me and he used to invite me over to his house to watch TV with him while his parents went bowling on Tuesday nights. His parents belonged to a bowling league that took place at the Chino Club bowling alley in Hurley. There were several teams that participated in the league and it was a popular weeknight social event for adults.

Bobby and I used to watch TV shows like "Route 66", "Dragnet", "Whirlybirds", and "Sea Hunt" while we snacked on Fritos and drank Pepsis for most of the evening. Sometimes we would wrestle on the living room floor or do crazy things like stand up on the couch and try to get light headed and pass out by hyperventilating. One evening, when I was about nine years old and he was about 13 or 14, we were hanging out in his living room and Bobby went to a closet and dragged out his mom's Hoover vacuum cleaner. He attached a metal pipe nozzle to the end of the hose, turned it on, and then put his hand over the end of the pipe to make sure he had good suction. Then he said to me, "Hey, have you ever tried this before?" and he unzipped his pants and pulled out his penis.

With the vacuum cleaner humming away, he stuck his penis inside the metal hose fitting and began moving the hose up and down. After a couple of minutes Bobby pulled the vacuum cleaner hose away and asked me, "That felt really cool. Do you want to try it?"

I was totally confused and puzzled about Bobby's exciting new idea. I remember thinking, "Why would anyone want to put a suction hose on their pecker? I hope I don't get weird like that when I get older."

I finally told him, "No thanks," and returned to the TV to continue watching "Dragnet".

Early Friendships

The first good friend I ever had was a kid named Tommy Bates. The Bates lived a few houses up the street from me and I used to go to his house quite often from the time I was four years old until I left for college. His parents, Lois and Oscar, were like a second family to my older brother and me. When I was about nine or 10 years old my brother gave Tommy the nickname of "Thomasido", which quickly morphed into the name "Sido". The name stuck and he was known as Sido for the remainder of his life.

Oscar was an avid hunter and would bring home fish and wild game for dinner. The first time I ever ate venison, quail, and fresh trout was at the Bates' house. In the summer of 1962, the Bates took me on a family vacation to Greer, Arizona where we stayed in a little cabin while Oscar fished in the nearby stream.

Photo 4-2: This is a photo of Sido Bates and I sitting on the steps of the cabin in Greer, Arizona. I am seated on the left and Sido on the right. Sido's father, Oscar, is looking out the front door of the cabin toward the camera.

In addition to hunting and fishing, Oscar was a sports fan and loved to watch ball games on TV during his free time. My brother and I used to go to the Bates' house and stay all day to watch the bowl games at the end of college football season. Oscar also enjoyed keeping an eye on the weather and had a homemade barometer hanging on the kitchen wall. He kept records of the barometric pressure and used it to help him forecast the weather and plan outings.

Lois was nice to all of Sido's friends and would often do little things for us. She always made root beer Kool-Aid in the summers and would drive us to places if we needed a ride. One time she heated up her scissors and used them to roll up our hair and make curls. She also fed us dozens of great meals over the years.

One evening she drove my brother and Sido to the Bayard Theatre to see the movie "Dracula". After they returned home from the movie, the three of them convinced me that Dracula was coming to Hurley. They said that I needed to get a cross, some garlic, and a metal spike to protect myself from having my blood sucked out and becoming a vampire. They even helped me make a cross to carry around in case I ran into a vampire. I became so scared from the hoax that I ran home crying. I was afraid to watch horror movies for over ten years because of that experience.

Lois also had a good sense of humor when she was around the kids. When I was about six years old, the Bates had a bird dog named "Double O" who used to jump on my leg and hump me when I walked into their back yard. Lois would always tell me, "Don't worry Jerry, he won't hurt you. He just wants to dance with you."

When Sido and I weren't out on the streets at night creating havoc, we used to spend hours at his house playing games and goofing around. We would play with his electric football game for a while and then read comic books. Sido also had an electric train that we played with at Christmas time, and we occasionally played the game of Mr. Potato as we sat around the kitchen table. To play Mr. Potato, you would transform a potato into a cartoon like character by sticking plastic body parts and clothing articles onto it. Each part had a pointed shaft behind it that you stuck into the potato to hold it into place.

Sometimes we played with his Viewmaster, which was a toy that resembled a pair of binoculars but was actually a hand-held slide projector. The Viewmaster had a slot where you inserted a round, cardboard disc that had numerous color slide photographs along the edge. You advanced to the next photo frame by pulling down a lever on the side. You always had to look toward a light or out a window to illuminate the slides. One of the coolest features of the Viewmaster was that the slides appeared to be three-dimensional, which made you feel like you were in the picture. I remember viewing some color slides of dinosaurs that looked like they could jump right out of the Viewmaster and devour you.

Sido and I used to invent games to play when we were at his house. One of my favorite games was called "Are You Ready Brother?" To play, we would get on his bed and stand on our knees and cover our eyes with a blindfold. Then, we would each roll up a newspaper in our right hand and hold each other's hand with our left hand. One of us would start the game by asking the other, "Are you ready, brother?" and the other guy would reply, "Yes, I'm ready, brother." Then we would beat each other over the head with the rolled up newspaper until someone either let go of the other guy's hand or fell off the bed.

There were always lots of comic books scattered around Sido's bedroom. Sometimes we would sit around and read through a small pile of them in one sitting before we got bored and went outside to do something else. The comic books usually had several advertisements for mail order products that appealed to devious kids like us and, once in a while, we would save our money and send off for select merchandise. For example, one time we ordered a karate instructional booklet from a comic book ad and spent several afternoons in Sido's front yard trying to figure out some of the moves. Since he was four years older than me and quite a bit bigger, I was usually the practice dummy. Another time there was an ad for an exercise program featuring Charles Atlas that said something like, "Are you a 95 lb. weakling? Don't let them kick sand in your face." We ordered the Charles Atlas exercise booklet and spent a few days trying to get muscle-bound. We never did get the instant results we were looking for, so we gave up on the program and threw the book away.

Our favorite comic book ads were for practical jokes. We ordered things like "fly in the ice cube" to put in people's drinks, "cigarette loads" that would supposedly explode when the victim lit their cigarette, a "fake nail" that you could stick into someone's car tire, "fake vomit" that was made of rubber and had little red chunks in it, and of course, the "poo-poo cushion", which we hid under the mattress of a chair or couch. When someone sat down, it sounded like a fart. We also bought "fake gashes" and "fake blood" that you could put on your arm or leg and freak your parents out. But, the best novelty item of all was the "fake dog shit". I'll never forget the comic book ad that showed a pile of fresh dog shit on the floor with steam emanating from it, while a dog with a dumb look on his face stood next to it. Next to the dog was an adult that appeared to be totally aghast at the situation. The caption above read, "Bad dog. Should have left him out."

I did manage to get a few laughs out of some of these pranks. One day I put the "fake dog shit" on my dad's plate when he came home for the lunch hour from work. When he sat down at the table and looked at his plate, he exclaimed, "God Damn, what the hell is this?"

My mother laughed as hard as I did.

Another time I put the "fake nail" in his car tire and told him there was a huge nail sticking out of it. He went outside to take a look and immediately began cussing as he pulled the jack and spare tire out of the trunk of the car. While he was setting the jack under the rear bumper of the car I pulled the nail out of the tire and showed it to him. I could tell that he wasn't overly amused about the prank as he threw the jack and spare tire back into the trunk.

Sido taught me how to survive and have fun in the streets of Hurley at night. In fact, we almost always found trouble while we were out and about. Stealing fruit out of people's yards was our main activity, although vandalism was pretty high up on our list as well. Once in a while, though, we found ways to cause trouble right there in his yard.

I remember one summer we were on a firecracker jag. By utilizing the "trial and error" method of scientific discovery, we determined that if you removed the seed from a ripe apricot and replaced it with a lit firecracker, the apricot would explode and blow a yellow mush all over the place. During the next phase of our research, we soon discovered that when an apricot is thrown with a lit firecracker planted firmly inside, the apricot would explode in mid-air. We deduced that if these steps were followed as a car drove by your house at night, the apricot would explode and make a mess on someone's windshield. We also determined that if we hid behind the thick mulberry hedges in Sido's front yard after we launched the apricot, the odds of getting caught would be greatly reduced.

One of the funniest things Sido ever did occurred one evening when Tubby Porkman and I went to the Copper Drive Inn movie theater with him. As we were sitting in his car watching the movie, Sido made the claim that if you held a match down between your legs when you farted, a flame would blow out of your ass like a blowtorch. Of course, Tubby and I just laughed at him and told him to prove it. Eager to accept the challenge, Sido lit a match, spread his legs, and lifted his butt up off of the car seat and farted. Sure enough, just as he had claimed, a flame shot out from his pants. Tubby and I laughed so hard that we had to throw open the passenger side door to roll around on the ground as we held our guts and gasped for air.

Butch Steyskal was my other good buddy when I was in elementary school and junior high. He, like Sido, was also four years older than me. I used to go to his house and play cars in the dirt in his back yard and we used to build model cars and airplanes in his living room. We also hiked and rode our bicycles all over town and the surrounding areas.

One time Butch made a four-wheeled pushcart out of scraps of lumber he found in his yard. You could sit on the cart and steer it by placing your feet on the front axle that pivoted back and forth. One of us would drive while one or two other kids pushed the cart down the street or sidewalk. We used to have fun pushing his young nephew, Johnny Menard, around the streets of Hurley when he and his parents came to visit from Santa Rita. Johnny was about five years old at the time and was easy to push because he was so small.

When I was in first grade, Butch got a little white dog and named it Rumple Stiltskin. For some reason, every time I left Butch's house to go home the dog would always follow me. The dog apparently liked me so much the Steyskals eventually gave the dog to me. I had Rumple until I was a senior in high school and he always followed me everywhere I went.

My parents refused to let Rumple in the house, so he consequently spent many cold winter nights sleeping out in the yard. Sometimes, when my parents would do something to make me mad, I would "accidentally on purpose" let Rumple into the house just to see them throw a fit and run him out. One of my favorite tricks was to let Rumple inside on days when it was raining or snowing, while he was sopping wet and muddy. This proved to be a surefire way to get my parents very animated. I always wondered what the neighbors must have thought when they heard all of the noise and commotion coming from our house when the dog was inside. I probably couldn't have generated a worse reaction from my parents if I had let a rattlesnake loose on our kitchen floor.

When I was about six years old in 1956, Butch and I would go with his mother to the old Hurley High School football field on Nevada Street on Saturday mornings. She was a member of the Ground Observation Core (GOC), and we would climb up onto the top of the press box with binoculars and look in the skies for unauthorized aircraft. Because of World War II, the Korean War, and the "McCarthy era of communist paranoia", GOC civilian volunteers helped keep a vigilant eye open at all times. After spending several Saturdays spotting aircraft, Mrs. Steyskal rewarded me with a small metal pin shaped like wings, with the initials GOC in the middle.

Butch was fascinated with cars and could name the year and model of just about any car that drove by. His family had a nice, brand new 1958 Ford Fairlane 500 that he was very proud of and sometimes his older sister would take us places in the car. One place we went on a fairly regular basis was to

Butch's grandmother's house in Arenas Valley. His sister would drive us there on the road that goes north off of Highway 180, now called Arenas Valley Road. We nicknamed the road "The Rollercoaster Road" because there were lots of dips and hills on it. We always begged her to go really fast over that section of road in hopes that we would go airborne as the car crested out on one of the hills.

When Butch and I went to his grandmother's house we would usually spend the night. She lived just northeast of the Copper Drive-Inn Movie Theater. Butch and I would walk across an open pasture to a little gas station next to the theater to get sodas and candy bars. We also used to go into her old garage and sit on her John Deere tractor and pretend to drive it. Sometimes she would have us do chores like shovel snow or chop fire wood and carry it inside for her old wood burning cook stove.

Hurley Junior High School Years

By the time I was in the seventh and eighth grade our classes were held downstairs in the old wooden two-story Hurley High School building. The main doors to the school faced the east and opened onto Third Street between Romero Street and Carrasco Street. The principal's office was the first door to the left as you entered the building and the gymnasium was straight ahead from the entrance. There were classrooms on the right and left of the gym, the library was upstairs, and there was more classroom space upstairs next to the library. The classrooms had large windows and hardwood floors. The gym had a second story spectator's balcony that ran along both sides of the gym. There was a stage at the west end of the gym and storage closets flanking the stage. We used to check out sports equipment for P.E. classes and the summer recreation program from one of the closets. At the north end of the gym was the boys' showers and locker room and the girls' locker room was on the south side. The band room was a separate building southwest of the gym, and directly to the west of the gym was a large dirt athletic field that occupied the remainder of the block.

As we transitioned from elementary school to junior high school, the major difference was that we had a different teacher for each subject rather than having only one teacher all day. The seventh grade math teacher was a pretty lady named Miss Burnette. She got along well with the kids and most of the boys in class had a crush on her. The eighth grade English teacher was an older, short thin lady with a bulbous red nose named Mrs. Thompson. She didn't take a lot of flack from anyone and was quick to use the paddle on troublemakers. She could really pack a wallop for a little lady. She had wrinkled skin, probably from being a chain smoker, and had a reddish complexion that reminded me of someone who drank a lot.

I was in Mrs. Thompson's class late one morning, and when I went home for lunch I learned that President Kennedy had been shot while riding in a motorcade in Dallas. It wasn't until I returned from lunch that afternoon that we learned he had died. I remember how unsettling and important this event was because the teachers seemed to be shocked and worried for the remainder of the afternoon.

Photo 4-3: The doors to the old Hurley High School faced the east. It was a nice two-story building but by the early 1960's it had become quite a firetrap. I thought it was a shame they tore it down. Photo courtesy of New Mexico State University Library, Archives and Special Collections.

Mrs. Appleton was the math teacher and, unlike Mrs. Thompson, she was much heavier and spent more time seated at her desk in front of the class. She always had a cough medicine bottle with her and she would take a little nip whenever she coughed. We always suspected there was more than cough medicine in that bottle and the rumor among the students was that she was usually half in the bag by mid afternoon. We enjoyed putting thumbtacks in her seat in hopes that we would get to see her jump up out of her chair, but for some reason she never seemed to react to them. Some students speculated that she never felt the tacks due to the multiple layers of fatty tissue that padded her posterior.

Mrs. Appleton was usually oblivious to the misbehavior that was going on in her class. There was always a lot of note passing and cheating when I was in her class, but one day an unusual incident allegedly happened during one of her other classes. An upperclassman told me once a boy in his class was masturbating while seated at his desk. The teacher was busy delivering the lesson and apparently never noticed. Meanwhile, the boys in the class were trying their best to keep from falling out of their desks from laughter.

Mrs. Wilke was the English teacher for many years until she retired in the early 1960's. By the time I was in seventh grade Mrs. Murphy had taken her place. I had known Mrs. Murphy since I was a little kid and she was always very nice to the kids. In fact, she was so nice we decided to push our luck during class with her on a few occasions.

I remember delivering a book report in front of her class in which I fabricated the entire story on the spot. Another time I was caught throwing a Thorndike Barnhart dictionary across the room to Troy Wakefield. Each dictionary weighed three or four pounds and if it had hit someone it would have certainly knocked them out of their desk.

I figured Mrs. Murphy wouldn't do anything to me for throwing the dictionary, but on this occasion I was sadly mistaken. She politely called Troy and I out into the hallway and calmly took us next door to Mr. Price's class and turned us over to him.

Mr. Price was a history teacher who stood about 6'3" and weighed around 220 pounds. He was popular with the kids but when he decided to dig out the paddle you knew you were in deep trouble. He would bend kids over his desk in front of the entire class and lay into them with his old size 13 U.S. Keds rubber tennis shoe sole. The canvas upper was removed in order to afford superior gripping power in combination with a smooth, aerodynamic flow as the shoe forcefully accelerated toward the posterior region of a nervous young lad.

One of his swats would subtly remind you that you were in big trouble. Two swats led to a declaration of emergency, and three swats would bring on the water works for most kids. And when he paddled someone, you could hear the swats echo throughout the hallways of the entire first floor of the Hurley School building. I think I got two swats that day and I can tell you with relative certainty it was difficult to sit down for the remainder of the afternoon.

Mr. Price didn't always have to resort to the tennis shoe when kids goofed around in his class. He had another weapon that was even worse, at least in my opinion. Being a history teacher, he had an old hand crank telephone on his desk. As he turned the crank, an armature would turn inside of several large, heavy horseshoe magnets, which generated electricity. He used the telephone as a prop in his history classes but on occasion he would ask an unruly student from the back of the class to come up to his desk. With the student standing in front of the class, he would say something like, "I thought I told you guys to stop talking back there."

After listening to a lame excuse from the young, behaviorally challenged history recalcitrant, he would tell him to reach out and grab onto the two wires protruding from the exposed guts of the telephone. Once the wires were firmly in the kid's grip, Mr. Price would start turning the crank slowly and then ask the kid, "Do you want me to turn it slow or fast?"

Any student in their right mind would always reply, "Slowly," as they felt the electrical current snake its way up their arms and into their spine.

"OK, no problem," Mr. Price would sincerely reply.

Then, all of a sudden he would crank the living hell out of the phone and the entire class would get to see a kid's hair stand on end for a few seconds. As I recall, there was a very low recidivism rate among troublemakers when the phone was on Mr. Price's desk.

During the boys P.E. class we usually played basketball and did calisthenics in the gym for part of the semester. When the weather was warmer we would play football or baseball on the dirt field. All of the boys had to dress out in gym shorts and tennis shoes every day and at the end of class we had to take showers in the locker room. That was when I first realized the huge difference in the maturity levels among us boys. It was quite embarrassing for us "late bloomers" to enter the showers with boys our age who had already undergone puberty and were well-endowed and ready for action.

Occasionally, the P.E. teacher, Mr. Dribbler, would take us down to the south end of Hurley to the old high school football stadium. The entire P.E. class would board the old Chevrolet school bus nicknamed "Fury" and head for the stadium. Even though the field hadn't been maintained or watered for several years, there were still the remnants of a black cinder oval track that circumvented the football field, and the pole vault and high jump pits still had sand in them. We usually played touch football, but once a semester Mr. Dribbler would organize an in-class track meet for us. All of the boys in class would participate in events such as races of various lengths, long jump, high jump, and pole vault.

I was still the class clown in seventh grade, but by now some of my old friends started to bully me a little because of my size. I even tried out for the seventh grade basketball team but I didn't make the cut. The team played games against the junior high schools from Bayard, Central, and Santa Rita. Our school mascot was the Hurley Apaches.

Once in a while after school, a small group of us would go over to Mike Strain's house on Santa Rita Street and play with his Ouija board. There were always a few girls and a few boys that showed up and we would ask the Ouija board questions like "Who does "so and so" have a crush on?" or "Will "so and so" go out with Jerry if he asks her out?"

It was amazing how accurate the Ouija board was when we asked it questions about dating and romance. I could never figure out how the guide piece slowly slid across the board and arrived at the correct answer every time. My best guess was that there was a connection between a person's hands and fingers and their subconscious thoughts and wishes. Hence, the guide piece always moved to wherever you thought it should go.

Another time, during my seventh grade school year, I remember going to Carla Gould's house after school so that she and Karen Hubble could teach me how to do the two-step and country swing dance styles. Carla played some 45-rpm records in her living room while the girls took turns dancing with me. At the time I had a terrible crush on one of the girls, but I was mortified at the possibility of her finding out about it. Several years after I graduated from high school I ran into her and she told me that she had a crush on me as well. If I had only known...

The schools did have some extracurricular activities that were fun, although they were few and far between. Once in a while we would celebrate a student's birthday in class and the kid's parents would bring cupcakes and Kool-Aid for the entire class. I also remember being in third grade when Richard Stevens' mother came to class to give a presentation on Africa. Richard's father had worked at a mining operation there and Mrs. Stevens showed us lots of artifacts and pictures from the continent. Mrs. Stevens spoke with a British accent, which made the presentation even worldlier. Richard's father was the Reduction Plant Superintendent at the time and, before coming to Hurley, the family had spent time in other countries.

A few times a year, the school would have an "all-school assembly" in the old Hurley High School gymnasium. All classes would be cancelled for the hour and some individual or duo performers would put on a one-hour show for the kids. We saw everything from jugglers to magicians to comediennes. The performers were always from out of town and performed for schools all over the country.

Hurley Junior High School and Cobre High School had a student volunteer organization called "Patrol Boys" who would staff crosswalks before and after school. In the evenings they would direct traffic at high school athletic events. Patrol boys wore a thickly woven white canvass strap that ran diagonally across their chest and up and over their shoulder. At the bottom it connected to another strap that went around their waist. They wore a "patrol boy" badge on the chest strap that gave them a sense of importance, power, and responsibility.

The seventh and eighth grades in Hurley would always go on an annual field trip somewhere close by. One field trip I enjoyed was when they took our class down to the mill and smelter at Kennecott. An employee of Kennecott ushered the group from one part of the operation to the next as they explained how things worked. It was always very noisy in the plant and I remember different areas having unique smells.

Another fun field trip was when we drove two or three miles west of Hurley to Cameron Creek. We spent most of the day there looking at prehistoric Native American sites and hunting for fossils in the rocks above Cameron Creek. We also visited a small cave and enjoyed the freedom of being outdoors instead of cooped up in a classroom all day.

Summer Recreation Program

During the summers, Hurley sponsored a summer recreation program for kids. A teacher and coach named Harold Stambach ran the weekday program at the Hurley High School gym until around 1958. Another teacher and coach named Frank Lopez took over the program and ran it until around 1964. Frank eventually became the principal of Cobre High School after I graduated. Lots of kids from both sides of the tracks, mostly boys, would loyally show up to spend the day playing various sports and games. Every morning we would go to the school and wait for Mr. Lopez to arrive and open up the gym. Once he let us into the gym, we would follow him to the little equipment room next to the stage. We were issued everything from balls, bats, gloves, bases, to footballs, basketballs, ping-pong paddles and nets for the morning activity.

The game we played most was Wiffle Ball (a game of baseball, using a lightweight plastic bat and a hollow plastic ball with big holes in it) inside the gym. I also enjoyed playing ping-pong and once in a while Mr. Lopez would let us bring our bicycles inside the gym and have bicycle time trials around the gym. Butch Steyskal and I usually had the best times because we both rode our bikes everywhere and were good riders.

On scheduled afternoons during the week, Mr. Lopez would check out golf clubs and balls to the kids and we would ride our bicycles across the tracks to the Hurley Golf Course on the north side of town. Sometimes, if the June afternoon winds were calm and the temperature was hot, the smelter smoke from the nearby smoke stacks would drop down and settle over us as we played our round of golf. The smoke was usually so bad that it made our eyes, nose, and throats sting. If we had a canteen handy, we would wet our handkerchiefs and put them over our noses and mouths to mitigate the stinging, although that didn't really help much.

Sometimes we would run to the clubhouse, which was located next to the road, to seek refuge from the smoke. There was a swamp cooler inside and we would cool off and hang around until the smoke subsided. An old man named Fidel Madrid always worked in the clubhouse and would sell us sodas and candy from the concession stand. Fidel didn't speak much English and could be grumpy on occasion, but we somehow managed to communicate fairly well with him. Fidel was Mr. Lopez's father-in-law.

Mr. Lopez organized a youth golf tournament every summer as part of the recreation program. The boys who usually won were Mr. Lopez's son, Doc Lopez, and another kid who lived near the golf course named Richard Garcia, a.k.a. "the Crow". Doc and the Crow went on to become outstanding golfers at Cobre High School and always did well at the New Mexico High School Golf Championships.

I was never a very good golfer and spent most of my time looking for my balls somewhere off in the rough. And when I say "rough", I mean, "rough". The wild grasses were mowed and the large rocks were cleared away on the fairways, but the roughs weren't groomed at all and we usually lost lots of balls.

The greens were round and made of black cinder instead of grass. Once you chipped your ball onto the green, you had to use a heavy metal drag to clear a smooth pathway from your ball to the hole. The drag was "T shaped", with a solid metal handle that was welded to the center of a heavy piece of pipe about two and a half feet long. There were also hand crank ball washers located near the tee boxes so you could wash the dirt off of your balls before you teed-off to the next hole.

It was during my junior high school years when I became good friends with Tubby Porkman. We not only played on the same little league baseball team, but we also went to PF (Pilgrim Fellowship, church youth group) together and remained good friends throughout high school and college. I must also confess that I drank a lot of beers with Tubby over the years.

I used to go to Tubby's house quite often after school or sometimes during the evening. When his parents were home we would usually hang out in his bedroom or go outside and goof around in his yard. We also took his motor scooter for long rides when the weather was nice.

When his parents weren't home, we usually hung out in the house and listened to records or searched for food in the family pantry. One time we were in his kitchen and he pulled out a jar of yellow jalapeno peppers that were soaking in vinegar. I made a bet with him that he couldn't eat ten of them without a drink of water. He took me up on the bet, and he easily ate them, one by one, until they were gone. Even though I lost the bet, it was worth watching him chomp down on each jalapeno and act totally unfazed as he ate them.

One day after school we were fooling around in Tubby's back yard. We were bored and looking for something to do when we noticed a neighborhood cat that frequently wandered into his yard. The cat always strutted around the yard like he owned the place, but Tubby's two dogs didn't find him overly amusing. We called the cat over to us and, as we petted it, we began to discuss various ways that we could have a little fun with it. Since we knew that his two dogs, Scooter and Carmon, didn't particularly care for the cat, we thought that it would be interesting to incorporate them into the fun as well.

We decided to throw a cord up over the hoop of his basketball goal and suspend the cat from the end of it. We rigged it so that when we pulled on the rope the cat would go up, and the cat would go back down when we gave the rope a little slack.

Once the cat was tied up and ready, we called his dogs into the back yard. As soon as they saw the cat they immediately lunged toward it, but we pulled the cord so that the cat was just out of reach of their snarling jaws. For quite some time we managed to keep the dogs fairly amused, but before long they became tired and retreated to the shade to lie down. The cat must not have had as much fun as we did because he didn't come around very frequently after that.

The other thing we used to do regularly at Tubby's house was pilfer his parents' liquor stash that was kept in a hallway closet. They would go to El Paso on occasion and buy liquor by the case because they saved a lot of money when they bought in volume. There were always several unopened bottles in the case boxes, so when his parents were gone for the evening we would take a bottle of gin or vodka and drink most of it. When the bottle was empty, we would refill it with water and return it to the box in the closet. I don't think his parents ever discovered our scheme because they never mentioned anything to Tubby about it.

Tubby and I spent many evenings talking about philosophy or girls, and we also listened to some great rock albums. Tubby had a passion for music and he was always eager to share his new music with me. Two new albums I remember listening to at his house were "Sergeant Pepper's Lonely Heart's Club Band" by the Beatles and "The Yardbirds Greatest Hits". Over the years, we spent lots of time discussing our musical interests, and we always had the radio blaring whenever we were in a car.

C.C. Snell Junior High School

In the fall semester of our eighth grade year (1963-64) we attended school in Hurley. For the spring semester we were bussed to a makeshift junior high school located at the old Bayard Elementary School north of the Town Hall. We joined students from Bayard, Central, Mimbres, and Santa Rita at this temporary location while the new school, C.C. Snell Junior High, was under construction. The temporary school was very overcrowded and chaotic, but fortunately we were there for only a semester. C.C. Snell was scheduled to open at the beginning of our ninth grade year.

During our eighth grade school year the Beatles had just stormed the U.S. and appeared on the Ed Sullivan Show. In fact, some of the kids already had a copy of the Beatle's album "Meet The Beatles", which had hit songs like "I Want To Hold Your Hand" and "I Saw Her Standing There". It was perfect "coming of age" music for young teenagers and some of the girls in Hurley were ecstatic. I remember one morning during a bus ride to school in Bayard when several of us were arguing over why we did or didn't like the Beatles. As I recall, almost all of the girls thought they were awesome and most of the boys didn't like them. I think the main reason why a lot of boys didn't like the Beatles at first was because they were jealous that the girls were interested in older guys who were worldly, had long hair, and wore funny looking shoes and bell-bottom pants. I was one of the few boys that were excited about their music.

My second semester of eighth grade in Bayard was interesting because I met lots of kids from other towns in the school district. One of the first kids I made friends with was a boy from Santa Rita named Willy Martin. His dad was the general manager of a smaller mining concern in the area and his mother was from a ranching family north of Cliff. Willy was a smart kid who always did well in school, although he rarely passed up an opportunity to participate in mischief.

Willy's parents liked to spend the weekends at their family ranch, and on a couple of occasions they invited me to go with them. Willy and I would do things like drive around the ranch in an old jeep, ride horses, or go hunting for deer and birds. Willy's mother was a nice lady, and I admired his dad because he was a Gringo who could speak Spanish.

The following year marked the opening of the brand new school, C. C. Snell Junior High School. Our freshman class was the first to graduate from there. All freshman classes prior to the 1964-65 school year attended Cobre High School.

Even though it was exciting to go to a brand new school with lots of new friends, there were a few groups of Hispanic boys who banded together and picked on individual Gringos as we walked down the halls or were in the P.E. dressing room. Before long, we wised-up and began walking to classes and hanging out in larger groups to keep from getting harassed.

While my Anglo friends and I were struggling to find our own identity, the Hispanic boys were doing the same. It was common to see a few of them in the halls of Snell or Cobre with taps on the heels of their black pointed-toe shoes, while wearing black plastic framed sunglasses with their hair combed straight back on the sides. You could always tell when they came down the hall because you could hear their shoes clicking against the tile floor. A few Hispanic boys used pungent hair tonics like "Tres Flores" or a greasy wax called "La Parot" (the parrot) to keep their hair slicked back. Many of the Gringo kids referred to them as "chucos" or "pachucos", although we didn't know anything about the real "pachucismo" movement in California a couple of decades earlier.

There were a few epic fistfights that first year at Snell, usually between one of the Hispanic kids and a Gringo, presumably because the different groups of kids were trying to establish dominance at the school. Later on, at Cobre High School we became friends with most of these same kids because we realized that we had a lot of things in common and weren't posing a threat to each other.

During my eighth grade year I became friends with some ranch kids and cowboys and decided to join F.F.A. my freshman year. I chose to raise sheep for a couple of years and I kept them at the F.F.A. pens (a.k.a. "the pig pens") south of Hurley on the pipeline road. I usually rode my bicycle down to feed them every evening after I finished delivering newspapers.

In the fall of my freshman year we took our animals to the New Mexico State Fair in Albuquerque and then to the Grant County Fair in Cliff a couple of weeks later. In the fall of my sophomore year, just a few days before we were to take our animals to the Grant County Fair, two dogs scaled the six foot high fence at the pig pens and either killed or mauled every sheep inside. Two of my four sheep were killed and the other two had so many bite marks around their neck that they couldn't eat for days. By the time I took them to the fair, they had lost a lot of weight and were in pretty bad shape. Consequently, most of our lambs didn't do very well at the fair and we made very little money from the livestock sale. Fortunately, the man who owned the dogs had an insurance policy that eventually paid all of us a fair settlement for the loss of our livestock.

I made enough money from that settlement to buy my first motorcycle, a Honda 90 c.c. Super Sport. The motorcycle was a valuable investment for me because I used it to deliver newspapers and it was my sole source of transportation throughout high school. About a week before I left for college I sold the motorcycle and used that money, plus my paper route savings, to pay for my freshman year of college.

One of the very first activities we did in our F.F.A. class at Snell was plant trees and shrubs all around the new junior high school. One day, while we were outside planting shrubs, Willy Martin and Troy Wakefield were spreading peat moss inside the holes that they had just dug. At some point during class they left to go to the bathroom for a few minutes and eventually strolled back to where we were working. No one paid much attention to their brief absence from class, and when we finished planting for the day we returned to our F.F.A. classroom.

While we were waiting for the dismissal bell to ring at the end of class, a voice came over the intercom that said, "Will Troy Wakefield and Willy Martin report to the principal's office immediately."

After they left, everyone in class began to wonder whether they were in some sort of trouble or if they were getting an award for something. As it turned out, they were definitely in trouble. These two outstanding young pranksters had taken some peat moss out of one of their bags, snuck into the janitor's lunchroom, and put the peat moss into their coffee pot. When the janitors returned to the lunchroom for their morning break, they poured themselves a cup of coffee and took one drink before they spit it out. It didn't take them long to figure out what was in their coffee pot and where it came from.

Another kid I became good friends with during my freshman year was a boy from Bayard named Tom Foy. I took to him right away because he had some personal characteristics that I found to be quite interesting. First of all, I could tell that he was really smart and was a good athlete. He was a "mover and shaker" type of kid that always had a scheme or a plan cooking in the back of his mind. He and I also seemed to share a healthy skepticism for boundaries, rules, and authority, and would do just about anything if it entailed having fun.

I actually met Tom once a couple of years before we went to C.C. Snell together, but I didn't know much about him. Then, one Saturday about a year later I was at the Cobre High School auditorium at a school carnival. It was some sort of fund-raiser and they had little booths set up where kids could pay to try to win cheap prizes. They also had a greased pole about 10 feet high that kids would try to climb and grab a $5 bill that was taped to the top. If you wanted to climb the pole, you had to put on coveralls so that you didn't get grease all over your street clothes.

Anyway, as I was walking out the back door of the auditorium to the dirt road behind the high school, I noticed a pack of about five high school guys chasing a kid. When they ran by me, I realized that the kid they were chasing was young Tom Foy. I think they eventually caught him and gave him a pink belly. A year or so later when we became friends, I asked him about that incident. He told me that the older boys chased him because he had mouthed-off to one of them and made him look dumb in front of his friends. Apparently his quick wit was getting him into trouble at a very young age.

After school Tom and I would go to his house and play all sorts of games that were modified to make them more fun. Tom's parents liked having his friends come over to play and they treated all of the kids really well. We played miniature basketball in his basement using a small ball and goals that were about five feet high. When we got bored with that we would play tackle football on our knees or have wrestling matches on the living room carpet. If that got boring we would invent a new game or just go somewhere looking for mischief.

Sometimes Mrs. Foy would drive us to out-of-town high school sporting events against teams like Deming, Las Cruces, or Gadsden High School. And when there were home games at Cobre High, Tom was always in attendance. Tom was a "gym rat" who loved to be around team sporting events.

Tom had a younger brother named Carney who would always play games with us. When it came to sports and games, Carney was just like Tom. They were the best "gamers" I had ever seen. Once they learned the rules to any game they would eventually dominate it. They always played fair and were fun to play with, but you really had to be on your toes to beat them if you were their opponent.

The Pinball Prodigies

The Foy boys were the kind of guys who could put a nickel in a pinball machine and play it all afternoon. They knew which bumpers to hit for a high score and they knew exactly how hard to bump the machine without tilting it. I never saw them play pinball when they didn't have 15-25 games racked up on the machine.

One time, when Tom was in sixth grade, he went to the Pénjamo Restaurant with his friend Joe Vencill to play the pinball machines. It was around dinnertime and Tom was supposed to be home with his family, but he couldn't resist racking up a few games on the machines before he headed home for the evening.

Not long after the boys dropped a few nickels into the pinball machines, Tom glanced out the window and saw his mother drive up in front of the restaurant. "Oh shit, he exclaimed. There's my mom. I'm supposed to be home right now. I need to hide somewhere so she won't know that I'm here."

The boys quickly looked around for a hiding place, but before Tom could make his move, the front door to the restaurant opened and in walked his mother. In a last ditch effort to hide, Tom squatted down underneath one of the pinball machines and signaled for Joe to stand in front of it to provide cover for him.

Tom's mother glanced over and noticed Joe standing in front of the pinball machines and immediately walked over to talk to him. With her hands on her hips and a tone of urgency in her voice, she asked, "Joe, have you seen Tommy?"

Joe shifted around a little to block her view and slowly replied, "Uh, no Mrs. Foy. I haven't seen him all afternoon."

Well, squatting under a pinball machine isn't exactly the best place to hide if you don't want to be seen by your mother. It didn't take Mrs. Foy more than a couple of seconds to realize that Tom was hiding behind Joe on his hands and knees and was avoiding her at all costs.

"Tommy, what are you doing trying to hide from me underneath that pinball machine? You know where you are supposed to be right now. Now, you get out from under there and get in the car."

As she began to leave, Mrs. Foy abruptly turned to look back at Joe while he stood helplessly by the pinball machines. She lowered her head and peered above her glasses at him for a second, and turned to walk away with young Tommy in tow.

Tom and his younger brother Carney shared a bedroom in the large basement of their house. We always went down there and listened to records or played our version of some sport. One afternoon, Tom and I decided to have a little fun and tie up one of Carney's friends with some cord. After we wrestled him to the floor, we removed his shirt and tied his right hand and foot to the posts of one of their beds and his left hand and foot to the posts of the other bed so that he was in a spread-eagle position. We then began to tickle him in the armpits with a feather while his arms were outstretched.

After a few minutes of our torture regimen, the kid was laughing and screaming so loud and uncontrollably that Tom's mother overheard the ruckus from upstairs. Out of curiosity, she came rushing downstairs to investigate. Once she walked into the bedroom and saw the boy tied up and shirtless, we could tell she wasn't very pleased with our idea of fun. She ordered us to cut him loose immediately and told me that I would have to go home. As it turned out, that was the only time I was ever sent home from the Foys' house in all the years I hung out there.

Another time in the Foys' basement, Tom and I were goofing around with a new chemistry set that he had been given for Christmas. I can't remember what chemicals he mixed together, but as he was holding the test tube in his hand it exploded and burned his hand. It also singed his face and eyebrows. Since his parents weren't home at the time and he was in need of medical attention, we hitchhiked from Bayard to Hurley to the Doctor's office on Chino Blvd. to get him treated for his burns. The doctor bandaged up his hand and gave him some ointment for his face.

One summer morning just before the school year began, I was at the Foys' house when there was a knock at the door. Tom's mother answered the door and found Carl Hyde, a Bayard Policeman, standing there. Officer Hyde was investigating an incident where someone had used spray paint to write graffiti on the press box at the Cobre High School football field. He went on to tell Mrs. Foy that he had reason to suspect that Tom and I may have had something to do with the graffiti incident.

Surprised, Mrs. Foy called Tom and me to the front door and stood by as Officer Hyde asked us if we knew anything about what had happened. The truth was that, for once, we didn't know anything about the graffiti incident. For some reason, officer Hyde didn't believe our story and tried to question us further. Finally, Mrs. Foy intervened and told him she thought we were telling the truth. After a few more questions, Officer Hyde realized he wasn't going to get anywhere with us so he left. He still had no suspects, tips, or clues as to who had painted graffiti on the press box.

After the cop left, Tom and I began to ponder who it could have been that painted the press box. We were upset with the Bayard cop for trying to blame it on us, but at the same time we were also miffed because someone was getting away with the graffiti job at our expense. In an effort to clear our names from the crime, we decided to do a little detective work and find out the identity of the culprits. By the end of the morning Tom and I had hatched an ingenious plan.

The following afternoon we set out for the Hurley Swimming Pool to begin our quest for truth, justice, and the American way. As kids came and went throughout the afternoon, we would strike up a casual conversation with them and inadvertently mention, "Hey, did you hear that someone painted graffiti on the Cobre High School press box? I don't know who did it but, whoever it was, they did an awesome job."

Then we would laugh and carry on for a few more minutes.

Eventually, as we continued our display of effusive admiration for the graffiti job to anyone who would listen to us, our good friend Jake Thompson was standing nearby and happened to overhear us. Before long he slowly meandered over and disclosed to us, wearing an ear-to-ear grin and beaming with pride, that, "It was Richard Gomez and I that did it."

We laughed with Jake for a while and repeatedly complimented him for his ingenious act of vandalism.

A few minutes later Tom and I walked over to the Chino Club to get an ice cream cone. We also asked permission to use their phone. Using a disguised voice and a handkerchief placed over the phone receiver, we made an anonymous call to our good friends at the Bayard Police Dept. and told them,

"The Cobre High press box was painted by Jake Thompson and Richard Gomez."

Then we hung up the phone before they could ask us any more questions.

A few days later, Tom and I were walking by the Cobre High football field when we happened to notice Jake and Richard chopping weeds near the bleachers. We went over to them and asked, "Hey, how come you guys are busting your butts out here in the hot sun? It's summer vacation."

One of the boys looked up as he was raking weeds into a big pile and responded, "We got caught painting graffiti on the press box. As punishment we have to cut weeds every day for a week."

Tom and I played dumb while we chatted with them but, by the time we were halfway across the football field, we were giddy with laughter.

One evening while I was at Tom's house I was invited to have dinner with the family. The Foys were a very gracious and generous family and over the years I ate dozens of fine meals with them. Tom's father, Tommy Foy Sr. was an attorney and politician in Silver City, and his mother was very active and prominent in local civic organizations.

As we sat down at the dinner table, I was subtly reminded that there was something quite unique and unusual in my pocket. This item was my most recent acquisition, and I knew Tom would get a kick out of it when I showed it to him. I also had a hunch that everyone in his family would find it very interesting and amusing as well.

A few days earlier I purchased a shiny new switchblade knife with a six-inch blade from a fine, upstanding young fellow from Hurley. He had acquired the knife in Juarez a few weeks earlier while he was "catting around" the backstreets with his buddies, but for some reason he needed to get rid of it. When he showed it to me, I became quite intrigued by how quickly the blade sprang into place when you pushed the little button on the side of the handle. The blade came to a sharp point at the end and it locked into place once it sprang open. It was truly a marvelous invention and I simply couldn't pass up the opportunity to become its next owner.

Servings of food were passed around and before long the table was overcome with near silence as everyone enjoyed their meal. After a few bites, it occurred to me how fun and exciting it would be to show off my new knife by using it to cut the piece of meat on my plate. While everyone was busy eating, I inconspicuously reached into my pocket and pulled out the switchblade. Then, I held it out in front of me and pushed the button on the handle. "Caawhaaak." The long, silver blade instantly sprang and locked into place. It worked like a charm and I was proud of my new knife as I began to cut the meat on my plate.

The dinner table suddenly became totally quiet. When I looked up from my plate, I was astonished at what I saw. Everyone's eyes were wide open and their jaws were nearly resting on their plates. Before I could figure out what was going on, Tom's dad yelled, "What are you doing with that knife? Switchblades are illegal in New Mexico. You could get arrested for carrying that thing around. You give me that knife right now before you get into trouble with it."

At first I thought he was kidding, but after a few seconds I realized he was dead serious. So, I reluctantly folded the knife up and gave it to him. It never occurred to me that carrying a switchblade knife in my pocket was a crime. As far as I was concerned, it was nothing more than a toy.

Later that evening I felt a little better about the switchblade ordeal when Tom offered to find out where his dad hid it so he could snatch it back for me. It took him a few months, but he did return it to me and I never heard anything else about it again.

Assorted Junior High School Mischief

During our freshman year at Snell there was a "TV-fueled" Duncan Yoyo craze going on with the kids. I learned several of the yoyo tricks and actually became quite proficient. I used to be able to do "Walk the Dog", "Rock-a-bye-Baby", "Around the World", and a few others.

It didn't take long for us to find a way to get in trouble at school with our yoyos. Occasionally a few guys with yoyos would walk down the hallway and follow a group of girls. Once they got close enough, one of the braver boys would flick his yoyo outward. As the yoyo returned it would catch the bottom of the girl's skirt and flip it up. It wasn't long before one of the girls told the principal what the boys were up to and yoyos soon became banished from school.

One afternoon my friend Willy and I got into a little jam when we were in P.E. class. Just as we were getting dressed at the end of class, a couple of boys in the locker room got into trouble with the P.E. teachers. Now, when a student misbehaved in P.E. class it was customary for the coaches to take them into the coach's office and bend them over the training table to beat their butt with a paddle. What made matters even worse was there was a big window in the coach's office and everyone in the locker room could watch the paddlings take place.

As Willy and I were leaving the locker room, we happened to walk by the window just as the two boys were taking their licks. Since school was over for the day and we were in a "clowning-around" mood, we stopped at the window and leaned against the glass to laugh and make faces at the boys as they got their swats. Then we quickly headed toward the exit door of the locker room and continued on our merry way.

All of a sudden one of the P.E. teachers came running out of the office and yelled, "So, you guys think it's funny, eh? Well, I need for you two boys to come on back into my office."

We looked at each other with a surprised look on our faces and returned to his office. Once we were inside, he bent us over the training table and gave us a little of the same medicine they had doled out to the other boys. The coaches got the last laugh on this occasion.

During junior high school and high school there were a few silly games the Hispanic kids used to play just to keep things lively. The games were so fun that the Gringo kids would get in on them as well. Somehow these ridiculous games helped us all to bond and become better friends.

One game was called "Sopitas". The game went something like this: If you asked a kid to do something without saying "please", then someone who overheard you would yell out "¡Mandando!" (the Spanish word for ordering or demanding).

Once everyone heard "¡Mandando!", someone else would immediately follow-up by yelling "¡Sopitas!", which entitled everyone nearby to mug you by slapping you on top of the head.

The only way you could call everybody off was by saying the phrase "Vuljer pee wee", and then whistling two short notes. The first note had to be about a third of an octave higher than the second note or it didn't work. The problem for the victim was, he would be laughing so hard while he was getting mugged that he couldn't whistle the last two notes. Sometimes a kid would get worked over for several minutes before the other kids would finally stop. It sounds weird, but everyone loved playing the game. One of the things that made it so fun was that no one was immune from getting "Sopitas". Even the bullies got worked over on occasion.

Another cool game was "Orejitas" (little ears), which went like this: Any time you were in possession of something new, you were subject to getting Orejitas. For example, if you walked into a classroom with a new pencil, a new pair of shoes, a new haircut, or whatever, someone would yell out "¡Zapatos nuevos!" (new shoes) or "¡Lapiz Nuevo!", (new pencil). Then, if someone responded by quickly yelling "¡Orejitas!", everyone nearby would get to yank and twist your ears.

"Madediao" (ma-de-dyow) was another fun word that was used frequently between classes, before and after school, and sometimes during class. If you were talking to someone and made a statement that appeared to be an exaggeration, one of the other kids would call you on it by blurting out, "Madediao".

Another phrase that was used in the same situations was "Neeeawww Stevie". Once in a while a teacher would state some fact during class, like, "Columbus discovered America in 1492," and some wise guy from the back of the class would yell out "Neeeawww Stevie". Everyone in class would break out laughing. The teacher usually got mad and would punish the wise guy, if they could ever find out who said it.

Once in a while the teacher would ask a student a question about a lesson and the student would reply with a ridiculous answer. One very popular "dumb answer" was "In Deming". For example, the math teacher might ask a question like, "Johnny, what is the square root of 947?"

Johnny, who was obviously unprepared for the lesson, would answer "In Deming".

Another popular "dumb answer" was "2,000". If the biology teacher asked a kid in the back of the room a question like, "Jimmy, explain the concept of osmosis."

Jimmy would then reply, "About 2,000, more less."

If you wanted to get kicked out of class, these answers were usually a great way to have your wish come true.

"Nucles" (nuke-less), or knuckles, was another fad type game we played at school. Nucles could get a little nasty at times. Guys would grow out the fingernail on their long middle finger and take turns trying to dig it into their opponent's knuckle using a motion similar to snapping your finger. To play, you had to double up your fist and let the other guy take a snap at your knuckle and then you would get to reciprocate. The object of the game was to play until someone drew blood. My brother used to come home from school with two or three bloody knuckles on each hand from a day of playing nucles.

Another juvenile game we played in Hurley when I was growing up dealt with farting. Anytime you farted in the company of friends you had to say "Vince" in order to avoid getting slugged in the arm. If your friend said "Pokes" before you said "Vince", he could slug you. If you said "Returns" to your friend as soon as he said "Pokes", but before he said "No Returns", you could slug him back after he slugged you. The only way to stop the slugfest was by saying "Returns and No Returns", which meant you could hit your friend back but he couldn't hit you again.

One time in the late 1950's, all of the schools from around the county were invited to go see the play "Rip Van Winkle" at Light Hall on the campus of New Mexico Western College. For some strange reason, the older Hurley kids felt like being disruptive during the play and were constantly making little noises and misbehaving. At one point, as Rip Van Winkle delivered one of his lines, one of the seventh or eighth graders from Hurley blurted out aloud, "Neawww Stevie" in the theater. Laughter from the Hurley section of the audience echoed throughout the theater. Finally, Rip Van Winkle had to stop the play and chastise the student audience for being disruptive. The next day at school the Hurley teachers did their usual teacher thing and threatened to take away our extracurricular activity privileges. Then, a couple of days later my older brother told me that the kid who disrupted the play was one of his classmates. I never did believe him, though, because the voice that yelled out "Neawww Stevie" sounded just like him.

Cobre High School

When Cobre High School opened in September of 1955, Hurley High School was closed for good. The students transferred to a Cobre campus that was much larger and more modern than the two story wooden building they were accustomed to. The old Hurley High School building then became Hurley Junior High School.

The first time I ever visited Cobre was probably within a year after it opened. Families from all over the school district went there to have the new Salk vaccine for polio administered to their children. I remember standing out in front of the high school in a huge line of people that extended onto the sidewalks and into the parking lot. Being a young boy at the time, I didn't realize what a historic accomplishment the Salk vaccine was for the field of medicine.

I attended Cobre High from the fall of 1965 until the spring of 1968 when I graduated. I can probably sum up my experience there by saying that, in general,

I hated it. From an academic perspective, Cobre High was better than average when compared to other high schools in New Mexico, but the culture at school was provincial and behind the times. The school administration was very traditional and conservative during a time when the rest of the country was on the verge of social revolution. Students would go home after school and watch television footage of the Viet Nam war and students rioting in the streets of major cities across America. "Pop Culture" was exploding with new music, fashion, and social norms, and Martin Luther King was kicking open the doors that harbored racial hatred and bigotry.

There were a lot of mixed messages floating around the school and community and it was difficult for students to find out what was actually true and what was myth. For example, the school would invite fat county cops with white cowboy hats to come into our classes to tell the students that marijuana was addicting and smoking it would lead to heroin use. Most of my friends had never seen or used marijuana in high school and it was easy to tell that the authorities were making a big deal out of nothing.

Before long some of the boys from Cobre and Silver schools began to change their haircut style from clean-cut flat tops to the more contemporary long hair, mop top haircuts. The Beach Boys also popularized the "surfer haircut" that some of the boys in Grant County began to wear. It was a little more clean-cut than the mop top style. The surfer cut was shorter on the sides than the mop top cut, and boys would comb their hair down over their upper forehead.

Unfortunately, long hair and other forms of self-expression were taboo in the area schools at the time. In 1965 the school administration at Cobre High School began cracking down on boys that had longer hair. As a result, several kids got into trouble at school and had huge hassles with their parents at home. The hair issue eventually became very socially divisive in Grant County for the remainder of my high school years and into the 1970's.

When I was a sophomore at CHS I grew my hair out in the style of the dreaded "surfer haircut". Two of my best friends also had haircuts similar to mine. One day we were called into the principal's office and told that if we didn't come to school the next day with our hair cut we would be suspended from school.

We came to school the next day without a haircut and, sure enough, were suspended. In fact, we were eventually suspended twice for our hair length, which made us hate school even worse than we already did. We soon realized that we were being singled out as martyrs for the rest of the student body to see. The message was quite clear: "We don't like nonconformists, and if you challenge our rigid rules, we're going to kick you out of here."

There was also social tension brewing between a small group of students who were growing their hair longer and listening to Rock music, and some of the cowboys who lived around Grant County. This particular group of cowboys detested the kids who had longer hair and there was constant harassment and hazing in the hallways at school and around town on the weekends. The cowboys called the longhaired kids "cat daddies" and "surfers" and the longhaired kids referred to the cowboys as "stomps", "goat ropers", or "shitkickers". If the kids with long hair ran into drunken cowboys at a dance on Friday night, there was a chance that someone would get into a fight. As I grew my hair out I began carrying a walnut "billy-club" in my coat sleeve in case I got jumped at the teen dances around the county.

I enjoyed being a member of F.F.A. during my freshman and sophomore years but I eventually quit because of the harassment from some of my fellow F.F.A. members. Sadly, some of the guys that hassled me were my friends who had turned against me because of my haircut.

Some of the high school aged cowboys also had problems with several of the Hispanic students. Since the longhaired kids and the Hispanics shared common social problems with them, new and unlikely friendships developed between the two groups. Consequently, whenever my friends and I ran into some of the Hispanic kids on a Saturday night, we would usually end up parked on some remote dirt road to drink and have fun.

If there was a silver lining to this socially challenging situation, I think that the long hair "movement" became a social litmus test for our small mining community. Prior to this issue, there was a fairly rigid and one-dimensional social hierarchy in the institutions of Grant County such as the schools, the courts, the police, the work place, and the churches. The choice to have a different haircut forced everyone to contend with a new social dynamic that we now refer to as "tolerance".

Another positive outcome was that the hair issue helped many kids in our community shape their social values and how they dealt with hatred, racism, and bigotry. Most kids with long hair learned, firsthand, what it was like to get judged by their appearance, not by their character or behavior.

While I can't say that Cobre High School condoned racial prejudice, there were a couple of situations that led some of my Hispanic friends to question whether they were being treated fairly. In the weeks leading up to our graduation, the seniors were required to meet with a school counselor to help make a plan for their life after high school. Many of the Hispanic kids were advised that their best option would be to join the military after graduation. To the contrary, a larger number of the Anglo students were encouraged to attend college. Although we had no statistical proof that this was happening, several students in my friendship circle made it a point to keep a close eye on these types of trends.

To some students, the counseling sessions seemed a bit superficial and phony anyway, since most of them had rarely set foot in the counselor's office during their entire three years at Cobre. The counselors didn't know the graduates well enough to be telling them whether or not they were "college material". They would look at your grades, your standardized test scores, and your behavior rap-sheet and then give you advice on what to do with the rest of your life.

Another race related incident occurred on the bus ride home to Hurley from Cobre High School one afternoon. The bus was an old Chevy with a three-speed transmission and the driver was a man named Mr. Simpson. Whenever he slowed down to make the left turn from the highway into Hurley, he always downshifted into second gear to help slow down the bus. As he forced the floor mounted gearshift lever into second gear, the transmission would make a loud grinding sound until the gears eventually meshed and the shift was complete.

The same thing occurred day after day. The driver would downshift as he turned into Hurley and the transmission would grind. After several months, the Hispanic kids sitting in the back of the bus decided to have some fun with Mr. Simpson's predictable routine. So, every day when he downshifted and turned into Hurley, someone from the back of the bus would yell, "Put the clutch, Simpson." To make matters even livelier, everyone in the back would then laugh and make all sorts of lewd comments, which usually had words like "pinche" or "cabron" woven into the cacophony and chaos.

After several days of this petty harassment, Mr. Simpson became increasingly irritated and upset. Finally, the situation came to a head one afternoon when I was sitting in the back of the bus with a few of my Hispanic friends. As we turned into Hurley, Mr. Simpson slammed the bus into second gear and the transmission barked out its usual grinding noise. Before anyone else could beat me to the punch, I yelled in my best Spanish accent, "Put the clutch, Simpson."

As soon as Mr. Simpson made the turn into Hurley, he abruptly stopped the bus on the side of the road. He then jumped up from the driver's seat and stormed to the back of the bus. In a very angry tone of voice he told all of the Hispanic students, "All right, I've had enough of your crap. You can just get the hell off of the bus and walk home."

After a brief exchange with Mr. Simpson, the Hispanic kids grabbed their belongings and began to exit the bus. As they stepped down onto the side of the road, they were laughing and making wise cracks because they had finally gotten the bus driver's goat. They also knew they had been singled out because of their ethnicity.

Another interesting situation developed during the pre-season football camp in the summer of 1967. The Cobre High football team was at Camp Thunderbird preparing for the upcoming season, when apparently there were several Hispanic players who felt they were not being given a fair shot at making the starting line-up for the football team. Finally, the Hispanic players had a private player's meeting and discussed the situation. They concluded that if they were to be chosen for any of the first team positions, they were going to have to substantially out-play the Anglo players with whom they were competing. As a group, they eventually motivated each other and worked their way into several of the starting positions for the duration of the season.

Beginning in the second week of December, 1967 Grant County had one of the worst series of snowstorms on record. The storms would dump enough snow to cancel school for a day or two and, just when it looked like the weather was clearing, another storm would move in and school would be cancelled for another couple of days. The storms continued until it was time for our Christmas vacation. By the time schools started again in January, we had been out of school for about a month. It was an exciting time because none of us had ever missed that much school before. There was, however, one small catch. Once the weather returned to normal we had to go to school on Saturdays to make up for all of the snow days that we missed.

I managed to have a few good times at Cobre in spite of its provincial approach to education. The lunch period was always fun because it was the biggest break from classes during the course of the school day. I would usually connect with my friends to go eat in the cafeteria or sit on the grass and eat a sack lunch. Sometimes we would walk across the highway to Al's Pastry and get a couple of tamales or go eat at the Sugar Shack next to the car wash. On Fridays the cafeteria always served good enchiladas and had quite a reputation among the students and the community. When I was a senior, I would occasionally skip lunch and go to the gym to play ping-pong with one of my favorite teachers, Mr. Aurelio Sandoval.

In my opinion, there were a few fine teachers scattered throughout the halls of Cobre High School, but some of the teachers and administrators were witless toads. As usual, the high achieving students received positive recognition and the low achieving students and troublemakers received the negative attention. The average students received very little encouragement and were given few opportunities to develop the self-confidence necessary to succeed after high school. If you weren't a jock or an honor student, there was a good chance you would slip through the cracks.

During my junior and senior years I had a P.E. class with a man named Mr. Erickson. He was a fun teacher and let us do lots of activities in class that were unusual and challenging. One year we did a unit in gymnastics and, once our class got good enough at tumbling and vaulting, we had a public performance one evening to show off our skills.

Mr. Erickson also let us chew some of his Red Man chewing tobacco whenever we played basketball in the gym. When we needed to spit we would walk over to the gymnasium wall behind one of the basketball goals and spit between the cinder block wall and the large vertical metal support beams that held up the roof. There were several occasions that my head was spinning when I left P.E. class.

Sometimes we would load our P.E. class into a bus and go swimming at the new Bayard indoor swimming pool. We learned different swimming strokes during class, but we also had a lot of free time to swim or dive. One morning Mr. Erickson said to me, "Hey Boswell, get up on the diving board and I'll teach you how to do a half gainer."

That was a scary dive because you had to throw your head back and kick your legs out in front of you as you jumped off of the board. I was afraid I would crack my head on the end of the diving board if I didn't jump far enough away from it.

After some brief instruction, I got up enough nerve to try it. I nervously made my approach and jumped up from the end of the diving board. I threw my head back just as Mr. Erickson had instructed but, the problem was, I didn't bring my knees up toward my chest as my body slowly rotated backwards. As a result, my feet never rose above my head and I crashed into the water, flat on my back. I hit so hard that it was the most painful dive of my life. Not only did my back turn bright red and sting in excruciating pain, but the impact partially knocked the wind out of me.

When I swam to the ladder to climb out of the pool, Mr. Erickson was standing right there. He looked down at me as I was gasping for air and said, "Get back on that board right now and try it again."

I immediately replied, "I can't. I'm in too much pain."

He looked down at me and told me again, as he pointed to the diving board, "Get your butt back up there."

So I went back to the diving board, still stinging and gasping for air, and tried it again. This time I was thinking to myself, "No matter what happens, I have to get my legs up over my head or else I will be in twice the pain I'm in now."

I took my approach and sprang off of the board again with my knees tucked closer to my chest. This time around I threw my head back with force and miraculously dove right into the water without any problem. When I got out of the pool again Mr. Erickson was laughing because I had done a nice half gainer on the second try. He told me as I was climbing out of the pool, "Whenever you fail the first time around, you have to try it again while you are still in pain. If you wait for the pain to go away, you will talk yourself out of doing it."

Learning a half gainer was indeed a painful lesson, but I will never forget it. I was the only guy in class who did it because everyone else was afraid to try it once they saw what happened to me.

At the end of P.E. class we routinely showered, got dressed, and returned to the gym to wait for the bell to ring. During that time, most of the boys would lean against the collapsed bleachers near our locker room and watch the girls walk by on the other side of the gym. Among the girl watchers in our class was one tall, thin boy who always leaned his back against the bleachers while standing on one foot as his other foot rested against the bleachers behind him. Whenever the girls came out of their locker room, this young man had a peculiar habit of reaching down and rubbing his crotch as he watched them from afar. No one knew if he did this intentionally or if it was a subconscious habit but, for several weeks, my friends and I would laugh as we watched him perform his morning ritual.

One morning we decided to have a little fun with this guy. As soon as he leaned back against the bleachers and began his crotch rubbing routine, a friend and I ran up the stairs to the balcony above the bleachers. Directly above where he was standing were some heavy canvass tumbling mats that the wrestling team had rolled up on the concrete balcony floor. The mats were probably four feet wide, eight feet long, about two inches thick, and weighed about 100 lbs. apiece.

My friend and I quietly lifted one of the rolled up mats onto the metal guardrail at the edge of the balcony and launched it overboard. The bulky mat accelerated downward and landed directly on top of the kid, instantly knocking him to the floor. By the time he crawled out from under the mat and figured out what had happened, he was fighting mad. Fortunately, we were long gone by the time he came to his senses. We apparently cured the kid of his case of "itchy testicles" because he never leaned up against the bleachers again.

Another teacher I liked was Miss Ranelle Hoover. She had a reputation of being a strict English teacher and many kids dreaded being in her class. On the first day of class she came across my name as she was taking roll and said to me, "You and I are going to have problems."

When I heard her say that, I knew right then and there that I was going to be in for a long year. But then, as the first couple of weeks of school went by, we somehow became good friends and I never had any problem with her. By the end of the school year she had become one of my favorite teachers of all time.

In her spare time, Mrs. Hoover was the choir director at the Methodist Church in Silver City. One morning after class, she invited Tubby Porkman and me to come listen to her choir the following Sunday. Tubby was also friends with her, so he and I dressed up and went to church to hear her choir. We could tell when we walked into the church that she was quite pleased to see us walking up the aisle in our sports coats, slacks, and ties.

When the services were over, she was delighted when we told her how much we enjoyed the choir. Then we hopped into Tubby's little International Scout and headed for home. Before we got to the outskirts of Silver City we popped open a fifth of Seagram's 7, spiked our ice-cold sodas, and loosened our ties for the ride home.

Mrs. Laura Espinosa was the Spanish teacher at Cobre High and she generally got along well with the students. Her class wasn't that difficult and most of the time the atmosphere in her room was casual. She always had a few "pet" kids in each class that ran errands and did little favors for her. Since my Spanish class was right before lunch, she would let one of her "pets" drive her car to the post office to mail a letter or go pick up a lunch for her at a local restaurant.

Mr. Harold Guildenberg was the Chemistry and Physics teacher. He was a strange bird but a good science teacher. He only threw me out of class once that I remember. I had been making monkey noises under my breath for several weeks as he was writing on the blackboard with his back turned toward the class. Finally, one day he turned around just as I was making my noises and he caught me in the act. I guess I can't blame the guy for finally getting fed up with my disruptive behavior, but darn it, I was just trying to make chemistry class a little more interesting.

Dr. Edward Linchman was a popular teacher and a nice guy who taught the upper level math classes. He was also my tennis coach. I never had him as a teacher because I had terrible study habits and was always enrolled in the lower level math classes.

Mrs. Brenda Jacobs was my Sociology teacher for one semester. She lived in Deming and drove to Bayard to teach. She was a nice lady and got along fine with the kids, but the one thing I remember most about her was her unusual behavior while the class was busy with a reading assignment. She would hike her bare foot up onto her desk and clip her toenails while the class was reading.

I had an older man named Mr. Raven for Biology as a sophomore. He was a nice man and a decent teacher but the poor fellow wore thick glasses and had fairly poor vision. His visual impairment became a green light for those of us seated in the back of the class to goof off and throw just about anything we wanted around the classroom. I learned very little in his class and my Biology grade proved it.

The Cobre High School Ag. Teacher, Mr. Walters, was well connected with the ranching and farming communities in southwest New Mexico. Under his tutelage, the students in FFA would take their livestock to the New Mexico State Fair in Albuquerque and then to the Grant County Fair in Cliff. Some students would also take their animals to a fair in El Paso as well. The New Mexico State Fair was always fun because the kids who entered their animals into the livestock show would get to stay in a dormitory on the fair grounds for several days and spend their free time checking out exhibits and going on carnival rides at the Midway.

There were other FFA travel opportunities as well. One year I made the FFA dairy judging team and we traveled to Arrey, NM, near Hatch, to compete in a dairy cow judging competition against kids from other FFA chapters in southern New Mexico. Our FFA chapter also had other teams that judged assorted livestock, and our FFA officers would travel to Kansas City every year to the National FFA Convention.

Mr. Walters knew the tricks of the trade when it came to showing livestock. He not only taught us how to show our animals in the ring but how to prepare our animals for the shows. It was common practice for the boys who raised sheep to spend a few hours shearing them just before we took them into the show ring. I don't know what other FFA chapters did to get their animals ready to show, but the Cobre FFA boys had a couple of additional secret preparation techniques in our bag of tricks. One of the more clandestine things we did in the tack room immediately before the show was place ice packs on the back of each sheep for about thirty minutes. The ice would make their muscles "tense up" and become hard. Since we knew the livestock judge preferred animals that had firm musculature, it gave our sheep a better chance of placing higher in the competition.

Another sly Cobre FFA trick that was practiced by the boys who raised hogs was to stick Vick's Vapo Rub up the hog's ass immediately prior to the show. This apparently caused the hog to hunch its back in response to the stinging menthol inside of them. Hogs with an arched back have better musculature and are considered more desirable than hogs with a flat back. The Vick's Vapo Rub application could turn an average hog into a better than average hog in about 15 seconds. One day I asked Mr. Walters if this technique really made hogs hunch up and he replied, "Well, what would you do if somebody stuck Vick's Vapo Rub up your ass?"

As it turned out, I'm glad I raised sheep instead of hogs because the thought of sticking my finger up a hog's asshole never did seem too appealing.

During my freshman year, my friends Randy Hampshire and Derick Borrows were raising hogs at some pigpens at the north end of Bayard. Derick's father drove him to the pens every day to feed, water, and exercise his hogs, but Randy had to walk across town to take care of his animals. Over a period of time Randy became disinterested and gradually began to neglect his hogs.

After a few weeks, Derick began to notice that his hogs were fat and healthy, while Randy's hogs were lean and falling behind in growth. Eventually, Derick felt so sorry for Randy's hogs that he began feeding and caring for them in his absence.

As the Grant County Fair approached, Derick continued to take care of Randy's hogs. With regular feeding and exercise, they had gained considerable weight and became healthy and strong again. Ironically, when Derick and Randy showed their hogs at the fair a few days later, one of Randy's hogs ended up winning Grand Champion and Derick's hog only won Reserve Grand Champion. I think that Derick was a little miffed about how things turned out, and Randy laughed all the way to the bank.

One of the fund-raising activities our F.F.A. chapter did was have some of our members work a concession stand at the roping arena down by B Ranch in North Hurley. Cowboys from around Grant County would come to Hurley on Sundays to have a "jackpot roping" competition. The arena was located on the west side of Whitewater Creek and northeast of the slag dumps.

One year my fellow FFA members Tommy Buckner and Lance Riggins volunteered to work the concession stand together for a few Sundays. They served sodas, hot dogs and candy bars from a concession trailer that was parked next to the arena.

The "ropin" always lasted for a few hours, and by late afternoon Tommy and Lance would get bored from standing around inside the concession trailer. Being typical 14 year-old boys, it didn't take long before they invented things to do to keep themselves amused. Since they were working in a concession stand, the obvious thing to do for fun was sabotage the food.

Photo 4-4: This is the old house that was located at B Ranch in Whitewater Creek. Photo courtesy of New Mexico State University Library, Archives and Special Collections.

When a hungry cowboy would come up to the counter to order a hot dog, the boys routinely placed a hot dog in the bun and then asked the customer if they wanted mustard, catsup, and/or relish. And depending on their inventory of freshly caught flies, they would add one or two to the hot dog as they slapped on the condiments.

If the customer ordered a soda to go along with their gourmet hot dog, Lance and Tommy would set them up for the "One-Two Punch". They would fill a cup with ice and soda and place it on the counter. As they reached across the counter to give the roper his change, they would accidently (on purpose) drop one of the coins onto the ground and say, "Oh, I'm sorry." As the cowboy bent over to pick up his money, they would either stick their slimy finger in the cup of soda or spit in it.

As their satisfied customers walked back toward the arena, Tommy and Lance would break out into hysterical laughter. In hindsight, I am absolutely certain they were lucky no one ever caught them doctoring-up the food. There is no telling what those cowboys would have done if they ever found out what the boys were doing in that concession stand.

I went out for Wrestling and Football while I was in high school, but I wasn't very good at either sport. I was, however, fairly decent at tennis and was a varsity letterman for a couple of years. There were always four or five guys on the team that were better than me but I always managed to make the varsity traveling team nevertheless.

My most memorable accomplishment in high school tennis came at a tournament in Las Cruces. I was playing doubles with a kid named Bobby Dominguez, a.k.a. "Angus", and our first match was against the number one tennis team from Silver High School. Bobby and I were the worst doubles team from Cobre and we stepped onto the court knowing the match was going to be a slaughter.

The first game began with the Silver High team serving to us. It would probably be more appropriate to say that they were serving rockets at us. Their serves were traveling so fast Bobby and I were lucky if we could just lob them back over the net. Whenever we did make an improbable return, they would scramble over and smash a kill shot right back at us.

It was obvious they were much better than we were, but, ironically, they were playing so aggressively that they began hitting the balls out of bounds and making tons of mistakes. My partner and I, realizing how lucky we were, began laughing and having a good time while the other team became increasingly frustrated and, before long, began "snipping" at each other. Eventually, they barely beat us, but that was probably the luckiest and most fun match I ever played.

Another memorable moment in my brief tennis career occurred in Deming. I was playing a singles match against some kid who was about my skill level. The court we were playing on had one of those old thick chord nets instead of the newer, stiffer, metal nets. After a couple of games into our set, my opponent and I had to switch sides of the court to resume the next game. Instead of walking around the net, I decided to take a shortcut and simply jump over it at mid-court. Somehow, as I threw my foot over the net, it became tangled, and I abruptly fell flat on my ass. After spending a minute trying to get my foot untangled, I stood up in a state of embarrassment and slowly looked around in hopes that no one had seen my blunder. Unfortunately, Coach Linchman and two of my teammates were standing at the back of the court, doubled over from laughing so hard.

If you received a varsity letter in a sport you were eligible to join the C Club. Almost all of my "jock" friends were veteran members of this elite club. One of the stipulations to joining the C Club was that all newcomers had to go through an initiation in order to be inducted. The initiation process was conducted by the student members and had very little oversight from the coaches who sponsored the club.

Not long after I received my varsity letter in tennis I was initiated and joined the club. The initiation was basically a day of hazing and harassment from the other members. For example, I had to carry a veteran C Club member's books to and from class for them during the school day. Then, during my lunch period I had to roll an egg down the hall with my nose. I know that rolling an egg down the hall sounds a bit like good clean fun, but there was one small catch. I had to roll the egg down some concrete steps. To add a little excitement to the task, we were informed that if the raw egg broke, we had to eat it. As you can imagine, my egg broke and I had to crack it open and slurp it down. I had never tasted anything as nasty as a raw egg before, and it was a couple of years before I could ever eat cooked eggs again.

At the end of the initiation day the new inductees were ordered to report to the locker room where we were given pink bellies. It was also rumored there would be one final secretive stage to the initiation that was to take place after the pink bellies were doled out. None of us knew exactly what the mysterious initiation entailed, but we had heard through the grapevine that the procedure involved the removal of some of our clothing, a blindfold, a raw hot dog, and possibly some Vaseline. Fortunately, that phase of the initiation never took place but it certainly created a little anxiety for the inductees throughout the day.

After-school practices for team sports were designed to toughen-up the athlete, similar to a boot camp. There was a mentality among the coaches at the time that you had to "make it hurt" to get into shape and be good at a particular sport. It wasn't uncommon to see fellow teammates run over to the edge of the football field to puke during wind sprints at the end of practice. When we did stretching exercises, like hamstring stretches, the coaches would have us bob up and down to stretch the muscle. We would also have to do sit-ups with our legs straight. And then there were lots of calisthenics like side straddle hops, toe touches, and squat-thrust that required the team to count, "One-two-three-four-two-two-three-four", and so on. Athletes weren't allowed to drink water during practice and there were salt tablet dispensers in the locker room so we could replace the salt we sweated out during practice. Athletes, especially football players, were encouraged to eat large portions of meat and potatoes to help them bulk up and build muscle mass.

When my friend Tubby Porkman was a senior, he was an outstanding fullback for the Cobre High football team. He was strong and fast and had a good instinct for finding open holes to run through. In addition to being a good football player, Tubby also was a budding young "rock and roll" musician and played guitar in a short-lived band called Tubby and the Turdmuffins.

One day, during a practice scrimmage, Tubby re-injured a knee that had bothered him from the previous football season. He knew that if he continued to play football he would injure it again and eventually develop a chronic knee problem.

In the few days after his injury, Tubby deliberated whether to continue playing in pain or quit the football team and spend his extra time playing music with his friends. He knew the coaches at Cobre High School highly discouraged athletes from quitting and there was an athletic culture where "quitters" were ostracized. Finally, after much thought and consideration, he got up enough nerve to go tell the head coach, Mr. Fred Byrd, that he was quitting the football team.

Although some kids would never relinquish an opportunity to be the star fullback on a good football team, Tubby had little interest in succumbing to the social pressure from his teammates and coaches to play football. He caught a lot of flack at school and in the community for his scandalous and rebellious decision, but in the end he stood up for himself and made the right choice. Consequently, Tubby's actions helped to embolden the rest of his close friends and challenged them to question some of the high school paradigms that were pervasive at the time.

In December of my senior year I had a rare opportunity to travel to Dallas to see the Cotton Bowl game between Alabama and Texas A and M University. One of my classmates, Larry Haskell, had family friends who lived there and we stayed at their house for a few nights. Larry, Eddie Mitchell, Marvin Harris, and I made the trip and we had a memorable time. Dallas was the largest city I had ever been to and I was impressed with the skyscrapers and the number of people walking about in the downtown area.

On the way to Dallas we spent the first night in Abilene, where we drove around town for half the night looking for whorehouses and trying to pick up high school girls at a local fast food drive-in. A couple of days later in Dallas we visited the site where President Kennedy had been shot and we also witnessed our first porno movie at some backstreet theatre. The trip proved to be a perfect outing for a group of seventeen year old boys.

High School Mischief

One day a boy from a local ranch family named Delbert Johnson brought a pair of cow eyeballs to high school for his science class to study. He brought them to school in a glass jar filled with some clear liquid, probably formaldehyde. Once his class had finished studying the eyeballs, the teacher gave them back to Delbert.

A few mornings later I was standing in the hallway talking to a friend when Delbert happened to walk by with his jar of eyeballs. Out of curiosity we asked him to show us what he had in the jar, so he came over and let us take a closer look.

The eyeballs were large and looked quite grotesque as they bobbled around in the clear liquid. Since they were of no further use to Delbert and my friend and I seemed intrigued with them, he offered to give them to us. At first we really didn't really want them, but after further consideration it seemed obvious that we could use them sooner or later for some kind of prank.

By mid afternoon we had figured out exactly what we were going to do with them. We searched around until we found an unlocked student locker full of books. When no one was looking, we opened the locker and poured the eyeballs, formaldehyde and all, over the student's books and quickly closed the locker door.

When the next class ended, we decided to stand around in the hallway a few feet away from the locker and wait to see if someone would come to get their books for the next class. Sometimes our pranks were just too easy to pull off, and in this particular case we hit the jackpot right away. Within a minute or so a student walked up to the locker and opened the door to throw her books inside. A strange smell quickly drifted into the immediate area. When she noticed the cow eyeballs sitting on top of her wet belongings, she gagged and jumped away from her locker. By the time she looked around to see who was watching, we were already walking by nonchalantly to our next class.

Once we were a ways down the hallway, we stopped to see what she would do next. By the time she stopped gagging, she flagged down one of the principals who was walking up the hall. The last thing we saw before we continued on to our next class was the principal reaching inside her locker and removing the eyeballs with his bare hand and dropping them, one by one, into a trash bag.

In the few days leading up to our high school graduation, a handful of seniors came to realize the importance of leaving an indelible mark in the mining district that would immortalize our senior class. We felt it was time to give back to the community and say "thank you" for the years of support and guidance that we received. After much deliberation and soul searching, we concluded it was now time to paint "Senior 68" in high visibility locations in Bayard and Hurley, without getting arrested.

The plan was to paint the Bayard water tank one night and the Hurley water tower the following night. On the first night, Marvin Harris, Toby Parker, and I departed from Toby's house and walked along the ridge behind Cobre High School to the Bayard water tank. The tank was situated on the ground and was very easy to paint. We simply walked around the perimeter with spray paint cans in hand and sprayed it wherever we wanted. When we were done we casually walked back to Toby's house and made plans for our assault on the Hurley water tower the following night.

The Hurley water tower presented a much greater logistical challenge and a higher risk of getting caught. First of all, the tower was located in an open area right next to a busy road near the railroad tracks. Then, we had to deal with the fact that the tank was about 40 feet off of the ground. The only way we could get to a paintable surface was to climb up a metal ladder that was mounted on one of the support legs.

To overcome these obstacles it was necessary to involve more people in the operation. We decided that two people would climb the long ladder to do the painting. We would also post someone at the bottom of the tower to keep an eye out for the cops, and another person would drive the getaway car.

Marvin and Toby decided to climb the ladder to do the painting while I stood guard at the bottom of the tank. Our friend Richard Newman drove the getaway car and Dolores Duran rode with him to help keep an eye out for the Hurley police. Richard and Dolores weren't seniors at the time but they were eager to participate in a little late-night mischief.

Our plan worked flawlessly until the painting was done and we were getting ready to leave the water tower. For some reason one of us thought the cops were coming and we got spooked. Marvin, Toby and I scattered in different directions, while the getaway car drove off to a residential street to avoid being seen.

I took off running to the south, along the railroad tracks on the west side of town. The dry grass next to the tracks was about waist high and would have provided ample cover in the event that I had to lie down to hide.

I sprinted past the railroad station toward a dark stretch of track when, all of a sudden, I found myself lying on the ground in excruciating pain. Tears swelled up in my eyes and after a few seconds I realized that my kneecap had a large gash in it and blood was running down my leg.

After lying on the ground for a few minutes, I somehow composed myself enough to stand up on one leg as I tried to figure out what had happened to me. While I was limping around in the tall grass, I stumbled across a vertical railroad marker sticking out of the ground. The marker was actually a section of steel railroad track that was about three feet high and was embedded in concrete. Although it was painted and had stenciled numbers near the top, the overgrown grass made it impossible to see. It was obvious I had slammed my leg into the marker while running by and was lucky I didn't tear my kneecap off. For the remainder of the evening it was impossible to put weight on my bad leg, and the only way I could get around was by hopping on one foot. Fortunately, the getaway car picked me up a few minutes later and we sped away from the scene of the crime.

The next day turned out to be very interesting. First of all, it didn't take a genius to figure out that whoever painted the tanks in Bayard and Hurley were seniors at Cobre High School. Secondly, every cop knew that whenever there was mischief in Bayard, the first person to question was Marvin Harris. They also knew that if there was mischief in Hurley, my name was at the top of their list of suspects.

Apparently, the Bayard cops called the Harris's home early in the morning and discussed the situation with Mr. Harris. Marvin was still fast asleep when they called. After hearing the policeman's story, Mr. Harris did an incredible piece of detective work that eventually led to the unraveling of our vandalism spree. He snuck into Marvin's bedroom while he was still asleep and took his wallet out of his pants. He then returned to the kitchen and enjoyed a leisurely breakfast.

Later that morning when Marvin strolled into the kitchen, Mr. Harris leaned back in his chair and told him, "Oh, by the way, the police came by here this morning to return your wallet. They said they found it up at the Bayard water tank."

He then handed the wallet to Marvin and asked him, "So, who painted Senior 68 on the tank?"

Busted...

Later that same day a Hurley cop named Lyncho Jaramillo came by my house to pay me a little visit. I had a pretty good hunch about the topic of conversation, so I rehearsed my alibi as I limped toward the front gate to meet him.

Once he got out of the patrol car and walked up to the front gate, he asked me, "Jerry boy, Do you know anything about the Hurley water tower being painted "Senior 68" last night?" (Lyncho always called me "Jerry boy". I had known him for years and I took it as a term of endearment.)

I looked him dead in the eye, and with heart-felt sincerity I responded, "No Lyncho, I don't know anything about it."

Then Lyncho asked, "Do you mind if I take a look at your hands?"

As I slowly raised them for Lyncho to examine, I noticed there was paint imbedded around the edges of my fingernails on both hands. I had failed to wash my hands thoroughly from the Bayard water tank job. "Oh, shit!" I thought to myself.

Even though I didn't actually paint the Hurley water tower, I knew it would be next to impossible to lie my way out of it. My only alternative was to take the rap for painting it so that nobody else would get in trouble.

Busted...

Toby Parker and I used to have lots of fun in high school. Not only was he a great person, he was also a talented athlete, artist, singer, impersonator, comedian, entertainer, actor, and all around hell raiser. One of the most interesting things about him was that he would never share his talents with anyone unless they were one of his good friends. Most teachers and students thought that Toby was a quiet and polite young man who never misbehaved in school.

When I sat near him during class he would draw cartoons and then pass them to me when the teacher wasn't looking. He would usually draw several frames in a sequence that told a story. The story I remember the most was a goofy, cartoon-like character sitting in a wheel chair, selling pencils on the street corner. In the next few frames a group of bullies would steal his money and pencils and then beat him up and leave him lying on the sidewalk.

If Toby wasn't drawing in class, he was moving his hand around as if it was detached or possessed by some demon that had a mind of its own. His hand would do crazy things while he wasn't looking. He could bend and contort the last joint of his middle finger and make it look as if it were a dog's head and nose. He used the other four fingers as the dog's legs. He would make his dog do things like sniff and piss on the student seated in front of him, or get into a dog fight with another dog, which, of course, was his other hand. One time he made me laugh so hard at his cartoons and dogs that the teacher kicked me out of class and made me go sit in the hallway. Meanwhile, Toby always kept a straight face and would never get caught disrupting class.

Toby and I used to spend lots of time at Marvin Harris' house when we were in high school. We would sometimes hang out there on school nights instead of doing our homework at home, and our grades proved it. We usually joked around with his sisters Bernice and Lisa and his brother Bobby until 10:00 p.m. or so before we would go home.

Once in a while Toby and I would spend hours recording different voices and accents with the help of Lisa's small, portable tape recorder. Our favorite thing to do was record a conversation in English, using a heavy Mexican accent, and then listen to the replay. Eventually our accents sounded so authentic that we used to make our Hispanic friends at school burst out in laughter as they listened to two Gringos carry on a conversation while speaking broken English.

One day Toby and I went to lunch in the school cafeteria. We got our trays of food and looked around for a place to sit down and eat. We noticed two girls sitting alone at a long table so we decided to go sit across from them. Once we were seated, we began eating our lunch and carrying on a fairly normal conversation.

As we were talking, Toby discretely and nonchalantly began to mix every food item on his tray into one big pile. First he stirred his vegetables and desert in with the main course, and then he got his Jell-O and mixed it in with the rest of the pile. The girls sitting across from us weren't paying much attention at first, but it wasn't long before they began to intermittently glance over to see what would happen next. Pretending not to notice them, Toby got his carton of milk and quietly poured the entire half pint over the pile of food sitting in the middle of his tray. He then got his fork and mixed everything up until it became a sloppy mush.

By this time the girls were totally captivated and looked on in utter astonishment. Toby and I continued to ignore them and resumed our casual conversation as we ate. Finally, Toby grabbed his paper napkin and dipped it into the soupy, foul colored pile of slop. Once it became saturated, he pulled it out of the mixture and raised it above his head. He then tilted his head back, put the end of the napkin in his mouth, and sucked the slop from it.

That was the last straw. The girls immediately gagged, grabbed their trays, and got up from the table and rushed away from us as quickly as they could.

Toby and I were always joking around and pulling pranks at school. In fact, we joked around so much our good friends referred to us as "Los Weasels" because we were so sly. We would do anything for a laugh and we were constantly on the lookout for an opportunity to create mischief.

One time the Drama Club had a school play scheduled in the high school auditorium for the following day. The club had just finished making the sets and backdrops for the play and had gone home for the evening. After school, Toby and I were snooping around back stage when no one was around and noticed that the large canvas backdrop for the opening act of the play had a living room scene painted on it. As we poked around a little longer we ran across a couple of cans of spray paint nearby that had been used to paint the backdrop. Realizing that the backdrop would make a great billboard, we took one of the cans and painted across it, in large block letters, "Los Weasels".

The next afternoon we were sitting in the audience anxiously awaiting the play to begin. Finally, the curtains slowly opened and the first thing that caught our eye was "Los Weasels" printed boldly across the backdrop. Fortunately, the only people who knew about our painting spree were a small handful of good friends who called us "Los Weasels". I'm sure we would have been immediately suspended from school if the Drama Club had known who it was that ruined the backdrop.

At one point, Toby and I thought it might be fun to be actors, so we joined the Cobre High School drama club called Masquer's Club. There was a play scheduled for later in the spring semester that we decided to try out for, and eventually we were given a couple of minor character roles. At first the rehearsals were sort of fun, but it wasn't long before we began to get bored.

Over the course of the next few weeks we both got called onto the carpet repeatedly because we were disruptive and made life difficult for the club sponsor, who happened to be the preacher at a local church in Bayard. Then, one afternoon a photographer for the Cobre High School yearbook came to take a group picture of the Masquers Club. We were instructed to simply smile for the camera, but Toby and I couldn't resist making goofy faces to liven things up a bit. After all, this was a photo of the drama club, not a staff photo for the library.

When the photos were eventually developed and delivered, the sponsor was furious. Toby and I were immediately called into the principal's office to be reprimanded. As we entered the office we were instructed to close the door and sit down. The Principal sat behind his desk and leaned back in his chair with his arms folded, while the Masquers Club sponsor stood nearby with a scowl on his face. It was clear from the beginning of the meeting that they weren't too happy to see us.

The Principal looked at us for a few seconds and said in a serious tone of voice, "You boys ruined the Masquers Club group photos by making silly faces. Now the entire club will have to do retakes because of you two."

Then, one of us replied, "How did we ruin the photos? We'd like to see them."

The Principal thought about it a minute and decided to make a little bargain with Toby and me. He glared across his desk at us and said, "All right.

We will show you the photos, but if we do, you will have to quit the Masquers Club."

Without wasting a second, Toby and I looked at each other briefly and responded to the Principal, "OK, no problem. Show us the photos."

The Principal glanced over to the preacher and then fixed his attention back on us. He then told us, "You guys are officially kicked out of Masquers Club," and never showed us the photos. He had double-crossed us.

As Toby and I walked out of the Principal's office, we struggled to control our laughter. Finally, I looked at him and sarcastically quipped, "Boy, they really punished us this time, didn't they?"

During the holiday season there were a few individual classes at Cobre High School that traditionally held a small gift exchange at the end of class. Students would draw names from a hat a few days beforehand and then bring a gift for that person on the day of the party. All gift donors remained anonymous unless they chose to disclose who they were.

One year Toby drew a girl named Suzie Johnston for the gift exchange. It just so happened that Suzie was a serious, college bound student who was a tad on the snooty side. She always studied hard and eventually went on to become the valedictorian of her class. Her father was a high-ranking administrator of Cobre Schools at the time and considered education to be a top priority for all of the kids in his family. Needless to say, a girl like Suzie didn't have much use for a couple of pedestrian pranksters like Toby and me.

On the day of the gift exchange, we all brought our gifts and placed them on a table in front of the class. Toby brought a nicely wrapped box with a label that said, "To: Suzie", but he chose to remain anonymous. When the class was nearly over, everyone gathered around the table to find the gift that had their name on it and they opened it.

Suzie found her gift and diligently tore away the wrapping paper and removed the lid from the small box. Meanwhile off to the side, Toby and I subtly fixated our eyes on her to see what her reaction would be to the gift. With a smile on her face, Suzie playfully reached inside and slowly removed the gift. At first she wasn't quite sure what it was, but as she moved it around in her hand her curiosity quickly turned to anger.

She quickly looked up and her eyes darted around the room to see if anyone was watching. Toby and I were too quick for her. By the time she looked our way, we appeared to be totally preoccupied with our new gifts and were chatting away with friends.

In a way, I can't blame Suzie for being so "bent out of shape". After all, she was now the proud owner of an old, very used bar of soap that had kinky, dried pubic hairs stuck to it. As she dropped the nasty bar of soap back into its box, I exercised every bit of self-control I could muster in order to avoid falling to the floor in a fit of hysterical laughter.

One day while Toby Parker was at Marvin Harris' house he noticed that some kid had left their bicycle leaning against the house near the driveway.

Toby was a daredevil and would do anything for a laugh, so he walked over and grabbed the bicycle and pushed it up a rocky hill directly behind Harris' house. He then got on the bike and rode it down the hill, bouncing over bumps and swerving between yuccas until he reached the Harris' paved driveway. From there, he accelerated and shot out over the edge of the road below. The hill dropped off sharply, which made Toby and the bicycle become airborne above the rugged terrain. He eventually crash-landed several feet below the driveway among the rocks and cactus. He hit the ground so hard that he was thrown from the bike upon impact. Miraculously, Toby emerged from the crash virtually unscathed, but the bicycle was totally demolished.

A couple of days later Toby showed me the bicycle and I don't think there was one part on it that wasn't bent or broken. We never did find out who owned the bike, but they must have been shocked when they returned to Harris' house to pick it up.

Another boy who became a good friend was a Hispanic kid from North Hurley named Gene Valles. I knew Gene when we were in elementary school but we started hanging around together when I was in about eighth grade. Tubby Porkman and I used to go over to his house on B Street and spend lots of time with him.

The thing I remember most about going to visit Gene was the hospitality that his parents and family extended toward us. The Valles family enjoyed having kids around and they treated Gene's friends as if they were part of an extended family. As soon as Tubby and I walked in the door, Gene's mother, Luisa, would offer us an enchilada or some other red chili dish.

As an eighth grade boy who knew everything, I considered Gene to be an expert at dating and schmoozing the girls. He was never afraid to talk to them and he always had a few smooth lines ready whenever he engaged in conversation with them. He used to offer me advice on how to put the moves on some girl who I was interested in, or he would tell me things to do to catch her attention. On a couple of occasions he helped me get up the nerve to call a girl on the telephone and then would coach me as I talked to her. He would tell me things like, "Ask her if she's going out with someone," or "Tell her that you love the color of her eyes," or "Tell her that you like her new hairdo," and so on.

Gene enjoyed playing baseball when he was younger and he had a good throwing arm. Later on I discovered that the reason he could throw so well was because he always loved to throw rocks when he was a kid. From time to time we used to throw rocks at a bottle or a clump of grass and he would always hit the target long before I did.

Gene was also a good swimmer. He would spend every day during the summer at the Hurley Swimming Pool because he was a good friend with the older lifeguards and would help them out around the pool or run errands for them. I don't know if he ever got paid, but he probably got to swim for free, and I'm sure the lifeguards bought him an occasional soda or ice cream cone.

Tubby and I also became good friends with Gene's dad, M.P. Valles. In the spring of 1964 MP drove Gene, Tubby, and I out to Lake Roberts to go camping for three days. The three of us had a great time at the lake, but one night a group of eight boys about our age came to our camp and robbed us. They threatened to beat us up if we didn't give them all of our money. We pulled out our wallets and gave them everything we had, but fortunately I had a couple of dollars stashed behind a leather flap in my wallet they didn't find. We were able to buy enough food at the Lake Roberts store to last until MP came to pick us up a couple of days later.

When we were in high school it became a tradition to go to Gene's house on Christmas Eve. Luisa enjoyed making lots of tamales and menudo for everyone who came by to visit. Later on in the evening we would have a gift exchange and then go to midnight mass at the Hurley Catholic Church. After mass we would return to Gene's house and stay up the remainder of the night drinking the beer we had stashed outside on his back porch. As the Valles Christmas Eve tradition grew over the years, there would sometimes be 15 or 20 kids celebrating until the wee hours of the morning. There were many Christmas mornings when I got home just as everyone in my family was getting out of bed.

Photo 4-5: This is a photo of one of our Christmas Eve parties at M.P. and Luisa Valles' home in North Hurley. Photo courtesy of Howie and Kathy Miller.

While I was attending Cobre High School I met a couple of brothers from Bayard Named Juan Carlos and Eloy Maldonado. Their father was a man named Chincho who managed one of the local grocery stores. Eloy worked at the grocery store after school and on weekends and Juan Carlos worked at the gift shop next door. Gene, Tubby, and I used to go to the Bayard shopping center to visit both boys at work on a regular basis and before long we developed friendships with several employees that lasted for many years.

Going to Juan Carlos and Eloy's house to pick them up for an evening out on the town was never quick and easy. First of all, they had a family of six kids and all of them became our good friends. It was difficult to simply walk into their home without a sit-down visit with someone, and it was virtually impossible to leave without joining the family for one of Mrs. Maldonado's red enchiladas.

It was interesting and amusing to go to the Maldonado house because all of the kids had nicknames that were funny and quite fitting. The youngest brother, Alfred, was always off playing at some neighbor's house, so the family referred to him as "The Stranger". Eloy supposedly looked like an owl so his nickname was "Tecolote". Juan Carlos was called "Melon" because his family said he had a melon shaped head. Mr. Maldonado's name was "Chincho", and I am fairly certain that "Chincho" was also a nickname. The two grandfathers of the family were called "Grandpa Gentes" and "Grandpa Venado". The youngest daughter was named "Kuki" but I don't know if that was a nickname or her given name.

For years I had a great interest in learning Spanish, and Gene, Juan Carlos, and Eloy turned out to be my "unofficial" Spanish teachers. I took Spanish classes at school, but these boys taught me the way things were said on the streets of Bayard and Hurley. In addition to helping me with vocabulary and sentence structure, they were also eager to teach me cuss words and vulgar phrases. Unfortunately, they occasionally failed to explain the exact English translations to some of their prized vulgar "dichos".

One evening I was at the Maldonado home watching TV and the entire family was seated in the living room. Grandpa Venado and his wife were also there. I was sitting on a couch and The Stranger was sitting next to me. He was about five years old at the time and he was a cute kid.

For some reason, The Stranger kept trying to grab something out of my hand or, perhaps he just wanted to get my attention. Since he was being playful with me, I decided to show off my Spanish and tell him something I had just learned from my rogue Spanish instructors. In a fun and humorous way, I wanted to tell him, "Quit messing around with me," so I said to him, "No me chingas, Stranger."

All of a sudden, every one in the room looked towards me and the room fell silent. Mr. Maldonado's eyebrows shot upward and his jaw dropped open before he quickly responded, "What did you say?"

Meanwhile, Juan Carlos and Eloy were biting their tongues to keep from exploding with laughter. Finally Mr. Maldonado told me that what I had said was an extremely vulgar phrase. In the midst of my embarrassment, I attempted to redeem myself by telling Mr. Maldonado, "Well, that's what Juan Carlos and Eloy taught me to say."

Slowly, grins began to appear on everyone's faces and, once Juan Carlos stopped laughing, he asked me, "Do you know what you really said? You just told The Stranger, "Quit F_ _ _KING around with me."

That was the last time I ever tried out my new Spanish phrases without researching their exact definition.

CHAPTER FIVE: GROWING UP IN HURLEY

"If you were my kid I would have beaten your little butt."

A Little Information About My Family

My family consisted of my parents and four children. We had a first cousin named James who lived with us for several years from the time I was in elementary school until I went to high school. I was the third child of four and I had an older sister, an older brother, and a younger sister. My parents started their family when they were fairly old because of World War II. Consequently, my dad was 44 and my mother was 42 when I was born. My older sister was always nice to me and was my social connection to what was happening around town and in Silver City. My older brother could become grumpy if we made noise while he was doing his homework, but I spent a lot of time tagging along with him as a kid because we both loved to play sports and create a little mischief in the neighborhood. My little sister was probably the nicest person in the family and always did well in school. My brother and I enjoyed teasing her when she was young because it was easy to "get her goat". James was my brother's age and was fun to be with, but he liked to get into trouble once in a while and gave my parents many headaches over the years.

My maternal grandmother lived in Silver City when I was very young, but she later moved back to her hometown of Belen, NM. She was divorced from my grandfather, who was an engineer for the railroad there. She was actually my step grandmother because my real grandmother died in the flu epidemic of 1918 in Belen. Both of my paternal grandparents died before I was born so I never knew them. They moved to Deming when my father was six years old and they raised their family there.

Once in a while in the mid 1950's, our family would drive over the Black Range to the town of Hot Springs (now known as T or C) to meet my grandmother from Belen. My big sister would ride back to Belen with my grandmother so she could visit our cousin Marsha. My sister was the same age as Marsha and she would usually spend a week or two with her. There were a few summers when Marsha came to Hurley and spend some time with us as well.

My first memory of the Black Range highway was prior to 1957 when it was still a gravel road. It had lots of curves and it was fairly steep in places. The steep grade caused automobile motors to overheat during the ascent to Emory Pass. It was common to see cars from the late 1940's and early 1950's pulled over on the side of the road with their hoods up and steam billowing out from their radiators. Many travelers brought extra water in their air-cooled canvass water bag and used it to refill their radiators. The bags were usually hung from the radio antenna of the car and rode against the front quarter panel near the door.

My Home Life

My family lived in a small three-bedroom/one-bath house on Elguea Street throughout my childhood. My brother, James, and I shared a bedroom, my sisters shared the second bedroom, and my parents were in the larger bedroom.

After I completed high school and left home, I realized that no one in the family really had much privacy in our small house. This was probably one of the reasons my older sister got married while she was still in high school. It was also the main reason why I spent most of my youth in the streets of Hurley. I felt cooped-up when I was at home and looked forward to playing outside with my friends whenever possible.

My mother was a "stay at home" housewife and always kept the house clean, provided three meals a day for the family, and made sure we all had clean clothes that weren't torn or tattered. She would occasionally do special little things for my siblings and me, especially if we were well behaved or did well in school. I always loved her chocolate fudge she made for us when we came home from school, and my all-time favorite dish was the strawberry shortcake she made on my birthdays.

When I was little, my mom would read storybooks to me and help me with my reading. On school nights, she and my father spent their time in the living room watching TV and smoking cigarettes while we studied. If we needed help with our homework, we would usually consult with my mother. My dad helped us too, but my mom was Salutatorian of her high school class and she was good with academic details.

Neither of my parents spent much time outside in the yard playing with us when we were younger. They were 15 to 20 years older than the parents of my classmates, and both of them were fairly heavy smokers. Rather than bug them to do things with me, I would go visit one of my friends or tag along with my brother and cousin James when they went to play team sports with their friends. The older boys usually let me play in their games, even though I was usually a few years younger than anyone on the team. Of course, the one drawback to playing team sports with older boys was that I was always picked last.

My father worked in the payroll office at Kennecott and barely earned enough money to support a family of six. If the kids in my family wanted spending money we had to go out and earn it because my dad was tight with what little money he had. I did yard work for neighbors, delivered newspapers, set bowling pins at the Chino Club, and raised sheep for the fairs. My high school friends were always amazed when I told them that my father was so tight he made me pay for my own haircuts. My siblings and I knew early on that if we ever wanted to buy a car or go to college, we would have to pay for it on our own.

When I was in high school, I always dreaded asking to borrow the car for the evening. My dad would usually throw a fit when I asked him for the car, and most of the time he wouldn't let me borrow it. He was even reluctant to let me borrow the car for something important, like taking a girl to the prom.

My dad had a pretty good sense of humor, although we sometimes didn't catch on to it until we were much older. For example, when we were young we were constantly running in and out of the house whenever we played in the yard. My dad used to tell us, "Close the screen door. You're letting the flies out."

For years I was baffled as to why he always said we were letting the flies "out" instead of "in". It wasn't until I was in junior high school that I figured out he was being sarcastic.

Back in the day it seemed like older people always came up with amusing sayings or clichés. Since my father was born in 1906, he had some great old sayings I never heard anywhere else. For example, if he was drinking beer and all of a sudden had to go to the bathroom, he might say, "That beer ran through me like shit through a tin horn."

Or, if one of his friends greeted him on the street and asked him how he was doing, he might reply, "I'm ahead of the hounds."

If it was getting late and he wanted my siblings and I to go to bed, he would tell us, "You need to get some sleep so you can wake up bright eyed and bushy tailed."

When he lectured us about being able to take care of ourselves, he would tell us, "It's kind of like being an old a mountain lion. If you don't catch nothin', you don't eat nothin'."

If someone tried to get him to do something he didn't want to do, he would reply, "Well you can just shit and fall back in it."

Sometimes we would be driving down the street and along the way he would see a brand new expensive car parked in front of a shabby, run down house or mobile home. He would point to the car and shake his head and remark, "Take a look at the car in front of that shack. That's like putting a $100 saddle on a $10 horse."

If he was doing something he really enjoyed and someone asked him, "How is it going?" he might reply, "I feel like a dog in a meat house."

Whenever someone in the room farted, he would ask them, "Did you just step on a frog?"

One of the funniest things my father ever told me was when we were walking out of a store after we had just purchased something. The cashier, who seemed like a nice lady, happened to have a large mouth and big buckteeth. As we walked toward the car, he remarked, "Damn, I bet that lady could eat an apple through a chain link fence."

It wasn't until I was in late high school and college when I realized my family had names for things that were different than mainstream America. In our home we always referred to the noon meal, which was usually the largest meal of the day, as "dinner". We called the evening meal "supper". And we always called the refrigerator the "ice box". We also ate different dishes than people from other parts of the country. Since I was from Hurley, I knew all about things like menudo, rellenos, tamales, and chicharrones but it wasn't until I was in college when I first ate a bagel, a bratwurst, quiche, yogurt, tortellini, or eggs Benedict.

My family frequently ate dishes like pinto beans and cornbread because it was cheap. It was also popular in the '50's and '60's to eat canned goods like vegetables or beef stew or spaghetti and meatballs. We ate tacos with canned salsa and enchiladas with canned red chili sauce. We ate cheap cuts of meat like round steak or pork chops, and occasionally had fresh green beans or corn on the cob.

We usually had bacon, eggs, and toast for breakfast and on Sundays my mom would cook a pot roast for "dinner". We would always make roast beef sandwiches for "supper" with the leftover pot roast. For the major holidays my mother would always cook up a nice turkey dinner and we would feed off of the leftover turkey for several days afterward.

Somewhere in our family lineage we may have had some southern roots because we ate dishes like bread and gravy, cornbread and milk (put a piece of cornbread into a glass of milk and eat it with a spoon), and once in a while we made a sandwich consisting of white bread, bread-and-butter pickles, and mayonnaise. Another common snack at our house was to put slices of butter on top of a piece of white bread and sprinkle sugar on top. My all time favorite snack though, were Cheez-its, which were a common fixture on our kitchen shelf throughout my entire childhood.

My dad had an unusual meal quirk. He would usually eat "supper" alone after the rest of us were done. Sometimes he would fry a steak and put mushrooms on it or open a can of something quite unusual, such as oyster stew or menudo. Then he would sit on a little stool next to the kitchen stove and drink beer as he tended to his dinner. It seemed like he needed the solitude and this was probably the only time during the course of the day he could find it.

Saturday Trips To Silver City

Like many families from Hurley, my parents would load everyone into our car once every couple of weeks to go shopping in Silver City. The boys went with my dad to the barbershop for haircuts while my mother and sisters would go shopping on Bullard Street. When we were done we would sometimes go out to lunch before we made the long trek back to Hurley in our 1949 Chevy two door hard top. My two favorite places to eat were the Ranchburger on College Ave. across from the mortuary, and the Silver Café on Bullard Street. Every once in a while we would also have lunch at the Chef's Grill on Texas Street, located behind the Murray Hotel.

In the later 1950's, the "flattop" haircut craze became popular for boys. As our hair grew out between haircuts my father would always tell my brother and I, "You guys need a haircut. You're starting to look like a couple of damn renegades."

Then he would take us to Silver City to Manny's Barbershop across from the Buffalo Bar to get a flattop. While we were getting our haircuts, my dad would climb up onto the shoeshine bench and get a shine as he read the newspaper or chatted with the shoeshine boy.

Getting a flattop haircut was always an interesting endeavor. First, Manny would cut our hair short on the sides and back. Next, he would take a wide, flat, metal comb with several long teeth and a handle on one end, and slide it onto the top of our head from front to back. Then he would take his electric clippers and run them across the top of the metal comb contraption from side to side to cut any hair that stuck out above the metal teeth. When he was done with the haircut he always plastered on a thick, greasy goop called "Butch-Wax" that kept our hair standing straight up all day long.

The main stores I remember in downtown Silver City were J.C. Penney's, Rasco's, The White House, Pennington's, Cosgrove's, Howell Drug Store, Rexall Drugs, Food Mart, Borenstein's, R.O. Schmitz Jewelers, Blackwell's Jewelers, Joe Welsh Men's Apparel, The Maxwell House, Home Furniture, Union Furniture Company, The Farmer's Market on Yankee Street, Colby's Sporting Goods, Johnny's Barber Shop and Manny's Barber shop, The Gila Theater and the Silco Theater, The Buffalo Bar, Gamble's, Clifton Chevrolet and the Chrysler dealership, The Army and Navy Store, Surplus City, Pete's Business Machines, Smith's Music & TV, The American National Bank, the Murray, Palace, and Bullard Hotels, Schadel's Bakery, the Post Office, an old shoe shop and welding shop on north Bullard Street near College Avenue, three gas stations, and a five and dime store. Sometimes Sido and I would hitchhike to Silver on Saturdays to go to the bowling alley to bowl or play pinball machines. The bowling alley was located just north of 12th Street and west of Pope Street.

It seems like back in the 1950's and 1960's a lot of people from Hurley never knew the physical addresses of any of the businesses in Silver City. For example, if someone asked, "Where is the Rexall Drug Store?" a common reply would be, "Right next door to the Food Mart." I never knew the names of any of the streets in Silver City until I was in college, but I could explain how to get to any store in town by referring to landmarks or commonly known stores or buildings.

Another interesting phenomenon I remember as a kid was how area residents talked about going to different towns in the area. If you were in Hurley, you would say, "Let's go over to Silver City", or, "down to Deming", or "over to Cliff", or "up to Bayard", or, "up to Reserve". If you were in Silver City, you would say, "Let's go out to Cliff", or "over to Bayard", or, "out to Hurley", or "up to Lake Roberts". If you traveled farther away, you might say, "Let's go down to Mexico", or, "up to Canada", or, "out to California", or, "over to Arizona", or, "up to Phoenix", or, "over to Tucson", or, "down to Las Cruces".

My Earliest Childhood Memories

When I was three years old I began fulfilling my destiny to explore and seek adventure. I hated being cooped up and always had a curious desire to leave the confines of my yard and wander off in any random direction, just to see what was out there. Unfortunately for my parents, I developed a knack of leaving my yard to walk around town without them knowing I was gone. When they would come to check up on me and realize I was gone, they usually enlisted the help of neighbors and the local police to come looking for me.

It wasn't long before my parents began hiding my shoes from me because I was running away so frequently. The lack of shoes, however, proved to be only a temporary setback for me because it wasn't long before I started sneaking into my dad's closet and putting on his work boots to wander the neighborhood. I had to drag them on the ground as I walked because I didn't know how to tie the bootlaces, and my feet and legs were so small that the shoes wouldn't stay on my feet. The boots had a definite impact on my range of travel, so I would usually walk nearby to the Bates' house and visit my new friend Sido.

When I was about five years old our family had a visit from my parents' good friends from Albuquerque, Jackie and Asher Smith. They were the couple who introduced my dad to my mom when my dad was stationed in Albuquerque during World War II. On this particular visit they brought their nice little Terrier dog with them. His name was Corky and the dog and I became good friends almost immediately. One evening during their visit, I took Corky for a walk around the neighborhood with a leash. Everyone was expecting me to be gone for about 20 minutes but for some reason I walked the dog all over town and was gone for over two hours. My parents became worried and eventually called the police to help search for me. By the time they found me, I still wasn't ready to bring him back home.

My urge to slip away from my parents and explore my surroundings intensified as I got older. A few months after my long walk with Corky, our family drove to Silver to visit my grandmother who lived near the corner of Kelly and Black Streets. After about a half an hour of sitting around in her stuffy little apartment, I decided to go outside for some fresh air. Once I was outside alone, it wasn't long before I succumbed to the temptation to explore my new surroundings. As usual, I didn't plan on being gone for very long and it never occurred to me to ask permission to walk around the streets of Silver City alone.

I walked down the driveway and out onto Kelly Street and headed south to the corner of Market and Black Streets. I hadn't gone very far when I noticed a large, empty lot with several kids playing baseball there. They looked like they were having fun so I walked over to check out the situation. Before I knew it, I had made several new friends and was having a grand time. About two hours later, the Silver City police eventually found me and returned me to my grandmother's apartment. I later learned that my parents had called KSIL radio station and asked them to broadcast a bulletin for a "missing child".

One of my greatest excursions as a young child came when I was in first grade. In the fall of that year I made friends with a classmate named Bob Stevenson who came from a Mormon family. Bob was a nice kid and one day he invited me to come with him to the Mormon Church in Silver City to attend an after school program for kids called "Primary". His mom picked us up after school in their green 1954 Chevy and drove us over to Silver City. The church was located on top of a hill at the west end of Market Street.

For some reason, after about a half an hour of the class, I became bored and wasn't having any fun. I remember walking outside of the church and thinking about whether or not I wanted to stay there until Primary was over. I knew that returning to class was not an option for me, and I also knew I didn't want to stay at the church. So, I did what any red blooded six year old kid would do and decided to sneak away and walk 15 miles back to Hurley. I was determined to walk well into the night.

I left the church and set out across the neighborhoods and busy streets of Silver City and eventually made it to the intersection of Highway 180 and the Pinos Altos highway. From there, I continued walking eastward up the hill along the shoulder of the highway. There was still a lot of daylight left and I knew before long I would be out of town and on the open road. I wasn't tired and my plan hadn't changed. I was walking to Hurley.

I had just walked past a large junkyard on the south side of Highway 180 and was not far from the top of the hill when suddenly the Stevenson's pulled up next to me in their car. The door opened and Mrs. Stevenson told me to get in. I don't remember what she said to me as we drove home but I know for sure that I never attended Primary at the Mormon Church again.

When I was about four years old I used to walk to the Chino Club to get a soda or a candy bar. Back in the mid 1950's sodas cost a whopping six cents and candy bars were a nickel. A few of my older brother's friends were always hanging around the Club when I was there and they used to call me over to their group and teach me every cuss word in the book. They would howl with laughter every time I repeated a certain word or phrase. Before long I became their primary source of entertainment.

The older boys would usually hang out in front of the Club near the stairway leading up to the front door. At the bottom of the stairs on each side were square concrete pillars that stood about two feet tall and were flat on top. When they saw an adult pull up in front of the Club in their car, they would have me climb up onto one of the pillars and cuss them out as they walked up the steps and into the Club. They would tell me, "Oh, here comes Mrs. "So and So". Tell her "f_ _ _ you" when she walks up the steps." Then they would go hide behind the pyracantha bushes as the lady approached.

At first, adults were caught off guard because they couldn't believe such vulgarity was coming out of the mouth of a little kid like me. Then they would respond to my vulgar tirade by telling me things like, "Why, someone ought to slap your little face," or, "Somebody needs to wash your mouth out with soap." Meanwhile, the boys snickered and choked back their laughter as they hid behind the bushes.

The boys had me telling the adults things they only dreamed of saying to them. They knew they would get their butts beat if they even tried. My Chino Club pillar performances eventually turned out to be a lucrative endeavor for a model young stand-up comedian like me. It wasn't long before they were buying me candy and sodas whenever they saw the adults become noticeably angry. The angrier the adults became, the more I was showered with rewards. One time I was even given a bite out of a chunk of hard chewing tobacco for cussing out some lady who went into the Club to get a six-pack of Pepsi Cola.

I had become a "childhood cuss word sensation" overnight. It wasn't long before I was notorious all over Hurley for my exceptionally foul mouth. I learned how to cuss so well I began using profanity on my own at a very young age, and without provocation. I even had a friend who lived up the street from me who once told me that his mother didn't want me coming over to play with him because I cussed too much.

Throughout my entire childhood, my brother's friends and many adults living in Hurley periodically reminisced about my vulgar monologues. In fact, many decades after I had become an adult I ran into an old Hurley friend named Ronny Wagner. Ronny used to drive a grocery delivery van for the Hurley Stores in the mid 1950's and he told me a story that happened one day when he was making a delivery. He said one day he was cruising down the street when, all of a sudden, he saw a young boy lying in the middle of the street in front of him. When he stopped to get out of the van to see if the kid was hurt, the kid jumped up and said, "Fuck you", and ran off. I laughed and thought it was a pretty good story and then I asked him if he remembered who the kid was. Ronny looked at me with a big smile on his face and replied, "It was you."

Cussing apparently wasn't my only strong suit when I was very young. When I wasn't rattling off profanities to make my friends laugh, I used to love getting into trouble and then doing whatever I could to avoid punishment. For instance, I might tease my sister or do something to make my parents mad, and then go hide under the bed in my sister's bedroom. In retaliation, my mother would come into the bedroom to spank me. She would tell me to get out from under the bed, but I wouldn't budge. Then she would get a broom and poke the broomstick under the bed to flush me out, but her technique didn't always work. Whenever I saw the broomstick coming I would grab onto the box springs underneath the bed and lift myself up away from the floor as the broomstick slid beneath me. I figured out at an early age that if I stayed under the bed long enough she would eventually calm down and I wouldn't get a spanking.

Once I got a little older and was too big to hide under the bed, my new strategy for avoiding punishment was to run out of the house and down the street. There were many times when I busted out of the back door in a full sprint with my dad in hot pursuit with a belt in hand. I knew if he caught me while I was still in the house I would be dead meat, but once I got outside I was in my element and was impossible to catch.

There were several reasons why running away from a spanking made perfect sense to me. First of all, I could outrun my parents. Secondly, I knew they would be too embarrassed to be seen chasing me down the street as they yelled at me and demanded that I come back. Lastly, I knew time was on my side and, if I stayed gone long enough, things would eventually cool down. With conditions like that, what kid in their right mind would stick around to take a genuine butt beating?

I continued my strategy of "fleeing from justice" for as long as I could get away with it, although once in a while things just didn't work out in my favor. One evening Sido and I were goofing around in my yard and my dad came out to hassle me about something I had done earlier in the afternoon. When it became apparent I was in for a spanking, I took off running, as usual. As I sped out the back gate and rounded the corner into the alley, I heard Sido tell my dad, "I'll go catch him for you, Mr. Boswell."

Sure enough, by the time I got to the end of the alley, Sido caught up to me with a huge, shit-eating grin on his face. He grabbed me and dragged me back to my dad, who was still standing in the back yard. I am certain that Sido didn't chase after me to please my dad. His only interest in being my father's bounty hunter was so he could see me get spanked.

I have to admit, both Sido and I used to get a tremendous amount of enjoyment when we eavesdropped on a nasty spanking. If we were outside playing and suddenly heard some neighborhood kid screaming and crying, Sido and I would hop the fence to their yard and sneak over to a window to listen to the beating from a few feet away. After the first few hits, we had to exercise a lot of self-control to keep from laughing aloud and getting discovered by an angry parent.

Late one afternoon Sido and I were playing with this kid in his yard when his father threw open the front door and screamed out in anger, "Jeff, you get your butt in this house right this minute."

Then he looked at Sido and me and ordered, "You two boys need to go on home."

We could tell by his father's tone of voice that Jeff was in big trouble. With fear in his eyes and his head hanging low, Jeff reluctantly walked up the steps onto the front porch and disappeared through the doorway.

Once Jeff and his dad were inside the house and out of sight, Sido and I snuck around to the side of the house under Jeff's bedroom window and waited for the fireworks to begin. Within a few seconds the party was in full swing. At first we heard the father screaming at Jeff. Then came the hits, the slapping of leather against flesh, the banging and thrashing of two people in a small room, and most importantly, the crying and screaming. Jeff's father was in a rage.

The beating was too good to be true, and Sido and I knew we had hit the jackpot on this one. The more Jeff howled, the harder we laughed. After a few minutes had passed, Jeff's cries turned to pleads for mercy. By now he was screaming and trying to catch his breath as he begged his father to stop, but his father just hit him even harder.

Finally, Jeff was crying at the top of his lungs and his pleads were incoherent. Then, something strange happened. As Sido and I were squatting below the window, we simultaneously and telepathically came to the realization that there was a big difference between a simple spanking and an abusive beating laced with anger and rage. We glanced at each other and, in near perfect unison, we jumped up and ran out of Jeff's yard as fast as we could run. As we ran up the street, we both knew we had just witnessed something that wasn't funny any more.

By the time I was in junior high school, getting a spanking had become a sport. One evening my friend Willie Martin dropped by my house for a visit. We were in my bedroom goofing off for a while, but we soon ran out of things to do and became bored. To create a little excitement and mischief around the house, Willie and I hatched a plan to provoke my father into spanking me while he listened from inside the closet. My father didn't know that Willie was in my bedroom with me at the time.

Once Willie was tucked away in the closet with the door closed, I walked into the living room where my parents were watching TV and intentionally did something stupid and outrageous to make my father mad. I don't remember what I said to him, but he quickly took the bait and came storming into the bedroom with a belt in his hand, ready to maneuver into a position to hit me. Just as he drew the belt back to swat me, we heard some banging around in the closet and suddenly the door popped open. One of the cardboard boxes Willie had been sitting on buckled beneath him, causing him to accidentally fall to the floor and crash into the closet door. Once my dad saw Willie roll out of the closet with a smile on his face, he immediately realized he had been duped into spanking me. He shook his head back and forth a couple of times and mumbled a few cuss words as he walked back to the living room to watch TV.

Getting Kicked Out of, Well, Just About Everything

Looking back at my childhood, I think I was a very independent and precocious child who loved to have fun and play pranks on others. Most of the time my behavior was entertaining, but once in a while I got a little carried away with my ability to make others laugh, which eventually annoyed the adults who were trying to mentor and shape us into compliant and obedient young citizens.

When I was 5 years old, I started attending Sunday school at the Hurley Community Church. One Sunday morning I went to Sunday school and a twelve-year-old girl named Sissy Duvall was delivering the lesson under the guidance of a woman named Billie Womack. Billie was the head Sunday school teacher for the Hurley Community Church.

When it was time for the class to begin she asked the children to please be seated. There were about a dozen or more small wooden chairs lined up in a couple of rows and we all scurried about to find a chair in preparation for the class. As I was getting ready to sit down, I noticed a young girl named Kitty Duvall had claimed the seat next to me. She was the younger sister of Sissy, our teacher.

I was in a rather playful mood that morning and, as Kitty began to sit down, I reached over and pulled her chair out from under her. Just as her butt landed on the floor, the back of her head banged against the edge of the chair. Once I heard her begin to cry, I knew I was about to get into trouble.

The teacher came over to make sure that Kitty was not hurt and then she scolded me for my bad behavior. As my punishment, Mrs. Womack kicked me out of Sunday school for the remainder of the class and sent me home.

On the way home from Sunday school I soon realized that my parents would know something was fishy if I showed up at home earlier than usual. I figured if I could just kill an hour and then come home, my mother would never know I was in trouble. So, I did what any normal kid would do in this situation; I hid out for a while.

When I finally arrived home, I walked confidently through the front door, business as usual. I paused for a moment to tell my mom I was home and then casually slid into my bedroom to change out of my Sunday school duds. My mom appeared to be in a good mood when she greeted me, which meant she didn't have a clue about the Sunday school incident. I quickly changed clothes and headed out into the front yard with a couple of my toy cars and found a nice patch of dirt to play in. I remember feeling a great sense of immunity and relief in the yard, knowing that the news of my bad behavior would never penetrate the confines of my Elguea Street sanctuary. Before long, my guilt faded away and life was normal and good again.

A few minutes later, while I was on my knees forging dirt roads and bridges for my toy cars, I heard a noise at our front gate. When I looked up from my corner of the yard I saw one of the most terrifying sights of my life. Billie Womack had opened the gate and was walking up the sidewalk to knock on our front door.

My mom came out onto the porch to greet Mrs. Womack and, almost immediately, her pleasant smile transformed into a look of serious concern. Then, as Mrs. Womack lowered her voice and conveyed vast amounts of information to my mother, their heads began to nod and repeatedly glance over toward my corner of the yard. I couldn't hear what they were saying, but I could tell by their body language that things weren't looking good for me. Those mean old women were terrorizing me, and they were doing it on purpose.

As it turned out, this was undoubtedly one of my earliest memories of the world crashing down around me. On that fateful Sunday morning I realized, firsthand, what it meant to grow up in a small town liker Hurley. I learned that there was a network of evil adults who knew everyone in town and were eager to gang up on kids like me and make our lives miserable. This was an epiphany moment for me. I realized that if I was going to have any chance of surviving in Hurley, I needed to be much sneakier and anonymous in my approach to mischief.

Getting kicked out of Sunday school was a harbinger of what was to come for the remainder of my childhood. I always felt a little bad when I got into trouble but, eventually, it became clear that "getting into trouble" was a human struggle that pitted kids against adults, and I knew which side I was on. I'd take a horsewhippin' if it was amusing to my buddies.

Over the years I've had my friends in tears from laughing at some of the stunts I pulled off. My street mentor, Sido Bates, used to grin from ear to ear when he heard about my latest shenanigans, and he would usually offer select tidbits of wisdom to me. He'd talk to me like a big brother and tell me things like, "Don't ever take any shit off of adults," or, "Rules were made to be broken," or, "Son, you were born to raise hell."

When I was in Cub Scouts, I was sent home from a pack meeting for continually goofing around. A couple of years later I got kicked out of Boy Scouts one night because I was being a nuisance and messing up some game we were playing. Then, when I was about 13 years old, there was an upstanding and righteous Mormon couple in Hurley named Mr. and Mrs. Walton who started a square dance class for kids. The class met weekly at the Chino Club ballroom, and Mr. Walton would call the dances while Mrs. Walton cued the records and worked with the kids on the dance floor.

For the life of me, I don't know how I got tangled up with the square dance class, but apparently someone above me in the family hierarchy thought it would be good for me. I didn't particularly enjoy being there because I found square dancing and square dance music to be old fashioned and boring compared to rock and roll, the twist, the jitterbug, and Elvis Presley music. Anyway, we learned how to listen to the calls and do the various steps and formations for several dances.

One day, the caller said, "OK, get yourself a partner so we can learn a new dance step."

All of the other boys followed directions and began asking different girls to be their partner, but by now I was getting fed up with square dancing. Instead of finding a partner, I walked over and stood on the side of the dance floor in hopes I could just sit this one out without being noticed.

Just as they were getting ready to start, Mrs. Walton noticed me and came over and said, "Jerry, we're getting ready to start the next dance and you need to find a partner."

Without actually looking around, I quickly replied, "Everyone is taken."

Mrs. Walton glanced over to where the girls had been standing and turned back to me and said, "No, there is a girl without a partner standing right over there," and pointed to a girl on the other side of the room.

In a last-ditch effort to avoid dancing again, I offered one final excuse. With an attitude of defiance seething in my voice, I responded, "What? I'm not going to dance with that pig!"

The next thing I knew, Mrs. Walton slapped me in the face and started to scold me. As you can probably well imagine, I was kicked out of square dance class.

Bicycles and Motorcycles

One of my earliest and fondest memories was my fascination with bicycles. By the time I was five years old I was dying to have mobility and was envious of the older kids who could ride a bicycle. The first bicycle I ever rode was a small girls' bike that belonged to my older sister. We called it "the little blue bike".

I learned to ride the little blue bike in my yard where I could land in the grass or soft dirt when I fell down. On my first trial, I kept my balance long enough to run into a trash barrel in our backyard but, little by little, I increased the distance I could ride until I actually made it completely around our house. Learning how to ride a bicycle was the biggest accomplishment in my life up to that point and it forever changed how I perceived the world.

Before long I became the primary owner of the little blue bike and rode it nearly every day. When the bike needed maintenance I would take it to an older man named Virgil Crow who lived on the west end of Pattie Street. He would help me fix a flat, tighten the chain, adjust the seat, or replace missing screws, bolts, and nuts.

Soon I was cruising all over the neighborhood and gradually expanding my riding domain. Then, one day, with my new sense of confidence and freedom, I rode the bike out to the highway and headed north across the railroad tracks, past North Hurley, and out toward the settlement of Quatro Milpas.

As I rode down the hill beyond Pena's roadside tienda I noticed some Hispanic children playing near the highway. Since I was already a long way from home, I decided to stop and play with them rather than continue my journey up the road toward Bayard. I didn't know any of the kids there but that didn't stop me from having a good time. Finally, someone's father came up to me and asked me my name so they could call my parents to tell them where I was.

A couple of years later I saw a chubby kid at school who looked familiar. He was about three years older than I was and his name was Cleo Lopez. After talking to him one day, he mentioned he was one of the kids that I played with the day I took my first long bicycle excursion. As I got older, I would see Cleo around at school and we always talked about the time I rode my bicycle all the way out to his house. Several years later Cleo became a patrol boy and I used to see him direct traffic with a flashlight in front of Cobre High School before and after sporting events.

When I was in elementary school, one of the fads among the Hurley kids was to take an old deck of cards and a few clothes pins and clip the cards onto the forks and frame of the bicycle so they would flap against the spokes as the wheels turned. The cards made our bicycles sound like a motorcycle.

In the late 1950's and early 1960's there was a local policeman and artist named Gilbert Carreon who used to paint small license plates for the kids to put on their bicycles. Gilbert took requests from us and would paint whatever we wanted. Most kids typically requested their favorite cartoon character or their first name or the logo to their favorite sports team. Each license plate was made out of a 6"x4" piece of particleboard that had a couple of holes drilled in the top corners for easy mounting. We would usually hang the license plate under the bicycle seat or at the base of the handlebars. Gilbert charged us something like fifteen cents apiece for each plate.

One of my best bicycle-riding buddies throughout elementary school was Butch Steyskal. We lived to ride our bikes. We always rode up to the Chino Club or the Sweet Shop to get candy and sodas, and sometimes we would make a sack lunch and take bicycle hikes down around the tailings or out to Cameron Creek.

One time Butch and I rode our bikes from Hurley to Arenas Valley to his grandmother's house, which was just north of the Copper Drive Inn movie theatre. On this particular trip we took water and sack lunches with us, and my dog Rumple followed us along. We took the dirt road to Cameron Creek and followed it north until it ran into what is now Racetrack Road. From there, we continued on to Highway 180 and crossed to the north side of Arenas Valley to get to her house.

We spent the night at his grandmother's house and headed back to Hurley the following day. For the return trip, we followed the old highway that ran from Arenas Valley to Fort Bayard. From there we rode through Central, then on to Bayard, and eventually back to Hurley on the old North Hurley Highway.

When Butch and I got to Fort Bayard, I realized my dog Rumple was no longer with us. We called for him and waited around for several minutes but he never showed up. We had come too far to double back toward Arenas Valley to look for him, so we decided to continue on to Hurley and have someone bring me back in a car to look for him.

That evening cousin James and I jumped into my dad's '49 Chevy and went back to the area in Arenas Valley where I last saw Rumple. We stopped at every house along the highway to ask people if they had seen my dog, but I soon realized that no one was taking me seriously. The problem was, my dog didn't look like a normal dog.

You see, a few days before we embarked on the notorious Arenas Valley bike trip I was spray-painting a plastic model car I had just glued together. (Building model cars and airplanes was one of my favorite hobbies when I was young.) When I was done, I had about a half a can of blue spray paint remaining, so I looked through my model collection for something to paint. As it turned out, none of my models needed a paint job, but the next best thing to paint just happened to be lying quietly under the table at my feet; my loyal dog Rumple.

Rumple was a small white dog with brown ears and a brown spot in his side. He was awfully cute as he was, but for some reason it occurred to me that he would look good with a little blue mixed in with his other colors.

After conducting a complete color analysis and studying the latest information on canine fashion trends, I decided to spray a blue stripe down his back and paint his tail blue. As I stepped back to admire his new paint job, it became obvious that there was still something missing. Even though the dog looked good in blue, he just didn't have a sense of identity. Fortunately, that was an easy problem to remedy. I simply painted my cousin James' name on his side. In less than five minutes I had transformed what was once a common, butt-sniffing, fire hydrant pissing yard dog into a spiffy, four-legged mobile masterpiece.

Things were going well for little Rumple and I until James came home from school later that afternoon. As Rumple ran up to greet him at the front gate, James noticed that his name was painted in large letters along the side of the dog. For some reason, he didn't find the same humor and aesthetic beauty in Rumple's new paint job that I did. In fact, he became so angry that he chased me around the yard and kicked my ass. I think he was mad because I painted HIS name on Rumple, not because he objected to the overall paint job.

Now we return to the Arenas Valley bicycle adventure. As James drove me to people's homes along the Arenas Valley road to inquire about my dog, I would knock on their front door and say something like, "Hello, I lost my dog in the area and I was wondering if you have seen him."

The obvious question everyone would ask me was, "What does he look like?" and my rehearsed response would be, "He is a fairly small white dog with brown ears and a brown spot on his side, and he has a blue stripe going down his back with a blue tail."

At that point, most people would either laugh or slam the door in my face.

Luckily, I left my phone number with a few folks along the way and by the next morning someone called to let me know they had Rumple at their house and I could come pick him up.

By the time I was in junior high there were several kids in Hurley who had motor scooters or smaller motorcycles. Tubby Porkman had a little scooter called an Allstate Piaggio that had three speeds and a passenger seat. He used to take me for cruises around town and once in a while he would even let me drive it. Another kid up the street named Red Necker had a red Cushman Husky and he would give me a ride once in a while as well.

One hot summer morning Red and I went cruising on the dirt road that went around to the east side of the tailings to the Bolton Wells pumping station. We were probably about three miles away from Hurley when suddenly his scooter broke down. I had to help him push it all the way back to town, but fortunately he was a big strong kid and we made it home by mid afternoon.

There were a few other motorcycle owners in town, too. Bill Archibald had a motor scooter/bicycle called a Moped. It didn't have a very large motor and you could actually pedal it to assist the motor when you were going up hills or wanted to go a little faster. Another kid named John Dempsey had a Honda Trail 90 that was really fun because you could take it out to the four-wheel-drive roads around Hurley and bushwhack in the rough country. Albert Kelly had a small two-stroke motorcycle made by Sears. It was cheaply made when compared to Hondas and Yamahas, and when he drove it around town people would comment that it sounded like "a bumble bee in a tin can".

The Pierpont brothers had numerous cars and motorcycles over the years and always cruised around town together on whatever vehicles they had up-and-running at the time. The older brother was a tall, lanky kid named Leroy. He was a skilled auto and motorcycle mechanic ever since he was a young boy. His younger brother, Tiny, was a very large, overweight kid who also piddled around with mechanics to a lesser extent.

Both boys were nice kids who wore dirty, greasy clothes and always had dirty hands and fingernails from working on engines. Their yard was filled with junk cars and vehicles they worked on over the years. One time I went over to the Pierpont's house to see Leroy about a mechanical problem and he took me into the family bathroom and showed me a motorcycle engine he had been overhauling in the bathtub.

The Pierpont boys enjoyed riding their motorcycles around the streets of Hurley together. Leroy would always be in the lead as he cruised on his large motorcycle. Then, big Tiny would cruise by a few seconds later on his smaller scooter. My mother used to sit out on our front porch swing from time to time, and whenever Tiny passed by she would chuckle and say, "There goes the caboose."

When I was a sophomore in high school, I finally saved up enough money from my sheep raising venture and my paper route to buy a new Honda 90 Super Sport motorcycle from Werner Tire Store in Silver City. I drove it every day to deliver newspapers, but it also became my primary source of transportation throughout high school.

During the three years I owned the Honda 90 I nearly killed myself a few times. I must say I am lucky to be alive today. Most of the wrecks and near wrecks were from being an inexperienced rider, although I eventually learned how to keep an eye out for things like gravel, ice, or oil on the road.

My friends and I loved to cruise around town at night on our motorcycles. Sometimes we played motorcycle tag, using the entire town of Hurley as our game course. We would race up and down streets and alleys with our headlights off in order to avoid being seen by the person chasing us. It was amazing no one ever got seriously hurt.

Another fun nighttime activity during the summers was taking girls for rides. My favorite motorcycle trick was to take a cute girl for a ride somewhere on a dirt road and then hit the "KILL" switch once we were a couple of miles from town. The motor would instantly shut down and the motorcycle would roll to a stop. Then I would tell the girl something like, "We need to wait a few minutes before we try to start the motorcycle again because it may be flooded."

Of course, my plan all along was to kill time so that I could flirt and hopefully have a little make-out session while we were alone together. Finally, I would "save the day" by using my ingenious mechanical skills to figure out how to start the motorcycle.

Motorcycles were also the perfect vehicles to launch water balloons at people. One afternoon I loaded three friends on my Honda 90 and we cruised all over town with an arsenal of water balloons and pelted anyone we saw along the streets. One kid sat on the handlebars, another on the gas tank, I drove, and another kid was sitting in the passenger seat behind me. You could drive up close to unsuspecting targets, pound them with the balloons, and drive away before they had a chance to pull you off of the motorcycle and kick your ass.

When the summer of 1967 rolled around, I had owned my Honda 90 for more than a year and my interest in motorcycles had grown. In the late spring of that same year, my friend Larry Benavidez purchased a new Bridgestone 175 c.c. Motorcycle. His motorcycle wasn't considered to be large by any means, but all of the motorcycle magazine reviews noted that it was really fast for its size.

When school was out for the summer, Larry used his new motorcycle to commute to a job at the Mimbres Ranger Station. He was a fire fighter with the Forest Service and had to ride about 25 miles in order to get to work. The roads were two-lane and paved all the way to the ranger station, and there were a few stretches that were fairly narrow and had curves.

One warm summer night in the middle of June, Tubby and I went to visit Larry at his parents' house on Aztec Street. Tubby and Larry were close friends because they had been teammates on the Cobre High track team. On this particular night Larry's parents and family were out of town, so the three of us hung out in his kitchen until around 3:00 a.m. At one point in the evening the discussion turned to motorcycles and Larry offered to let me take his new motorcycle for a ride. I was thrilled at the opportunity to ride the new Bridgestone 175 because I had read the reviews about it and was quite impressed with the horsepower that the small motor delivered.

At around midnight, I hopped on his motorcycle and drove it to Bayard and back to Hurley. The Bridgestone 175 was indeed an impressive motorcycle. It was lightweight and handled well but it also accelerated quickly and could easily cruise at highway speeds. After I returned from the ride, Larry cooked us some scrambled eggs and chorizo and Tubby and I eventually went home.

One morning a few days later I was cruising around on my Honda 90 and I pulled into Ted Carr's Exxon gas station on Carrasco Street. My friend Eddie Mitchell worked there during the summers and I used to stop in and visit with him when I was in the neighborhood. I was feeling confident and cocky on my little Honda as I screeched to a halt next to the gas pumps in front of the office.

Before I could get off of my motorcycle, Eddie came out of the office and said, "You better be careful on that thing. Larry Benavidez wrecked his motorcycle this morning on the way to work and was killed."

I was silent for a moment as I tried to gather my wits. At first I thought Eddie was kidding. I asked myself, "Why would Eddie bullshit me about something as serious as this?"

Then I reasoned that perhaps Eddie had been misinformed and didn't have his facts straight. I thought to myself, "It wasn't Larry in the accident. It must have been someone else. It was probably someone with the first name of Larry or the last name of Benavidez, but not Larry Benavidez."

I tried every denial tactic I could think of before the news actually began to sink in. This was the first time I ever had to deal with the loss of a personal friend and it was a difficult concept to accept. By the time I read the article in the newspaper and heard all of my friends talk about the accident, I finally realized there were no other possible outcomes. The truth of the matter was I had just lost a good friend.

Larry's funeral was held at the Hurley Catholic Church on another beautiful June day. By the time I arrived, the church was totally packed with family and high school kids from Cobre High School and throughout Grant County. I had never seen the parking lot of the church so filled with cars.

Once the church services were over, there was a funeral procession to the burial site at the Catholic Cemetery west of town. Cars were lined up bumper-to-bumper as they drove slowly away from the church. There were so many cars in the procession that it extended from the church to the cemetery about a mile away. Larry's funeral served as a final validation of the fact that you had to be extremely careful on a motorcycle.

Musical influences during My Childhood

My very first memory of being interested in music was when I was a preschool toddler. My mother listened to KSIL radio station from Silver City while she did housework in the mornings and I would sit near the radio and listen to the various programs. I remember listening to songs like "The Tumbling Tumble Weed" by the Sons of the Pioneers and "House of Bamboo" by Earl Grant in the mid 1950's.

KSIL radio also had an afternoon program called "Mexican Serenade" that was hosted by a DJ named Bill Acosta. Bill would play popular Mexican tunes and a little Salsa type music, which I really enjoyed. (Speaking of KSIL, they also aired a "call-in" program in the mornings called "The Mousetrap", where people discussed local issues and politics. I was young when that program was on the air but for some strange reason I enjoyed listening to people complain, whine, and argue about things.)

When I was in first grade I heard a tune called "Hound Dog" by Elvis Presley that became my first favorite song. My sister had the tune in her 45 r.p.m. Record collection. I used to go into her bedroom when she was at school and listen to that song as well as "Teddy Bear" and "Love Me Tender" by Elvis. She also had records by other popular artists such as Fabian, Johnny Horton, Chuck Berry, Little Richard, The Everly Brothers, Richie Valens, and Peggy Lee.

By the mid 1950's, teenagers were buying records and cruising around listening to the latest hit tunes that blared away on the AM radio in their car. The music of that era was instrumental in helping forge an identity for an entire generation and, even though I was very young at the time, I felt as though I was a part of it. I learned at a young age that music was a social medium that helped me make friends.

During the 1950's and 1960's, radio reception in Hurley was fairly limited. Fortunately we could pick up two AM radio stations that played Top 40 popular music. The daytime station was KGRT from Las Cruces and the nighttime station was KOMA from Oklahoma City. I spent most of my childhood listening to these two stations because they were our only connection to the outside world.

Once in a while there were other interesting AM stations that faded in and out of the local airwaves at night. Sido Bates and I used to sit in his '53 Ford at night and scan the radio dial in search of the gruff voice of Wolfman Jack out of Del Rio, Texas. He was quite a talker and eventually went on to become a nationally famous DJ. Wolfman Jack was by far the coolest DJ we had ever heard. As I remember, he always played great music and there was quite a bit of howling going on between songs. And, whenever we were hanging out with our friends we used to impersonate Wolfman Jack and get lots of laughs.

There was also a high-powered Mexican radio station out of Juarez called XELO that played top 40 tunes. XELO played some great music, but what we really found amusing was the Spanish speaking DJ. Between songs he would play a prerecorded radio ID that consisted of a huge explosion followed by a crowing rooster and then, in Spanish he would say "¡Radio X E L O!"

Listening to records and the radio were enjoyable, but when I heard live music for the first time my interest rose to another level. An older boy named Joey Allen, who lived directly across the street from us, had a band that practiced in their front yard on summer evenings. I used to love going over there to watch them play. They did a song called, "I'm Gonna Find Me A Bluebird" that was the first song I ever heard being performed by a live band.

Later on I went to see a band called The Rhythm Wranglers play country tunes at the local dances. I also used to walk down the street to listen to a couple of local boys named Fred Mason and Mike McGee play their guitars on Fred's front porch. Mike eventually became quite an accomplished guitarist and played in regional bands in the 1960's and 1970's.

By the time I was in fifth grade and had a limited income from delivering newspapers, I began buying records at the Hurley Stores and at the Rexall Drug Store in Silver City. The first Record I ever bought was "Greenback Dollar" by the Kingston Trio, and not long after that I bought "Fingertips, Part II", by Stevie Wonder. That song influenced me a lot because Stevie Wonder was exactly my age (12 years old) when the record was released.

Eventually, my musical interests led me to the Motown Label, where I fell in love with R & B and Soul Music. By the time I was in Junior High and High School I was listening to Marvin Gaye, James Brown, Aretha Franklin, Dionne Warwick, Sam and Dave, Smokey Robinson and the Miracles, Wilson Pickett, Martha and the Vandellas, The Four Tops, The Temptations, James and Bobby Purify, and Arthur Connelly, Archie Bell and the Drells from Houston, Texas, to name a few. Then, when the British music invasion hit the U.S. in about 1963, I started listening to The Beatles, The Rolling Stones, Chad and Jeremy, The Animals, the Who, Herman and the Hermits, Freddy and the Dreamers, Manfred Mann, Van Morrison, The Beau Brummels, The Kinks, The Yardbirds, The Dave Clark Five, and Paul Revere and the Raiders. Some of the American bands I liked then were The Buffalo Springfield, Jimi Hendrix, The Birds, Jefferson Airplane, Vanilla Fudge, The Loving Spoonful, The Beach Boys, The Ventures, Jan and Dean, Mitch Ryder and the Detroit Wheels, Neil Diamond, Johnny Rivers, and one of my all time favorite bands, The Young Rascals.

When I was in elementary school my friend Butch Steyskal used to point out drum parts to songs when they came out on the radio. That's probably when I first became interested in becoming a drummer. I eventually developed my own knack for picking out drum parts and years later I used to bang on the dashboard of everyone's car as I listened to the radio. My favorite song to play on the dashboard was "Wipeout" by the Surfaris.

One time when I was in high school my friend Juan Carlos Maldonado rented his drum set to me for a week for $10. It was in the middle of February when I brought the drums home and my parents wouldn't let me play them in the house because they were too loud. Since I was determined to get my money's worth out of Juan Carlos' drums, I set them up and played them outside in our back yard at night in the freezing weather. I had to wear a heavy jacket and a winter hat to stay warm when I played.

By the time I was about 14 years old I listened to lots of music and knew almost all of the artists who came out on the radio. To be honest, I actually thought I was fairly good at keeping up with the latest releases and the up and coming artists. Then, one evening I went to the Chino Club to play ping-pong and spend a little money listening to the jukebox. At this point in time I had been listening a lot to "Papa's Got a Brand New Bag" and "This Is a Man's World" by James Brown. He was my new favorite artist.

As I put a quarter in the jukebox and began selecting some tunes I wanted to hear, I noticed a song called "Pop a Top Again" by James Ed Brown. I wasn't sure whether James "Ed" Brown was the same guy as James Brown or not, but I decided to take a chance and play the song anyway. Once the song started, it took me about one second to realize I had made a huge mistake. "Pop a Top Again" turned out to be a twangy country song instead of the funky R & B tune I had hoped it would be. I still laugh whenever I hear that song, and it is one of my favorite country tunes to this day.

Influence of Television

Oscar and Lois Bates were the first family in the neighborhood to purchase a TV, which must have been about 1954 or 1955. My brother and I were good friends with Tommy "Sido" Bates, and we used to head up to the Bates' house after school and on weekends to watch TV. We watched a lot of baseball games at their home. Oscar was a semi pro baseball player when he was younger and was a big fan of major league baseball. At one point in his career the Detroit Tigers had an eye on him as a potential player.

The only TV channel we could get in Hurley had the baseball "Game of the Week" with Dizzy Dean and Pee Wee Reese. The sponsor for that show happened to be Falstaff Beer. I'm fairly certain I remember seeing commercials of Dizzy Dean as he sat in the press box and poured a bottle of Falstaff Beer into a glass. Then he would always sing some country song as he announced the remainder of the game. In fact, after several beer commercials Dizzy and Pee Wee appeared to be having a pretty good time.

It was claimed by some baseball viewers that during the late innings of a particular game, Pee Wee Reese mentioned to Dizzy that there was a man and a woman kissing frequently in the stands.

Dizzy then turned to Pee Wee and asked, "Why are they kissing so frequently?"

Pee Wee quickly replied, "It looks like he is kissing her on the strikes and she is kissing him on the balls."

My brother and I went up to the Bates' house every holiday season and spent hours watching every college football bowl game that was broadcast. Sometimes we made bets with each other and the person who lost would usually get really mad. To make matters even worse, the winner would "rub it in" until the loser was livid. And when the Yankees and the Chicago White Sox played, there was always a good chance my brother and I would get into a fight because he was a White Sox fan and I was a Yankee fan.

During the weekdays after school we watched shows like The Mickey Mouse Club and Rin Tin Tin, and on weekends we watched Lassie, Walt

Disney, Roy Rogers, Hop a Long Cassidy, Wild Bill Hickock, My Friend Flicka, Captain Kangaroo, and lots of cartoons.

Not long after my family got our first TV in about 1957, we watched shows like The Ed Sullivan Show, The Red Skelton Show, Leave It to Beaver, Dennis the Menace, The Three Stooges, I Love Lucy, Amos 'n Andy, The Honeymooners, The Jack Benny Show, Arthur Godfrey, I've Got a Secret, What's My Line, George Burns and Gracie Allen, Perry Mason, and The General Electric Hour with Ronald Reagan. The Bullwinkle Show was my favorite cartoon show, although I enjoyed Foghorn Leghorn, Yosemite Sam, The Roadrunner, most versions of Bugs Bunny, and Mighty Mouse with the villain Oil Can Harry.

Two of my favorite shows in the mid 1960's were The Wild, Wild West and The Saint, starring Roger Moore as Simon Templar. I also enjoyed watching a talk show called the Joe Pine Show because he liked to interview kooks and weirdoes. He typically interviewed people who claimed to have been abducted by UFO's or who had some other far fetched story, but one night he had the Governor of Georgia, Lester Maddox, on his show. Gov. Maddox was quite a kook in his own right, but Joe Pine got the Governor so wound up and mad that he got up and walked off of the stage in the middle of the interview.

By the time we finally got our TV, Hurley could still only receive the CBS channel from El Paso with the call letters KROD. A short time later we began to pick up NBC and eventually ABC out of El Paso. The first TVs made were black and white, but by the late 1950's people were ditching their old TV sets for color TVs. Initially, color TVs weren't that great and the screens were small, but within a few years the screens became larger and the image quality vastly improved. Some brands had much better picture quality than others, but everyone still had to spend a little time adjusting the color knobs to get the best picture. Sometimes we would have to go outside and adjust the direction our TV antenna was pointing so we could improve the quality of the picture. If someone's TV ever developed a problem and was in need of repair, there was a man who lived on Carrasco Street in Hurley named Nick Kennedy who knew the basics of TV electronics. He would come to your house and tear the TV apart right there in your living room. Depending on the problem, he would be at your house for several hours until he fixed and reassembled it.

Family dynamics were definitely affected by television. It was quite common for family members to argue or get into big fights over which TV programs they wanted to watch. Parents used to come up with TV rules for the kids like, "No TV after 10:00 p.m.", or "No TV until you get your homework done", or "No TV for a week until you bring up your math grade". Many times an entire family would sit around the living room together to watch shows that had broad appeal to young and old alike.

I remember many Sunday evenings when we would be playing touch football out in the street or alley and someone's mother would yell out the door, "The Walt Disney show will be on in 5 minutes." Everyone would scramble home and that would be the end of the football game. Then, about halfway into the program, I would eat my dinner on a TV dinner tray as I watched the remainder of the show.

In the mid 1960's I liked to watch the teen music shows that aired on Saturday mornings. First there would be American Bandstand with Dick Clark. He would play some Top 40 hits off the charts and always had a guest band perform live on the show. It looked to me like the bands would mimic or lip-sync their tunes in front of the camera, while the sound engineers played their record off-stage. The dancers on the show were mostly clean-cut, white, middle to upper class kids who showed off the latest fad dance moves.

After American Bandstand came a regional teen music and dance show out of El Paso called "Crosno's Hop". Steve Crosno was the MC and most of the kids on the show were Hispanic kids from El Paso. Many of the boys would have their hair slicked back on the sides and sometimes wore sunglasses in the studio. Crosno mostly played soul, R and B, and Tejano/Tex-Mex music on his program.

A few years later "Soul Train" burst onto the scene and featured the latest hits from urban Black America. The music was R & B and Funk. I always loved the music on this show more than the others. The dancers were almost all black kids, dressed to the nines, and did dance moves that made the white kids from American Bandstand look stiff and clumsy.

A couple of other shows that were produced out of El Paso are also worth mentioning. On Saturday mornings there was a cartoon show called "Cartoon Carnival", hosted by Marlin Haines. Immediately before each cartoon he would say, "One, Two, Three, Daffy Fuddlebug" and the cartoon would begin. Also airing on Saturday mornings was a kid's show called "Saturday Circus", hosted by Red Brown and Anna Lee. As I recall, Red Brown and Anna Lee were a couple of country hicks. The show was a tad too folksy for me, but they did have local and regional kids appear on their program.

Popular Toys

Television helped generate a market for toy sales to kids all across America in the late 1950's and 1960's. The cartoon shows on Saturday mornings had advertisements that informed us about the latest "must have" toy of the day. For example, the Slinky was a coil of wire shaped like a spring that could do cool tricks, like walk down your stairs. Silly Putty was a putty-like material that came in a plastic eggshell. Kids could flatten the putty over a color comic book page and, when you peeled it away, it would have a copy of the comic book picture on it.

Then there was the Hoola Hoop craze that stormed the country. Kids all over Hurley were out in their yards spinning a hoop around their waist, ankles, knees, and elbows. Some families even had the Wham-O Slip and Slide rolled out onto their lawn during the summer months. Kids would run and dive onto the water-soaked, slippery, plastic runway until they slid off onto the grass at the other end of the strip.

And who can forget the Pogo Stick. It was a metal pole about four feet long with a spring-loaded rubber foot that was about two inches wide. The bottom of the vertical pole had foot pegs and you held on to the top as you jumped around your yard like a kangaroo.

I was always a sucker for contraptions like the Pogo Stick. I got good enough to hop all the way around my house on the spring-loaded monstrosity with only one foot and one hand clinging to the pole. Most kids had to hold on with both hands, while keeping both feet on the foot pegs. I thought I was pretty "bad-ass" on that thing until one afternoon I nearly broke my tailbone when the Pogo Stick slipped out from under me on a wet sidewalk. I fell so hard that I cried for two days.

The Etch-A-Sketch was a great drawing toy and, with a little practice, I quickly mastered the art of drawing pornographic pictures to make my friends laugh. And no child in Hurley was left behind when the Duncan Yoyo craze hit town. Several of us spent weeks learning how to "walk-the-dog" or do "rock-a-bye-baby". Pick-Up-Sticks was another toy that kept kids busy on cold winter afternoons. They consisted of about two or three dozen colored plastic sticks about eight or ten inches in length and the diameter of a toothpick. Players would first dump the sticks onto the table into a tangled up pile. Then, each player took turns extracting their colored sticks from the pile without moving the other sticks. When I was very young I also enjoyed playing with Tinker Toys. They were round wooden sticks and blocks of wood with round holes. You could stick the sticks into the blocks and build things like windmills or crude automobiles.

Another popular game among boys was Electric Football. The football field was a thin piece of sheet metal that was about 30 inches long and maybe 18 inches wide. It was painted green with white yard lines marked every 10 yards and there were upright goal posts at each end zone. There was a small wall or bumper that surrounded the circumference of the board. Kids would place their small plastic men on the board in whatever formation they chose, and play began when someone flicked a switch to an electric vibrator underneath the metal football field. The metal field and the electric motor in the vibrator made a loud, low-pitched drone sound that was actually quite annoying.

One of the small plastic players would carry a felt football about the size of a split pea and would be tackled whenever a player on the opposing team touched them. The players had a flat base beneath their feet and two small strips of a photographic film-like material extending beneath the base. The vibration of the board slowly propelled the players in a forward direction. Kids were continually trying to make their players go faster by experimenting with the angle of the film-like strips beneath the players.

For field goals, there was a special player with a little spring-loaded kicking leg. You would cock the little leg back and let go of it to propel the felt football toward the opponent's goal post.

Two other toys that were specifically marketed to girls were the Barbie Doll and the Easy Bake Oven. They were off limits to us boys but I remember seeing a lot of girls playing with them.

There were also a couple of other toys that I spent many hours playing with on my living room floor. Lincoln Logs were miniature wooden logs that had notches cut out at each end so you could stack them to build a log cabin. Many kids also had an Erector Set, which enabled them to build things out of various shaped metal pieces. The pieces had holes in them so they could be bolted together to make everything from buildings to heavy equipment replicas like cranes.

Lastly, there were a couple of really cool toys some of the kids in Hurley owned but they weren't as well known as the toys I just mentioned. One toy was a hollow plastic rocket that flew high into the air and was propelled by pressurized water. To make it fly you had to hook up a garden hose to the plastic base. Next you attached the rocket to the top of the base and turned on the water. Once the rocket was full you turned off the water. You then increased the water pressure inside of the rocket with a hand pump that was built into the base. Once the rocket had lots of pressure you would slide a lever to launch it into the air. If you weren't paying attention during the launch, the nose of the rocket could hit you in the head going about 1,000 mph and mess up your face. Sometimes we launched the rocket horizontally instead of vertically in hopes of hitting a particular target several yards away. Moving targets such as a neighborhood dog were always fun to aim for, although I don't recall actually hitting one. I'm not sure, but I think they eventually stopped selling this toy because of safety concerns.

I remember one other toy that was quite simple but was perhaps the most historically significant toy of all. There was a cartoon show in the mid 1950's that was broadcast on Saturday mornings called Winky Dink. In every cartoon episode, a character named Winky Dink would get into some sort of jam and would need your help. If you were a Winky Dink fan you could order, for a small fee of course, a clear plastic film that rolled across your TV screen. The film stuck to the TV screen with static electricity. Once the film was in place, you could draw on it with a crayon. So, for example, if Winky Dink needed to cross a river to get away from a villain, the cartoon would freeze momentarily while you drew a bridge across the river. Then, Winky Dink would walk across your bridge to get to the other side of the river. Winky Dink was probably the first television cartoon that was considered to be interactive with the TV viewer.

As long as we're on the subject of toys, there was one homemade toy we used to make out of a wooden clothespin that is worth mentioning. We took the clothespin apart and carved a slot on the side of one of the legs and reconfigured the metal spring. We would then reassemble the clothespin so the spring became a trigger of sorts. When you slid a wooden stick match down the middle of the clothespin and pulled the trigger, it would ignite the match and shoot it several feet away, sort of like a miniature flamethrower. Kids will be kids, and it was never long before one of us had a small burn hole in our shirt or jeans from one of the match projectiles.

Introduction to Adulthood: The Dating Scene

Coming of age in Hurley and Grant County in the 1960's was quite interesting. I'm sure every adult who reads this book can tell plenty of stories about their dating life. Generally speaking, the kids in Hurley learned about the birds and the bees just as early as kids from other parts of the country whether they came from a city or a rural area. We all went through the same progression. When we were in fourth grade, boys and girls started having crushes on each other. By sixth grade many kids were undergoing puberty and were actually holding hands and kissing. A very small percentage of sixth graders were doing more than just kissing. The seventh and eighth grade girls and boys had boyfriends/girlfriends who usually lasted all of two weeks. By high school, my buddies and I had become full-blown girl watchers and had the social skills to make things happen. The rest is history.

With that being said, Hurley boys had some local dynamics at work that influenced their dating habits. For example, our first crushes were usually on local girls who were in our classes at school. Then, there were situations where some cute girl from out of town would come to Hurley to visit her grandparents or some other relative during the summer. Whenever that happened, my friends and I homed in on these girls like "a cop on a one-legged shoplifter". First, we would see them around town or at the Hurley Swimming Pool and do a little detective work to find out where they were staying. Then, by nightfall we would inadvertently stroll by grandma's house a few times over the course of the evening. Sooner or later we would see them out in the yard and welcome them to town with a friendly "hello".

You know where it went from there.

The next stage we went through is what I refer to as the "grass-is-greener" syndrome. For some reason the girls from Hurley weren't doing it for us anymore and we started paying serious attention to out-of-town girls. We were suddenly getting all worked up over junior high and high school girls from Bayard, Central and Santa Rita.

Next, it was the girls from Silver High School who triggered our fantasies. We would see them at high school athletic events or when they cruised up and down Bullard Street in Silver City in their parents' car. Our testosterone was raging and we were continually looking for ways to get to know them.

Inevitably, one of our friends would meet a girl from some far away "dream-land" like Deming and, the next thing you know, a carload of Cobre boys would be driving down there to rendezvous with her and her friends. The Deming girls were our first experience with the dating category known as "long-distance-romance".

Back on the home front, some girls were considered better catches than others based on long established local social norms. For example, there were the "goodie-goodie" girls who appealed to some of us because they made good grades or joined the Rainbow Girls or became the prom queen or came from a rich or prominent family or their father was a "big-shot" at Kennecott. Other girls were just downright good looking and made themselves more desirable by going to the local dances and looking really hot in tight jeans or short skirts. Then there were the party girls who became our good buddies and were fun to be with, but you had to be careful who you ended up with as the evening wore on.

To be fair, the girls also had their social parameters to consider when selecting a boy to go out with. I can only speculate about what the girls looked for in a boy back in our high school years because I am a guy and I will never fully understand the inner workings of the female mind. I did notice, however, that girls usually liked older guys. By the time we were sophomores at Cobre High School, most of the girls in my class considered my friends and I "chopped liver" because we were immature and very unsophisticated. While they were schmoozing with the junior and senior boys, we had to look for cute eighth or ninth grade girls at the junior high school.

Naturally, most girls liked boys who were handsome. But they also liked guys who had certain traits such as confidence, politeness and good manners, and were clean-cut. They also liked guys who were stud athletes or did well in school but weren't nerds. And it surely didn't hurt a fellow if he came from a family of wealth and prominence, lived in a big house or on a large family ranch, or drove a nice car.

Some girls had romantic fetishes and would only date certain types of guys. For example, some Anglo girls would only go out with Hispanic boys and some Hispanic girls would only go out with Anglo boys. There were other girls who wouldn't give you the time of day unless you were a jock or a cowboy or a "big-man-on-campus".

Then there were the girls who only went out with "bad boys". These girls were romantically aroused by boys with resumes that included but weren't limited to such characteristics as bad grades, repeated skirmishes with local law enforcement agencies, fast driving habits, personal drama, a reputation as a fighter, an inclination to indulge excessively in alcohol, greasy fingernails, or always having a group of guys from another high school mad at them and wanting to beat the shit out of them.

The Alamogordo Girls

During the summer after my ninth grade school year, Gene Valles and I went camping at Lake Roberts. Late one afternoon we noticed a couple of girls about our age who were camping with their parents. Being the fine, upstanding, courteous boys we were, it didn't take us long to figure out a way to approach these girls as they were walking innocently around the lake. After a brief introduction, a little flirting, and a few cornball jokes, we somehow persuaded them to sneak away from their camp later that evening and meet us near the boat ramp.

Gene and I showed up at the boat ramp at the agreed upon time and waited for them. Before long they showed up and the four of us spent the evening visiting and flirting. Both girls were cute and we could tell they were becoming more interested in us as the evening wore on. We eventually paired up and Gene took one of the girls for a walk while her friend and I continued to visit near the boat ramp.

A few minutes later we decided to take a walk of our own. We walked up the road a ways and eventually climbed up a rocky hill overlooking the campground below. We looked around and found a fairly level spot near the east end of the lake where we sat together and enjoyed the view. For the first few minutes we joked around and giggled a lot, but that situation somehow evolved into long embraces and wet kisses. Even though I was very excited and aroused about being with a girl, I also felt somewhat clumsy and stressed. But hey, don't get me wrong. It was my first romantic experience and it was quite fun.

Later that evening we all met up again and Gene and I walked the girls back down the road towards their camp. Before we parted, the girls gave us their phone numbers and addresses and we kissed them goodnight. We were somewhat excited to find out they were from Alamogordo and wanted us to come visit them some time.

Everyone knows that all good romances have their obstacles, and this brief encounter with the Alamogordo girls was no exception. First of all, summer vacation was nearly over and school was scheduled to start in a few days. Secondly, Alamogordo was a long way from Hurley and if we were going to go visit them, we had to figure out a plan to get there and back without telling our parents.

Most 15 year old kids would have been discouraged about our dilemma, but Gene and I were a couple of confident young whippersnappers who knew everything about everything. We weren't about to let a little thing like logistics get in our way.

A couple of weeks into the new school year, Gene and I called the girls and told them we would like to come see them sometime. They seemed quite excited about our call and told us we should come see them soon. In fact, they told us we should come over the following Friday night. They gave us a street address and directions to their house and, before we knew it, we had one foot out the door to Alamogordo.

The girls were expecting us and we didn't want to let them down. At the time we didn't really know how we were going to pull this trip off. There was one small detail that had to fall into place before anything was going to happen. We had to get our hands on an automobile for several hours without arousing parental suspicion.

The automobile issue didn't turn out to be as much of a problem as we had anticipated. The next day, Gene and I pitched our situation to Tom Foy and Tubby Porkman. These two adventurous young men became intrigued by our predicament and, before we knew it, we had a car and a plan to get to Alamogordo.

A couple of nights later Tom borrowed his parents' car and told them we were going to Silver to "cruise around for the evening". Instead, we jammed the Foys' station wagon into D-R-I-V-E and flew to Alamogordo with the car at full throttle. There were some stretches of road where we were cruising at well over 100 mph. We knew we had to get to Alamogordo and back quickly in order to make it look like we had spent a casual and uneventful evening cruising around Silver City. Never mind the extra 375 miles on the odometer.

Once we pulled into Alamogordo nearly three hours later, we went to a neighborhood and started looking for the girl's house. We followed the directions we were given and before long we found her street. We slowly began cruising back and forth as we looked for her address. To complicate matters, the street was dark, which made it difficult to see everyone's house number.

We didn't know it at the time, but for some strange reason the residents of Alamogordo didn't have much of a tolerance for slow moving station wagons that cruised back and forth in their neighborhoods late at night. Thus, it didn't take long for someone to call the cops after we drove by their house three or four times over a five-minute period of time. In a matter of minutes an officer had us pulled over in front of a residence with his lights flashing and a spotlight zeroed in on the back of our car.

To make a long story short, it didn't take the Alamogordo cops long to figure out we were young kids from Silver City who were three hours away from home on a Friday night without our parents' permission. They immediately took us to the police station and called Tom's parents to let them know that we were in Alamogordo. We were busted.

At first the cops wanted the Foys to drive from Bayard to Alamogordo to pick us up. After some negotiation and legal wrangling, however, the Foys eventually got the cops to agree to let us drive back to Bayard on our own. It was a long and dreadful drive home and we finally pulled into Bayard around 2:00 a.m. Tom got into quite a bit of trouble with his parents over our grandiose stunt and, unfortunately for Gene and me, we never saw the girls again.

CHAPTER SIX: STORIES FROM THE STREETS

"By today's standards, you guys would be considered juvenile delinquents."

With due respect to the town of Hurley and the many fine families who lived in the community, it would be difficult to name all of the adults who volunteered to serve in youth leadership roles throughout my childhood. During the school year it was popular to join Boy Scouts, Cub Scouts, Brownies and Girl Scouts, and in the summers most younger boys played Little League baseball. In addition to participating in some of those activities, I also attended the Pilgrim Fellowship (PF) youth group at the Hurley Community Church for several years. The Sunday night PF meetings were usually fun, although there was a "goodie-two-shoes" religious vibe that didn't do much for me at the time.

In spite of the generous efforts by these many wonderful people, I found Hurley to be a fairly boring place to grow up. While it is true that organized youth activities kept kids busy and off of the streets, Hurley was one of those places where you had to invent your own fun when there was nothing else going on. You either had to call other kids and organize an activity or lie around the house and watch TV.

When my friends and I didn't have anything else to do, we usually rode our bicycles or walked around town. In the evenings and on weekends we spent a lot of time at the Chino Club. During the summers we did things like play sand lot baseball, go swimming, go hiking, or hunted rabbits with a 22-caliber rifle. In the fall we would organize pick-up games of touch football in the streets, at the old Hurley High School football stadium, or at the vacant lot across from the Chino Club. In the late fall and winter we would organize games of basketball on the tennis courts next to the Chino Club. I also used to enjoy roller-skating and playing tennis there as well.

On warm summer nights we would occasionally get together with a group of kids and play games like Red Rover, Ollie Ollie Oxen Free, Kick the Can, Hide and go Seek, and Tag. Another game we played was called Mumblety Peg (we referred to it as "Mumbly Peg"), where two people would face each other about three feet apart and place their feet about shoulder width apart. Each person would take turns throwing a pocketknife into the grass. If it stuck, the opponent would have to move one of their feet to the knife. The objective was to make your opponent move their feet wider and wider apart until they could no longer reach the knife. Kids who had long legs or could do the splits usually did well at this game. As we got a little older, all of these games eventually gave way to our new game of choice, which was Spin-the-Bottle. Unfortunately, we didn't play Spin the Bottle as much as we wanted because we were usually too chicken to call girls up to participate.

Even though I did most of my devious deeds on the streets of Hurley, I did enjoy stirring things up around my family's home on occasion. One year my parents bought me a Gilbert Chemistry Set for Christmas (the one that came in a hefty metal box that included various chemicals, test tubes, and rubber stoppers inside). It didn't take me long to figure out that if you put sulfur and a little wax into a test tube and heated it up, you could create a rank odor that rivaled the smell of a bad fart. By mid-afternoon on Christmas day I had inserted the end of the glass tube into the keyhole of my sister's bedroom door and heated my fart mix with a cigarette lighter. A few minutes later my sister came storming out of her bedroom to go complain to my parents that her bedroom smelled like sewage.

Another time, when I was very young and empathetic toward the hungry children in our close-knit community, I remember putting some dog shit on a biscuit and attempting to convince my sister's friend that it was peanut butter. I spent several minutes trying to persuade her to take a bite but, unfortunately, she didn't go for it. I eventually fed the biscuit to some neighborhood dog.

When my friends and I weren't doing something constructive, which was most of the time, we were usually creating some sort of mischief around town. For example, when I was in my early teens I had an older friend named Mikey Bailey who lived across the street from the tennis courts. Mikey used to drive his dad's old Chevy pickup around town and would occasionally take some of his friends for rides. The truck was probably a 1951 model and had a couple of features that his friends found to be quite amusing. For one, the gearshift knob on the end of the floor shift lever was covered with the dried skin from a deer testicle. The truck also had a "suicide knob" on the steering wheel that had a picture of a naked woman embedded inside the clear plastic cover.

One cold winter night Mikey took me cruising around with him on the snow packed and slippery streets of Hurley. We had a great time sliding around street corners and spinning donuts in parking lots all over town. Mikey was a responsible driver but he did know how to have fun in that old truck.

Another night he took cousin James cruising up and down Aztec Street to roust out a large dog that would chase cars and bark feverishly whenever anyone drove by. The crazy mutt would run alongside the passenger door of the car and bark like hell until he reached the end of the block. Then he would stop and walk proudly back to his yard.

The dog's routine was so annoying and predictable that Mikey and cousin James decided it was time to help break him of his bad habit. Being the responsible community-minded young lads that they were, they concocted a dog training curriculum that was not only humane, but had the best interests of the dog in mind during every step of the remediation process. They referred to their plan as "The Streets of Hurley Canine Behavioral Modification Program".

Later that evening they went back to Mikey's garage and found a heavy metal bar that his dad used for digging postholes. Since the truck had a homemade rear bumper made from a three-inch diameter steel pipe, they slid part of the digging bar into the hollow bumper but left about three feet of it sticking out from the side of the truck. With the "modifier" in place, they drove back to Aztec Street where the dog lived.

Just as they had anticipated, whenever they drove up the street the dog came running out and began to chase Mikey's truck. At first the boys slowed down so he could run alongside the truck next to the passenger side door but, as soon as the dog started to show signs of fatigue, Mikey began to speed up. As the dog gradually lagged further and further behind, the "modifier" eventually caught him from the rear and caused him to trip and tumble, end over end, in the middle of the street.

In order to lend validity to their dog-training methodology, these two accomplished young behavioral scientists paid a couple of follow-up visits to the dog later that night but were never chased again. Apparently their training regimen was successful and the dog graduated from the highly coveted program with flying colors.

Fun at the Railroad Tracks

The ore train from Santa Rita came to Hurley loaded with thousands of tons of ore from the pit. The metal wheels of the ore cars would easily flatten anything that was lying on the steel train track because the cars were so heavy. When I was in fourth or fifth grade we used to go up to the railroad tracks between North and South Hurley and place objects like nails, pennies or nickels on top of one of the tracks. The next day we would return to retrieve our objects after they had been flattened and elongated. Sometimes our coins still had most of the facial image of the president intact and we would take them to school and show our friends. We also would file the edges of the flattened nails to make a small knife blade or a miniature sword.

When I was in high school we used to drive to one of the railroad crossings west of Hurley and let about half of the air out of each car tire. Then we would put the car on the tracks and take a ride south of Hurley to the Grant County Airport crossing or to the crossing by the cattle-loading corral at Whitewater. Riding the tracks at night was especially fun because you could turn off the headlights and cruise about 20 miles per hour. The tracks were as smooth as glass and the ride was very quiet. The driver never had to touch the steering wheel because the tracks guided the car tires in a perfectly straight line.

Rail riding also proved to be a great beer drinking activity since no one had to pay attention as the car floated down the tracks. Another advantage was that an oncoming train could be seen from miles away, which gave us plenty of time to get to a railroad crossing before the train got too close. When our ride was over, we would drive back to Hurley and go to one of the gas stations to inflate the tires back to their original pressure.

One afternoon when I was in high school, Toby Parker and I went down to the railroad tracks behind Snell Junior High School in Bayard and jumped onto a moving train as it passed by. Toby was an experienced train hopper and gave me a brief lesson on how to run alongside the train and grab the vertical handle on the side of the ore car.

Once we were on the train and headed southbound for Hurley, we stood between the cars so that no one would see us. The trickiest part of our free ride was jumping off of the moving car as we approached the Hurley rail yard. With the train still moving along at a pretty good clip, we had to land on the rugged ground alongside the track without falling down.

Halloween Stories

Halloween was always a great time in Hurley. Every kid in town would put on a costume and go out for a night of trick-or-treating to as many homes as possible. There were always a few houses that turned off their lights to indicate they weren't home or didn't want to participate in the festivities, but the majority of houses gave away treats until they ran out. A few ambitious kids would fill an entire grocery bag full of treats, take the bag home and empty it, and go back out on the town for even more goodies.

There were some people who had a reputation for giving better Halloween treats than others. Most homes in my neighborhood gave away pieces of hard candy, nuts, fruit, or suckers, but there was a lady named Mrs. Harland Smith who always gave the kids her famous popcorn balls.

A few of us were keenly aware when Mrs. Smith was doling out her delicious Halloween treat. We loved her popcorn balls so much that we would go to her house in the earlier part of the evening before she ran out. Then, we would swap masks with our friends and return to her house again and again. By the time we were on our third or fourth visit, she would finally catch on to our game and tell us not to come back.

Halloween was also a superb time to create a little mischief around town. Sido and I spent many Halloweens roaming around town looking for mean things to do. Two of our favorite evil deeds were to scribble on car windows with a bar of soap and cover cars with toilet paper. Most people knew better than to leave their cars parked on the street on Halloween night, but there were always a few folks who would either forget or were too lazy to park their car in their back yard.

Every Halloween you would hear stories floating around town about larger kids who were stealing candy from smaller, defenseless kids. In spite of all of the mean and rotten things Sido and I used to do, we had enough dignity and moral ethics to refrain from stealing candy from young trick-or-treaters. We were not thieves. Instead of stealing candy, we would walk up and slit their bags open with a knife, just to watch everything spill to the ground.

Halloween provided many innocent, well-intended school kids in Hurley the perfect opportunity to get even with the mean-spirited principal of the Hurley Schools for all of the unfair paddlings and constant misery he dealt out to us during the school year. The principal lived on Pattie Street in a nice bungalow home with a porch leading up to his front door. One Halloween night, some friends and I procured a burlap bag and walked up and down a couple of alleys to collect several fine specimens of fresh dog shit. Once the bag was partially full, we poured a little gasoline on it and took it to the principal's front porch. While one of us knocked on his front door, someone else lit the burlap bag with a match and threw it onto the porch. We ran down the street a ways, and when the principal answered the door, he saw the burlap bag burning in front of him. He rushed out and began stomping on it to put the fire out and then looked around to see who the culprits were. Sadly, none of us stuck around long enough to watch him clean the dog shit off of his shoes.

Halloween was also a special night for the Pilgrim Fellowship youth group at the Hurley Community Church. While most kids in town were trick-or-treating or causing trouble, the kids in our youth group would go door to door with small cardboard containers and collect money for UNICEF (The United Nations International Children's Fund). UNICEF used the money to buy food and medicine for disadvantaged children in third world countries. Our youth group usually generated quite a bit of money for the program and the pastor at our church beamed with pride every year as we made our selfless donation to the needy children of the world.

One evening a few weeks after Halloween, I was hanging out at the Chino Club with my friend Troy Wakefield. I was telling him about all of the money our PF youth group made for UNICEF by simply knocking on doors and asking for donations. (Now, it should be noted that neither Troy nor I were what I would refer to as "angels", and it should be further noted that neither of us were foolish enough to pass up an opportunity to participate in an occasional entrepreneurial endeavor on a microeconomic level.) With my financial guidance, coupled with Troy's tenacity and strong work ethic, we soon concocted a rather simple but devious plan to generate a little disposable income for ourselves that evening.

Our brilliant idea was to parlay the concept of "collecting money to help feed the starving children overseas" into "fattening Jerry and Troy's wallets here at home". The first thing we did was go to the snack bar and ask Carrie Dodson to dig a couple of empty one-quart ice cream containers out of the trash and loan us a felt tipped marker. In large block letters, we wrote "UNICEF" on each container and cut a slot in the lid so people could easily drop money inside. We then walked a couple of blocks down the street with our containers in-hand and selected a few houses that we thought would be relatively easy marks.

In order to increase the odds of a successful entrepreneurial venture of this nature, we typically targeted our visits to the homes of elderly couples or widows who didn't know us and were unable to chase us down the street once they realized we had just swindled them. As it turned out, our money collection scheme served us well. Before long we had acquired enough "disposable income" to return to the Chino Club and feast on sodas, candy, nuts, and beef jerky for the remainder of the evening.

The Story of Morgan Watson
***

Young Johnny Barfield was a seventh grade kid who lived in one of the smaller Hurley homes on the south side of town. He was basically a nice kid who had lots of friends in his class at school. He also knew a few of the older boys in town because they would hang out at the Chino Club together during school nights. Sometimes this led to trouble for Johnny and his friends because these boys would influence the younger ones to do things they would not have ordinarily done on their own.

Johnny could have done well in school if he applied himself, but for some reason he didn't like to study and became increasingly dissatisfied with his teachers at school. Instead of completing his assignments, he would always tell his parents his homework was done so he could get permission to go to the Chino Club to visit his friends. It was during these weeknight evenings at the Chino Club that Johnny and his friends were vulnerable to the temptation of creating mischief or getting into some sort of trouble around town.

One night Johnny was playing ping-pong with an older friend named Tommy Cooper when a high school kid named Morgan Watson walked into the ping-pong room. He was a senior at Cobre High School and was several years older than Johnny. Morgan was sort of a country hick and, even though he didn't do well in school, he never picked on other boys and was generally quite shy. He combed his shaggy blond hair straight back on the sides and one of his front teeth was slightly crooked. Most of the time he had a Marlboro cigarette hanging down below his lower lip and usually kept the red and white flip-top box rolled up into the sleeve of his dirty white short-sleeved t-shirt. Some of the jocks at school teased Morgan occasionally but he ignored them and spent a lot of his time alone.

Morgan wasn't involved in sports or other school sponsored activities, but he loved to fix up older model cars and trucks as a hobby and drive them around town. The neighbors near his house complained regularly about the junk cars that sat in the family's front yard, but nobody seemed to be able to get the town of Hurley or the local police to do anything about it. As long as Morgan didn't bother anyone personally, he could continue to yank engines out of cars and clutter up his parents' yard with car parts until his heart was content.

Morgan exchanged greetings with Johnny and Tommy and sat down in a folding metal chair next to the ping-pong table. He rocked back in his chair and took one last drag off of his cigarette before he flicked it with his greasy fingernail into a sand filled coffee can resting on the floor. Johnny and Tommy were in the middle of a close game when Morgan says, "Hey, I'm getting ready to go to a chick's house and, if you guys want, you are welcome to jump into my truck and go with me."

Tommy and Johnny continued playing for a couple of points before they finally stopped to consider Morgan's offer. Neither of the boys knew Morgan well enough to trust his word, but the possibility of meeting a new girl was an opportunity they couldn't ignore. After a brief discussion of their options for the evening, they decided that playing ping-pong would probably not be as fun as going to a girl's house and hanging out. Consequently, two minutes after their ping-pong game ended they found themselves climbing into Morgan's old, black 1940's-something pick-up truck that was parked in front of the Chino Club.

Morgan's truck was a mechanical work in progress. It was chock-full of idiosyncrasies and lots of little things that didn't work. The door on the passenger side didn't close unless you slammed it shut, the windows didn't roll up, and Morgan had to pump the gas pedal a few times before he punched the start button on the floorboard with his right foot to get the old slant-six motor to run.

Rrrr...Rrrr...Rrrr...Rrrr, then a pause. Morgan pumped the gas pedal three more times and then, Rrrr, Rrrr, Rrrr until the truck jumped to life. He backed out of the parking space and ground the stick shift into first gear, slowly let out the stiff clutch, and off they went. The three boys bounced their way down the one-way street along the big ditch until they came to Pattie Street on the south end of town. With a big grin on his face, Morgan looked over to the other boys and said, "I've got a couple of beers down here on the floorboard if either of you guys want one."

Then he reached down and grabbed one and opened it with a can opener that he took from the ashtray. Tommy and Johnny looked at each other, but neither of them said anything.

Morgan turned right on Pattie Street. He cruised up a couple of blocks and then turned left on a side street and made another quick right into a dark alley before he coasted to a stop and shut off the engine. Morgan chugged the rest of his beer and let out a loud belch before he turned again to the boys and said, "OK, follow me. Suzette lives just a couple of houses away and we can go into her yard through her back gate. It's dark back there and no one will see us."

The three boys walked down the alley and hopped over a gate into Suzette's back yard. Confused, Johnny said, "I thought we were going to Suzette's house to visit her."

Morgan quickly responded, "Shhhhhhh. Don't make any noise. We are going to peep through her window. Maybe we can see her get undressed."

Morgan led the boys farther into the back yard as they cautiously approached the house. While tiptoeing across the patio near a fairly large living room window, they noticed Suzette sitting on a couch in the center of the room. It was easy to tell from her animated gestures she was having a conversation with someone.

Morgan signaled, and the other boys advanced to within a couple of feet of the window. Suddenly, Suzette must have heard or seen something because she quickly looked out the window and saw three faces staring at her from outside. She panicked and jumped up from the couch and rushed into another room.

Realizing they had been seen, the boys turned around and began walking away from her house as quickly and quietly as possible. When they got to the alley, they broke out into a sprint back toward the truck. Tommy and Johnny jumped into the truck through the passenger door and had to slam it three or four times to get it to shut. Meanwhile, Morgan slammed his door shut, turned on the ignition, and pushed in the clutch as he hit the starter button with his foot.

Rrrr...Rrrr...Rrr...Rrr... nothing. Rrr...Rrr...Rrr... nothing again. "Oh shit," exclaimed Morgan, as he frantically pumped the gas pedal.

Rrr...Rrr...Rrr again. Nothing. Tommy finally looked over to Morgan with a look of panic on his face and said, "C'mon. Get this fucker started before we get our asses caught."

Morgan pumped the gas pedal a few more times, and finally, Rrr...Rrr...Vaaarrrrroooooommmm. The truck started. Morgan slammed it into first gear and sped up the dark alley with his lights off. At the end of the alley he turned right at the paved street and headed north. Morgan leaned forward and slapped the metal dashboard of his truck with his right hand and shouted, "C'mon baby. Just a few more blocks and we're home free."

No sooner than he had spoken, Morgan noticed a reflection of light flickering in the rear view mirror that was vibrating on the outside of the driver's-side door. "Oh shit," he exclaimed. "We're being followed." He frantically slammed the shift lever into third gear and punched the gas pedal all the way to the floor.

Morgan took a quick right and then a left as he sped around the corner onto another side street. Tommy looked around through the cracked rear window of the cab and exclaimed, "Oh fuck. They're getting closer. What are we going to do?"

Suddenly, Morgan slammed on the brakes and yanked the steering wheel to the right and slid into an alley. He downshifted into second gear and floor-boarded the old truck, but the car behind them continued to gain ground.

Just as the speeding car behind them passed under a streetlight, Morgan happened to glance into his rearview mirror. Quickly, he turned to the other two boys and barked-out in a state of panic and fear, "Oh shit. That's Suzette's boyfriend and he has a carload of guys with him. We're gonna get our asses kicked."

Once Morgan realized he couldn't ditch the car, he turned and sped directly toward his parents' house on Carrasco Street. He veered into the alley, shot through his back gate and into his back yard, and came to a screeching halt near the back door of his house. Within few seconds, the boys in the pursuing car came roaring into the yard and slammed on the brakes as they pulled up directly behind Morgan's old truck.

Tommy and Johnny had nowhere to run, but Morgan quickly flung open the driver's side door and ran into his parents' house before the carload of high school guys could climb out of their car and catch him. Meanwhile, Tommy and Johnny remained inside of Morgan's truck as they anticipated the onslaught of angry teenagers and the inevitable ass kicking that they were about to take.

As the car in pursuit came to an abrupt stop, all four doors flew open and six Cobre High School guys, some of them football players, ran past Morgan's truck toward the house. Then one of them yelled, "Get your ass out of that house, Morgan, you chicken shit mother fucker."

As the two boys sat in the front seat of the old truck in a state of terror, they heard Morgan respond from inside his house, "Get the hell out of here or I'll shoot your ass."

By now, a couple of back porch lights from the neighboring yards began to flick on. A full-blown public disturbance was in high gear and Johnny and Tommy were sitting right in the middle of it. Meanwhile, the high school guys were standing near the house as they continued to yell at Morgan.

Finally, Tommy looked over to Johnny and said quietly, "I don't think they even know we're here. They are only after Morgan. Let's jump out of the truck and head for the alley."

Tommy's hunch paid off. The other boys were totally preoccupied with their screaming match and never bothered to look inside Morgan's truck. As soon as Tommy and Johnny slipped into the alley, they took off running and didn't stop to catch their breath until they were a couple of blocks away from the fray.

While they were standing in the dark alley with their hands on their knees and gasping for air, a gunshot suddenly rang out from off in the distance. There was no doubt as to where it had come from. Instantly the boys broke into another run for several blocks and didn't stop until they could run no more. When they finally did stop, they were totally exhausted and scared and felt a sick feeling deep down in their guts. It was obvious things had taken a turn for the worse.

Off in the distance they could hear the siren and the revving motor of a police car as it sped off in the direction of Morgan's house. Johnny's heart jumped into his throat as he tried to catch his breath. "What do you think we should do now?" he asked Tommy.

"Let's just try to make it home and hope like hell that we don't get tangled up in this mess."

The next day at school Johnny waited for the other shoe to drop. He was worried and scared throughout the entire school day. Every time a teacher looked at him, he expected to hear her say something like, "Johnny, the principal needs to see you in his office immediately," or, "Johnny, there is a police officer here to see you."

Miraculously, by the end of the school day Johnny never heard a word about the incident from the night before. Nevertheless, he knew he wasn't off the hook yet. As he walked home from school he was still filled with anxiety because there was a chance the police could be waiting for him at home.

When he got home from school the coast was clear. His parents were acting normal and didn't seem upset about anything, so he knew the police hadn't been in contact with them either, at least for now. Then, just as he was sitting down to eat dinner, he glanced through the kitchen window and his eyes nearly popped out of his head. A police car pulled up in front of his house and a uniformed officer with a clipboard got out and strolled up the sidewalk toward the front door. Instantly, the smoldering sensation in his gut intensified and his appetite turned to nausea. The first thought that crossed Johnny's mind was that Morgan had shot one of the high school boys and the cop was coming to arrest him and take him to jail.

Johnny's worst nightmare was now a reality. First came the knock at the front door. Then he saw his mother get up off of the couch to see who was there.

As Johnny sat at the dinner table he could hear the officer tell his mother, "Hello Mrs. Barfield. I'm here to get some information about an incident that happened last night and we think Johnny may have been involved. Is Johnny here?"

Surprised and somewhat worried, Johnny's mother called out from the living room, "Johnny, there is a police officer here to see you."

Johnny suddenly had to pee so bad he was having trouble holding it in his bladder. He slowly slid his chair back and reluctantly walked to the front door where the officer was standing.

The Hurley cop started by asking, "Johnny boy, were you with Morgan Watson last night?"

Johnny sheepishly looked down and stalled around for a minute before answering, "Yes sir."

By now both of Johnny's parents were standing by the front door as the police officer continued with his questioning. "Did Morgan have some beer in his truck?"

Johnny then replied, "I think so."

"Did you know you were trespassing in Suzette McCalister's yard?"

"No sir. I thought that we were going to visit her."

"Where were you when Morgan fired the rifle?"

"We were running down the alley to get away. We didn't want to get beat up by the high school guys in the other car."

The officer went on to explain to Johnny's parents that an altercation had taken place at Morgan's house. A shot from a rifle was fired, but as it turned out, nobody was injured. The policeman then informed Johnny's parents that he needed to report to the juvenile probation officer at the Grant County Courthouse the following day to make a statement about what had happened. Although Johnny was relieved to hear that no one was shot or hurt, he still wasn't out of the woods with the law.

The next morning Johnny's father came to school and checked him out of Mrs. Snodgrass' Social Studies class about 10:00 a.m. and took him to the courthouse in Silver City. They were scheduled to see the juvenile probation officer, Mr. Bartley McDonald, at 10:30 a.m.

Mr. McDonald was a Mormon gentleman with a straight-laced and stern demeanor and had a reputation for not putting up with any nonsense from aspiring young juvenile delinquents. The word on the street was you wanted to avoid seeing him at all cost. Some of Johnny's older friends from Hurley already had the pleasure of getting to know Bartley McDonald during their previous court appearances, and regularly cautioned the younger boys by telling them, "Don't be dumb shits and get caught."

As Johnny and his dad settled into their chairs in Mr. McDonald's office, the officer began his well rehearsed pitch. "Now, son, I'm going to ask you a few questions about what happened the other night and I expect you to tell me the truth. If I find out you are lying, you could be sent to reform school for up to two years. Now, I've already talked to the other boys involved and if your story doesn't match what they have already told me, you could end up in big trouble."

With that said, Mr. McDonald began his interrogation by asking Johnny,

"Did Morgan Watson have any beer with him last night?"

Johnny nervously responded, "Yes. He had a couple of cans."

Next, the probation officer asked, "Did he drink any beer while you were with him?"

Again, an intimidated young Johnny responded, "Yes sir."

Then Mr. McDonald asked, "What did he use to open the beer?"

Johnny thought for a minute and then replied, "He used a church-key."

"With a WHAT?"

Again Johnny replied, "With a church-key."

All of a sudden Johnny noticed that both Bartley McDonald and his father were trying to hold back their laughter. Johnny didn't understand why they thought his response was so funny until later when his father pointed out that he should have replied, "The beer was opened with a can opener, not a church-key."

He went on to tell Johnny that Mr. McDonald was a religious man and had never heard someone refer to a can opener as a "church-key" before.

By the time the questioning was over, Johnny realized he wasn't really in trouble after all. They just wanted him to make a few statements as a witness. Since no one got shot or injured, the big issues seemed to be that Morgan was a minor in possession of alcohol and he discharged a gun inside the city limits.

The dark cloud hovering above Johnny's head soon evaporated away. Not only did he get to miss half a day of school, but as an added bonus his father took him by the Ranchburger Drive-in on College Avenue for a hamburger before their trip back to Hurley.

And, the best part of it all was, when Johnny got back to school he was the center of attention from all of his seventh grade classmates. Everyone was dying to find out why he went to court. The other kids were intrigued to hear stories of high speed chases through the alleys and streets of Hurley, gun shots being fired, boys running from the cops, high school guys bursting into someone's yard to beat them up, juvenile probation officers, beer, church-keys...

Prowling Stories

If we weren't hanging around the Chino Club during the evenings we were usually goofing off in someone's yard or walking around town with friends. We spent a lot of idle time doing things like poking and chasing each other, wrestling, telling dirty jokes, smoking or chewing tobacco, or playing silly games that we just invented. Of course, once we were old enough to drive we spent less time in Hurley and more time cruising all over the county with our friends.

On most of the nights when we were out and about town on foot, we would eventually end up prowling around looking for mischief. If today's laws were on the books back then, we would have been considered juvenile delinquents for doing some of the things we did. We kept the Hurley cops fairly busy as they responded to our shenanigans and chased us all over town.

By the time I was in high school, one of the local cops named Billy Reynoso made it a point to pick me up off of the streets at night and take me riding around with him in the patrol car just so he knew where I was. In spite of all of the crazy things I did over the years, I became pretty good friends with Billy and Lyncho Jaramillo, who shared the job with Billy.

On rare occasions we would sneak away from home in the middle of night to carouse around town. Tubby Porkman used to come by my bedroom window to roust me out of bed around 2:00 a.m. for our late evening activities. Instead of trying to wake me up by tapping on my window or making strange noises, we developed a clever system that was quiet and very effective. I would tie a long string to my thumb before I went to bed. The string ran through my bedroom window and hung down on the outside of the house. When Tubby showed up at my window he would simply pull on the string to wake me up. When my hand started bobbing up and down, I would quietly get dressed and sneak out my bedroom door.

One night we were stealing peaches from one of our favorite trees on Aztec Street when a neighbor from across the alley heard us rummaging around. He came out into the alley as we were leaving and yelled something like "Hey, what the hell is going on out here?"

As we were running away, we reached into our bag and pulled out a couple of peaches and turned to pelt the man to discourage him from coming after us. We were laughing so hard we had trouble catching our breath as we ran away.

Another memorable fruit/vegetable stealing story happened when Tubby and I were walking down an alley off of Carrasco Street at around 10:00 p.m. Earlier in the summer we had noticed a vegetable garden in someone's backyard, so we hopped over the back fence to forage around and see what was ripe and ready to take. The property had a garage located next to the alley, and the large doors to the automobile entrance had been left open.

Shortly after we entered the back yard, a car turned into the alley and slowly cruised our way. It was impossible to tell who it was, but we knew better than to remain out in the middle of the garden where we were exposed. We quickly looked for a place to hide, but the only cover we could find nearby was behind one of the open garage doors. We both quickly ran over and hid between the door and the garage so that the lights of the car wouldn't shine on us.

Apparently someone had seen us prowling around and reported us to the police. Officer Reynoso rolled to a stop in the middle of the alley directly in front of the garage entrance and got out of the patrol car. The homeowner then came out of his house and strolled to the back fence to talk to Billy. Tubby and I were about 20 feet away from the two men and we were now trapped behind the garage door. Luckily, the headlights of the patrol car were shining away from where we were hiding.

After about a minute of being pinned down, Tubby and I looked at each other and decided our only option was to make a break for it. We knew if we stayed behind the door much longer, there was a good chance one of the men would eventually notice us. We had to make our move before anything else went wrong.

We quickly pushed the door out of the way and took off running up the alley as fast as we could. As we were running away we could hear someone say,

"There they go," and the cop jumped into the patrol car and peeled out after us. By the time we were halfway down the alley, the cop had turned on his red lights and was in full pursuit. Shit had just hit the fan and Tubby and I knew we were in for good old-fashioned game of "cat and mouse".

Fortunately, we had a game plan already in place in the event something like this was to happen. Our first move was to split up and force the cop to make a choice as to which one of us he would pursue. Secondly, we would make the cop chase us up and down the alleys and through people's yards. That way, the cop would have to get out of his car and chase us on foot in the dark if he wanted to catch us. Lastly, we agreed to eventually meet back at my back yard on Elguea Street once we had ditched the cop.

We gained some time on Billy right away because we ran up the alley in the opposite direction his car was facing. Billy now had to drive around the block before he could come after us. By the time he came out of the alley we had already split up and were running down Romero Street. Once we saw him coming toward us, Tubby hopped over the fence to one yard and I headed off in a different direction.

With his red lights flashing, the cop chose to come after me. As he sped in my direction, I ran around a house and into the back yard, jumped another fence, and ran south into the next alley toward Aztec Street. To counter my move, the cop zipped around the block and came into the alley where I was making my getaway.

I quickly jumped another fence and ran into another backyard. As I ran through this particular yard, I caught a glimpse of a man sitting in an old, early 1950's, Dodge truck with the driver's side door open. He was smoking a cigar and listening to the radio as he enjoyed the pleasant summer evening. I flew by him as fast as I could run and juked around his house into the front yard.

From there I darted across Aztec Street and into another yard and then another alley. I crossed Elguea Street and ran through one more yard before I finally reached the alley leading to my house. I made one final push into my back yard and immediately hid so I could catch my breath and wait to see what would happen next.

I had only been home for about three minutes, when, suddenly, Tubby came tearing down the alley and into my back yard. He was also exhausted from the long chase and was still full of adrenalin as he leaned over and gasped for air. Once we regained our composure, we laid down on the grass near the corner of my house so we could keep an eye out for the cop.

We remained on the alert for about another 20 minutes until we could relax enough to begin debriefing each other about our escape routes. We laughed as we recounted our separate journeys from the time we split up until we reached my house. As it turned out, Tubby also had run through the yard with the man smoking his cigar. We found it quite amusing to speculate about the thoughts that must have run through the man's mind as he sat in his truck and listened to the radio: Just as he opened the door to relax and smoke his cigar, someone out of the dark of night came running through his yard. As he sat there wondering whether he was imagining things, someone else came running by, and finally a cop car came flying up the alley with his red lights flashing. It all happened so fast that the poor gentleman must have quickly put out his cigar and returned to the confines of his living room to watch TV. At least there he would be safe.

Sometimes when we were out raising hell around town at night we would swing by the house of a crazy elderly widow named Mrs. Bronson. She was never very friendly to the kids in the neighborhood and it didn't go unnoticed by my friends and me. In our efforts to exact a little revenge on her, my colleagues and I empirically developed, through extensive study of U.S. military ballistics data over a period of several years, a very effective and entertaining way to elevate her blood pressure. Since she lived in a house with a corrugated tin roof that made loud noises when hard objects landed on it, we used to pelt her roof with golf ball sized rocks in the middle of the night. Then, we would hide in someone's yard across the street and watch her flip on her porch light and come running out of the house, yelling and screaming in a fit of hysteria.

Cousin James and Sido, who were my mentors in mischief early on, were kind enough to share one of their favorite late night pranks with me. They would climb inside of an unlocked automobile that was parked in front of a house, put it in neutral, and roll it to the next block and park it in front of someone else's house. The next morning the owner would head out the door to go to work, lunch bucket and coffee thermos in hand, and stand in front of their house in a state of anger and confusion. As an added entertainment bonus, the owner would usually be late to work by the time they finished walking around the neighborhood looking for their car.

My mentors had a couple of other pranks up their sleeve as well. One night they went out and wrapped toilet paper on some cars around town. Now, at first glance the act of "toilet-papering" a car may appear to be a fun, lighthearted prank that would probably be a minor annoyance to most car owners. But these creative young men decided to take their youthful and harmless act of mischief to another level by lighting the toilet paper on fire.

For some strange reason, the police immediately took a keen interest in the novel activities of these boys. Sadly, by the time their rampage was over and done with, they ended up paying for about four paint jobs on neighborhood cars. While some folks may have considered it a stretch to suggest that my cousin was a budding young pyromaniac, he did manage to burn his parents' garage to the ground when he was five years old because he was playing with matches in the alley.

You know, we all got busted once in a while as we were growing up, but I suspect that Sido and James had some sort of sick, psychological need to get into trouble and get yelled at by adults. Sometimes I think those boys actually liked to get caught. The following story is yet another fine example that further demonstrates their propensity to articulate negatively with local law enforcement agencies.

One summer night these daring young lions decided to push over and destroy a brand new cinder block fence a man had just built around his yard. Since the man's home was located on the corner directly across from the Hurley swimming pool, every kid in town saw the destruction the following day. Within a few days the cops easily found out who the perpetrators were by simply talking to a few kids in town. All they had to do was follow the trail of bragging and bravado right back to James and Sido.

Since Sido and James didn't have enough money to pay for the damaged fence, the Hurley cops made them perform public service in order to generate the money they needed. The boys were given some buckets of yellow paint and told to paint the parking lanes and street dividing lines on Cortez Avenue in front of the Hurley Post Office and the Chino Sweet Shop. They were directed to work off their debt every Sunday for a month. To make matters even worse, they were on display for all of Hurley to see. They weren't very happy about that, but it was the only way they could repay the victim of their crime.

One Sunday I rode my bicycle up to Cortez Ave. to pay Sido and James a visit and see what their punishment entailed. I carried on a conversation with them as I watched them paint, but before long I became bored and found myself taunting and teasing them as they worked. They apparently didn't appreciate my snide comments or my sense of humor because they simultaneously put their paintbrushes down, walked over and pulled me off of my bicycle, and kicked my ass right there in front of the post office.

For most of my days in Hurley, our family car was a two door 1949 Chevy coupe, and my father usually parked the car inside our garage in the alley. On a couple of occasions before I was old enough to have a driver's license, Tubby and I "borrowed" the '49 Chevy and took it out for a cruise. The only time we could take it was in the middle of the night while my parents were sound asleep. I'm actually amazed we were able to unlock our garage doors, roll the car out of the garage and down the alley with the motor off, and start it up without ever waking my dad.

Stealing the car was the easy part. Returning it to the garage at the end of our foray was the tricky part. As I approached the garage I would have to gather up some speed and turn off the motor at the last minute so we would coast silently into the garage. That was always risky because the garage doors were narrow and, if I miscalculated, I would smash the car into the side of the doorway. Fortunately, I never put a scratch on the car.

One night we took the car all the way to Camp Thunderbird on the upper Mimbres. We were gone for nearly three hours and used over a third of a tank of gas. I never heard a word about it from my dad though, so I know he slept like a baby all night long.

Once in a while cousin James would take me to Silver City in my dad's '49 Chevy and do crazy things just to make me laugh. Sometimes he would drive down a residential street on the wrong side of the road or run stop signs at intersections that weren't very busy. If he saw a pedestrian walking along the side of the street he would honk the horn as he approached them. When the pedestrian would wave to us, James would look the other way and wave to an imaginary person on the opposite side of the road. Another time we were parked in front of a store and a lady walked in front of our car. When she got directly in front of us, James honked the horn for about five seconds and scared her half to death. And, perhaps the craziest stunt he ever pulled off was when he put the car into reverse and backed all the way up Hudson Street going about 25 miles per hour. He had the gas pedal floor-boarded and the engine was ready to blow a gasket. If a cop had seen him do that, he would still be trying to get out of jail.

Another fun, late night activity was making garbage can barricades. We used to go up and down the alleys and take people's metal garbage cans and build a barricade that would block the entire street. The bottom row of cans would stretch from one side of the road to the other and we would build a pyramid structure that was three tiers high with a total of 15 to 20 garbage cans.

We had to be especially careful when we built a barricade because things could get a little noisy if the cans were banged around as we carried them down the alley. We enjoyed building barricades because we would get to watch the Hurley cop dismantle the stinky mess the following morning. And of course, the local traffic was temporarily disrupted until the cop cleared the way.

Even though it was quite an engineering feat to build large barricades across the streets of Hurley, we soon discovered the barricades alone weren't enough of a thrill. There simply had to be something else we could do to push the envelope a little further.

One night, an inquisitive young man named Sido Bates took me behind the American Laundry building on Cortez Ave. and showed me a large pile of grey powder that the laundry regularly discarded onto the ground. I think this powder may have been a bi-product of the dry cleaning process, although I'm not sure about that. As we stood next to the pile of powder, Sido says to me, "You've got to check this shit out. You're going to love it."

He looked around for a second and found an old coffee can lying in the weeds nearby and scooped up some of the powder into the can. Next, he sprinkled the powder onto the ground in front of us and formed a straight line about two feet long and six inches wide. He then took a cigarette lighter and held it to the powder. After a few seconds the powder slowly caught on fire. As the fire grew, we tried to put it out by stepping on it but, when you removed your foot, the powder would slowly reignite.

As we watched the powder burn I looked up at Sido and noticed a gleam in his eye and a smile on his face. I knew exactly what he was thinking. At that moment, we had just crossed the threshold into a new frontier in the sacred art of small town vandalism.

Over the next few minutes we scrounged up another couple of containers nearby and filled them with the powder. Then we took the cans and walked a few blocks to Third Street, directly in front of the main entrance to the old Hurley High School. We set the containers down by the sidewalk near the entrance and went up and down the nearby alleys to gather a few garbage cans for our new "science project".

After about 20 minutes we had a nice, three-tiered barricade built in front of the school. Next, we took the cans of grey laundry powder and sprinkled a nice, fat line all the way around the barricade and set it on fire. We then ran down the alley and hid behind someone's garage and waited for the Hurley cop to show up.

About 15 minutes later, the cop pulled up and got out of his patrol car in front of the flaming barricade. He immediately realized he couldn't dismantle the barricade until he first put out the fire. Since he wasn't familiar with the material that was burning away beneath the garbage cans, he instinctively began to step on the powder to try to extinguish the flames.

Every time he removed his foot, the powder slowly flared up again and continued to burn. We were in stitches from laughter as we watched the cop try to put out the fire. It must have taken him 30 minutes to eventually put out the flames and dismantle the garbage can barricade. By then, we were long gone and off to another vandalism project.

In our early teens we spent a lot of time walking around town in the evenings. There were certain streets we frequented more than others in hopes of running into a cute girl from school, or perhaps an out of town beauty who was visiting relatives in Hurley during the summer. Sometimes, if we were friends with the girl, we would go into her yard at night and tap on her bedroom window and visit. Consequently, there may have been a few occasions where we inadvertently saw more than we probably should have as we approached someone's bedroom window.

One of my classmates named Kitty Duvall started dating my best prowling buddy, Tubby, in junior high school. Once in a while Tubby and I would stop by and visit Kitty at her parents' house on Cortez Ave. In the early part of the evening we would pay her a legitimate visit and hang out in her living room and listen to records. If it were after bedtime, we would sneak into her yard and knock on her bedroom window. We were especially careful during our late night visits because we obviously didn't want to wake her parents or get her into trouble.

Late one spring night we were prowling around town and went to pay Kitty a visit. As a matter of routine, Tubby and I always walked down the alley behind her house and scaled the six-foot high cinderblock fence surrounding her back yard. Once we jumped down into her yard, we would walk around to the side of the house to her bedroom. Kitty always knew who it was when she heard a knock on the window or a scratch on the screen.

On this particular night, Tubby and I followed our usual routine without any variation. We came down the alley, climbed up onto the cinderblock wall, and jumped down into her yard. Everything seemed fine until the moment we landed on the ground. For some reason, our landing was much softer than usual. We were momentarily puzzled, but it finally occurred to us we were standing ankle deep in mud. We figured that Kitty's dad had just watered the back yard so we continued onward to Kitty's window for our visit.

The next day when we saw Kitty, she told us her father was quite upset with us. He had spent several days putting new topsoil in the back yard and had just planted a new lawn. When he came out to check on his freshly watered yard the following morning, he noticed two sets of deep footprints that led from the cinderblock wall to Kitty's bedroom window. It didn't take him long to figure out Kitty was having late night visitors, and he knew exactly who they were.

One night we were walking down an alley and noticed an enormous pair of panties hanging on the clothesline in someone's back yard. We were so amazed at their sheer size that we strolled into the yard and pulled them down from the clothesline and took them with us as a conversation piece.

On our way down the street we noticed a Dodge pickup truck parked in front of a residence. The truck was set up as a utility vehicle and had a metal grill/headlight guard welded above the front bumper. Once we saw the grill we knew exactly what we were going to do with our new trophy. We were actually able to stretch them from one side of the grill guard to the other without tearing them. While some modern day automobile enthusiasts put a bra on the front of their new car to protect it from rocks and road tar, we were able to achieve the same affect at a fraction of the cost by using a pair of panties.

Another time, my dog Rumple and I were with a couple of friends down at the Hurley ballpark. We were in the bleachers watching a baseball game but soon became bored and decided to go walking around town. It was a warm and beautiful evening in late June as we walked through the streets of Hurley, and off in the distance we could hear firecrackers going off all over town. It was fairly easy for kids to buy fireworks back in the mid 1960's and, as one can imagine, the firecracker activity always picked up as the fourth of July approached.

One of the boys I was with had a few firecrackers in his pocket but he also had a large, round, red explosive called a "cherry bomb". Cherry bombs could be dangerous if you weren't careful with them. They had the explosive power of about 10 firecrackers and made a huge sound when they blew up.

The three of us turned into an alley at the east end of Aztec Street and began looking for a place to set off my friend's firecrackers and the cherry bomb. As we strolled down the alley we noticed the back door to one of the houses was open and someone was sitting at the kitchen table eating dinner. Since we didn't want to disturb anyone, we continued to walk down the alley a bit further until we found a good spot to make some noise.

It just so happened that all of the boys in our group came from good families and possessed a genuine concern for the welfare of the residents in our neighborhood. We considered ourselves to be good citizens and had every intention of using our fireworks responsibly. Furthermore, as we contemplated where to set off the cherry bomb, our top priority was safety.

After we kicked the issue around for a few minutes, it was decided that we would get "the most bang for our buck" if we gently lobbed my friend's cherry bomb into the kitchen of the house a couple of doors back. After all, the kitchen door was wide open and the only thing we lacked was a written invitation from the guy who was sitting at the dinner table.

So, we snuck back up the alley and walked to his back door, lit the cherry bomb, and tossed it inside. We would have preferred to stay for dinner, but instead, we sprinted out of his yard and headed down the alley toward the Big Ditch. Just as we ran past the man's garage we heard a huge "Ca-whaaaaam" coming from inside the house, and we knew our mission had been accomplished. By the time we got to the end of the alley we were laughing so hard we could barely run.

A few minutes later the three of us came dragging into the Chino Club, gasping for air and laughing uncontrollably. When we eventually recovered, we treated ourselves to some sodas and peanuts from the snack bar and settled down to celebrate the evening's accomplishments.

I had just emptied a bag of peanuts into my Pepsi and took my first swig, when the lady who worked behind the snack bar called out, "Jerry, you have a phone call."

I glanced around at my friends for a second before I walked over and picked up the phone. I planted the receiver to my ear and cautiously answered, "Hello?"

I immediately recognized the voice on the phone. It was my father. With more than a hint of anger in his voice, he asked me, "What the hell have you been doing?"

In an effort to appease my dad, I replied, "Nothing, just hanging out at the Chino Club."

Then he said, "Some guy down the street just called me and said you threw an explosive into his kitchen and nearly blew the windows out of his house. His wife damn near had a heart attack."

I then replied to my father with complete confidence, "Well, he must have mistaken me for someone else. I've been here at the Chino Club all evening long."

Once my dad heard my big lie, he quickly lost his civility and yelled, "Oh yeah? Then what the hell was Rumple doing in the guy's back yard when he came running out of his house?"

You know, some of these pranks just don't end up the way you planned them. Maybe that's why it was so exhilarating to wreak havoc all over Hurley. The element of the unknown...communing with the dark side...the suspense...the fear of getting caught...the euphoria of pulling off yet another act of mischief. Many times over the years I've had to ask myself, "Why do I do these things?"

In all honesty, as I close my eyes, take a deep breath, and attempt to descend inward in search of that profound level of meditative introspection where truth resides, I find myself frantically yet thoroughly scouring the bowels of my psychological DNA to find the answer to this perplexing question. And, when I emerge back into the glaring daylight of human reality, I always bring with me the knowledge that, in my heart of hearts, I do these things simply because they are so much fun.

A Few of My Favorite Practical Jokes

I would be a liar if I told you I didn't like to joke around and have as much fun as possible when I was a kid. I not only enjoyed telling jokes to my friends, but I also enjoyed being involved in practical jokes. Over the years there were a couple of jokes we pulled on other kids that stand out in my memory. As many folks know, the mark of a good practical joke is to either make everyone laugh or make the victim really mad.

In every group of boys who hang around on the streets of a small town, there is usually one kid among them that is young, naïve, or new in town and has a need to impress the other boys in order to become accepted by the group. Inevitably, the kid will make a statement that is typically grandiose, fictitious, or just downright hard to believe. The other boys will quickly cast doubt on the validity of his statement and an argument will ensue. A person passing by on a nearby street would inevitably overhear some of the boys in the group say things like, "Bullshit," or, "Yeah, right," or, "You're full of shit," or, "You're a dumb ass," or, "You don't have enough sense to pour piss out of a boot."

After several minutes of arguing, the situation usually deteriorates until one of the elder statesmen of the group, usually a high school kid, will tell the know-it-all kid, "Oh yeah? I bet you don't even know your ass from a hole in the ground," to which the "know-it-all" kid will always reply, "The hell I don't!"

The stage is now set. The older, street savvy boy will jump up and draw two circles on the ground with a stick. Using the stick as a pointer, he will point to the circles and say, "OK, if you're so damn smart, take a look at these two circles. Now, this circle over here is your ass," and he would point to the left circle. Then he would point to the other circle and say, "This circle is a hole in the ground. Now, my question to you is, which one of these two circles is your ass?"

The boastful kid, being eager to prove he knows what he is talking about, will always point to the circle on the left and say, "This one is my ass."

Then, one of the other boys in the group will step back and say, "No stupid, your ass is right here," and kick the kid in the butt. The other boys will then laugh and chide the naïve kid for falling for one of the oldest practical jokes in the book.

One summer afternoon I was in my yard with a couple of other kids and I offered them a glass of ice water. Shortly after I returned with the water, I told the other boys, "Hey, do you guys want to see a cool trick that is really hard to do?"

The other boys, who were somewhat bored and looking to be entertained, replied, "Sure, why not."

I went into my bedroom and came back out into the yard with a coffee can that had both ends cut out of it and was slightly flattened into an oval shape. I held up the coffee can and said, "I bet you a dollar you can't balance a quarter on the end of your nose and let it fall into this coffee can while it is stuffed down your pants."

I then stuffed the can between my bare stomach and my belt to demonstrate the move. (Hint: The trick is actually very easy to do.)

Once I was done with my demonstration, one of my friends said, "Oh, that looks really easy. I'll take you up on that bet. Let me see the can."

I gave the can to my friend and he quickly stuffed it down into his pants. As he tilted his head back to balance the quarter on his nose, I poured my glass of ice water down into the coffee can, which acted as a funnel. The front of his pants instantly became sopping wet while he still had his head tilted back. He jumped back and looked down at his wet pants, and his once-cocky demeanor instantly turned to rage. He lunged at me, but I quickly jumped away and took off running. He yanked the can out of his pants and chased me around the block, screaming, "I'm going to kick your ass, you son of a bitch".

Once in a while, when someone's parents were gone for the afternoon, we used to have fun making prank telephone calls. We would pick someone at random out of the phone book and call them up and say something like, "Hello, my name is "so and so" from KSIL Radio Station in Silver City and your name has been selected to participate in our monthly trivia contest. You are on the air, and if you can answer the following question you will be our grand prize winner for this month."

Then we would ask them some stupid question like, "Who was the first President of the United States?"

Once they gave us the correct answer, we would tell them, "Congratulations, Mrs. XXX. That is absolutely correct. You have just won a brand new Amana refrigerator, and as an added gift to you and your family we have fully stocked your new refrigerator with a burlap bag filled with fresh horse shit." CLICK…

When we were in junior high school, we used to go into a grocery store or tobacco shop in Silver City and ask the clerk standing behind the counter, "Do you have Prince Albert in a can?" and the clerk would reply, "Yes we do."

Then we would tell them, "Well, you better let him out before he suffocates."

By the time I was in high school, our practical jokes became slightly more complex and creative. Kids were a little older and smarter and they didn't fall for the youthful pranks we got away with in junior high school. The following story is a good example of how our practical jokes evolved as we transitioned into young adulthood.

Tom Foy used to have an occasional party at his parents' home on the hill behind Cobre High School every school year. There were always lots of high school kids at his parties, especially pretty girls. My friend Harry Horseyset and I showed up to one of Tom's famous parties one night and he and I had a practical joke ready to play on someone when the time was right.

About half way into the party I was standing around talking to a group friends in the living room. During our conversation I casually mentioned to a large football player named Albert Kline, "Hey Albert, if you want to hear a really funny story you should go ask Harry Horseyset about his sister's ballet lessons. It's a hilarious story."

Harry just happened to be standing a few feet away and was talking to a different group of kids. He pretended to be preoccupied in conversation but he was actually waiting to help me play our joke on someone.

Albert didn't know Harry very well but he was in a good mood and took the bait nevertheless. He walked over to Harry's group wearing a big grin and said, "Hey Harry, what's this I hear about your sister's ballet lessons?"

Harry slowly turned toward Albert with an insulted look on his face and responded in a very serious and somber tone of voice, "Hey, my sister is paraplegic and can't walk," and then turned his attention back to the group of kids he had been talking with.

Within a five second period of time, the look on Albert's face changed from a playful smile to an outward expression of shock and embarrassment and then to fury and rage. All of a sudden, he pivoted toward me and screamed and charged like a rhinoceros, ready to tear my head off. Once I saw him coming, I darted out the front door and ran to the far side of a car that was parked in front of the house. Albert chased me around the car several times while hysterically yelling over and over again, "I'm gonna kick your ass, you little bastard."

Finally, Harry came outside and told Albert that he was just kidding and it was only a joke. Harry and I had to spend the next few minutes buttering him up with humor so he would calm down and not hurt anyone. If Albert ever had gotten his hands on me that night, I wouldn't be here to tell this story.

During the school year the busses dropped off students in front of Cobre High School every morning about 30 to 45 minutes before classes actually started. We would use the extra time to walk around the halls with friends or go hang out on the grass in front of the school.

Once in a while we would get a group of six or eight guys together and create a little mischief. One of our favorite pranks was to walk the halls until we found a small group of girls socializing with each other and minding their own business. Our group would approach them in a rather casual manner, although we actually were planning to create a scene that would embarrass the hell out of them in front of as many people as possible. We would set the stage by acting very friendly with the girls and would spend several minutes chit chatting, joking around, and flirting with them. Then, when a teacher or another group of kids walked by, every guy in our group would simultaneously grab their nose with one hand and fan his face with the other. As we briskly backed away from the girls, we would make a big scene by pointing toward them and saying things like, "Oh my God, who farted?" or, "Gross me out!" or, "How smelly!"

We always got a lot of laughs from some of these pranks, but I don't think we impressed the girls enough to get a date with any of them.

One of my all time favorite pranks in high school took place in the Vocational Agriculture shop class of Mr. Arnold Walters. At the end of each class, the students were instructed to put their tools away and clean up their work area. When we were done, we would wait by the door of the shop for the dismissal bell to ring.

A couple of minutes before the bell, my friend and I would casually walk over by the welding area and throw a couple of quarters onto the concrete floor, in plain sight. Then, when Mr. Walters wasn't looking, we would grab an oxygen/acetylene torch, light it, and dial in a nice hot, blue flame. Next, we would heat the quarters until they started to turn orange. When we were done we would put the torch back on the welding cart and return to the door and wait for the dismissal bell.

Shortly after the bell, kids from the next class would begin arriving and entering the main area of the shop. Meanwhile, we would stick around by the shop door and keep a casual eye on the hot quarters. Before long some unsuspecting kid would notice the quarters on the floor and walk over to pick one up, thinking it was his lucky day. After a split second the quarter would go flying out of his hand and he would start screaming and thrashing around as he waved his hand frantically in the air. At that point, we would take off running to our next class before our victim figured out that we were the ones who heated up the coins. It was always difficult to make it to the next class on time because we were laughing so hard as we ran away.

Another time when I was in high school, I discovered that my friend Travis Longspray had an unusual and extraordinary skill. In fact, his skill was so unbelievable that we actually made bets with skeptical friends and won money from them. Somehow, Travis had the ability to piss farther than anyone I had ever seen in my life. I never could figure out how he did it, but my guess was he either had an abnormally strong urinary sphincter muscle that somehow propelled urine like a bullet, or perhaps he pinched the end of his pecker and let pressure build up inside before he quickly removed his fingers.

One evening Travis and I were sitting with a small group of boys on the steps of the Chino Club and I casually mentioned that Travis had a unique gift I had witnessed firsthand. With a captive audience, I confidently made the claim that, "Travis can piss an unbelievable distance. In fact, the other day I saw him piss over 20 feet from where he was standing."

One kid in the group obviously thought I was kidding and absolutely refused to believe me. "Bullshit," he exclaimed. "There's no way in hell that anyone can piss that far."

Then Travis smiled and said, "OK, fuckhead, you go stand 20 feet away from me and stay there. I'll piss on your fucking leg."

The other kid laughed and shook his head as he retorted, "Yeah, right. You guys are full of shit."

Then I jumped back into the fray and told the kid, "OK. If you're such a wise-ass, I'll bet you a dollar Travis can piss on your leg from 20 feet away. The only stipulation is that you have to stand still until his piss hits the ground."

With a big grin, the kid says, "You're on," and paced off 20 feet and turned around to face Travis.

Travis unzipped his pants and got into position. Wearing a big, shit-eating grin, he pointed toward the kid, leaned back, and thrust his hips forward to work his sphincter magic. Suddenly, a projectile of piss burst out from the end of Travis' pecker and sailed through the air like a yellow water balloon. Once it finally came to rest it had splattered on the kid's pant leg about half way between his foot and his knee.

The kid was so surprised he didn't know whether to laugh because he had just witnessed a miraculous event, or be angry because he had piss all over his pant leg and had just lost a bet.

"God damn you, you son-of-a-bitch," he yelled at Travis. The rest of the boys laughed in utter astonishment.

After a few seconds, the kid reluctantly reached into his pocket and pulled out a dollar bill and handed it to me. Travis and I went into the Chino Club and bought a couple of sodas and some snacks and had a good laugh. The kid went home to clean up and change his jeans.

Meet Mr. Mohawk
***

RRRIIIINNNNNGGGG. Ah, at Last. It was the bell for C-lunch at Cobre High School. Eduardo's stomach was growling and he was hungry. He grabbed his books and stormed out the door of Mrs. Hoover's English class on his way to the cafeteria. Along the way, he stopped to throw his books in his locker and wait for his good friends Freddy and George who had lockers nearby. The three of them then rushed to get in line at the cafeteria so they could meet up with Ruben and Pete, who were coming from Biology class at the other end of the hallway. The five boys were nearly inseparable at school and spent a lot of time together after school and during the weekends.

Whenever the boys were in the lunch line they usually joked around and engaged in horseplay, or perhaps flirted with girls who were standing nearby. They were always friendly with the cafeteria ladies in the kitchen and were generally well behaved while eating in the dining area. After lunch the group would routinely walk to Al's Pastry shop across the highway to buy a snack or a candy bar. If they still had time left in the lunch period they would go to the Bayard Shopping Center or Sugar Shack to visit with friends.

Shortly after the boys met near the entrance to the school kitchen, George happened to glance up the hallway and noticed Jimmy walking toward them with a smile on his face. Jimmy had just moved to town and, like any newcomer, was eager to make new friends. For the past few days Jimmy made it a point to meet up with George and the gang and tag along with them for the entire duration of the lunch period. Although Jimmy seemed like a nice kid, some of the boys in the group were becoming slightly annoyed with him because he followed them around every where they went, even when he wasn't invited.

Before long, the other boys began exploring ways to let him know he was becoming somewhat of a pest. At first, the group tried to meet off campus for lunch in hopes that Jimmy wouldn't be able to find them. That strategy worked for a day or two, but Jimmy eventually hunted them down and joined them for the remainder of the lunch period.

Another time, as Jimmy approached the group after lunch, they all turned and ran away from him as fast as possible. When they got about a block away, they stopped to see if they had eluded Jimmy but, to everyone's surprise, he came huffing and puffing up the sidewalk after them. By now it was apparent that Jimmy was oblivious to the fact they were trying to ditch him.

As the days went by, Jimmy continued to seek out his new friends. When the group walked up to Al's Pastry shop, Jimmy would always be right there behind them. Then, one day Pete told Jimmy, "Hey Jimmy. Would you run inside and get us some candy bars?"

Being eager to please the group, Jimmy smiled and replied, "Sure. The candy bars are on me."

The boys waited outside while Jimmy went in to buy the candy. As soon as they saw Jimmy walk up to the counter they took off running up the street. A few minutes later, as they stood laughing in front of the Bayard Drug Store, here came Jimmy around the corner with a handful of candy bars.

The boys continued to provide hints to Jimmy that he was becoming more and more of a nuisance, but he just wasn't getting the message. As their frustrations grew, their hints were becoming more direct and obvious.

One day at lunch the boys were standing in line at the cafeteria and Eduardo said to the group, "Hey, let's go to the movies on Friday night."

Eduardo intentionally directed his statement to the group and not to Jimmy, hoping he would get the hint he wasn't invited. Before anyone could respond, Jimmy replied, "Sounds great. Let's take dates."

The boys looked at each other in amazement and immediately dropped the subject for the time being.

Then there was the Mohawk incident. It began one day after school when the boys got together to discuss what to do about Jimmy. They had tried several approaches to get him to "bug off", but he never would get the hint. After some discussion about how frustrated everyone was becoming, a brilliant plan suddenly jelled in Freddy's mind. He raised his finger and said to his friends, "I've got an idea. I can't believe we didn't we think of this before. OK, here's the plan. Tomorrow when Jimmy comes to the cafeteria to join us, we're going to pretend ......"

The next day the boys were standing in the cafeteria line, business as usual. A couple of minutes later, just like clockwork, here came Jimmy walking down the hallway. As he approached the group, the boys were engaged in a conversation about their disagreement with Cobre High School's hair length policy for boys.

George quipped, "What a bunch of assholes. They made me go get a haircut because the hair on the sides of my head touched my ears."

Freddy chipped in and said, "Well, my friend Juan got hassled for letting it touch his collar."

At last, Eduardo said, "That's a bunch of bullshit. You know what we should do? We should mock their stupid hair policy by getting really weird haircuts."

All of the boys chuckled in approval. "Yeah, no kidding, exclaimed Pete. "Maybe we should all go get Mohawk haircuts and leave a little ponytail sticking out of the back of our heads."

Everyone laughed again, and then George challenged the other boys further by saying, "Hey, that's not a bad idea. If you guys will do it, I will."

Everyone smiled and looked at each other as Freddy said, "What a great idea. You can count me in."

Next, Eduardo declared, "Me too."

Ruben briefly grinned and laughed at the idea and then threw in his support.

Pete held up his clinched fist and said, "Let's do it, baby."

Picking up on the enthusiasm of the group, George smiled and quickly exclaimed, "Wow, this is going to be cooler than hell."

Everyone's eyes finally turned to Jimmy. As he looked back at the other boys in the group he had a gleam in his eye and a huge grin on his face. "What a great idea," he said. "I'll do it, too."

As soon as George heard Jimmy's response, he immediately leaned forward toward the others and said in a low and confidential tone of voice, "All right then, vatos. Here's the plan. After school today everyone will go to a barbershop and get their haircut. Later this evening I will call and check up on you guys to make sure you are ready for tomorrow."

All the boys laughed and vowed once again to follow through with the plan. Then they turned and went into the cafeteria for lunch.

As they were getting their cafeteria trays, Pete laughed once more and told the boys, "We're going to blow everyone's mind tomorrow when we show up with a Mohawk and a pony tail."

At about 7:30 p.m. that evening, Pete, Freddy, Ruben and George showed up at Eduardo's house in North Hurley. One by one they filed into Eduardo's bedroom where there was a telephone extension set up on a nightstand next to the bed. As the boys anticipated the phone call they were about to make to Jimmy, the suspense in the air made everyone giddy and on the verge of laughter.

"He is going to shit a brick when he finds out we didn't get our hair cuts," said Ruben.

"I know," exclaimed Freddy. "I hope he doesn't get all pissed off at us and want to fight us."

"Yeah, but what if he didn't get his hair cut off? What are we going to do then?" asked George.

George picked up the phone and, as he dialed Jimmy's number, the boys fell silent and huddled around to put their ears as close to the phone receiver as possible. "Hello. May I speak to Jimmy please?" said George.

The woman's voice at the other end of the phone line responded, "Yes. Just a minute please."

By now you could cut the tension in the room with a knife. The moment of truth was now before them. The unanswered question was, "Did Jimmy get the Mohawk haircut?"

A few seconds ticked by, and Jimmy came to the phone. "Hello?"

George cleared his voice and began, "Hello, Jimmy? This is George. How's it going?"

A brief pause came over the phone line until Jimmy responded, "Well, not too good."

George raised his eyebrows and promptly replied, "Oh, really? What happened? Did you get your haircut?"

In a sad and despondent voice, Jimmy said, "I've got some bad news for everyone. When I came home after school with my Mohawk haircut, my mother was so mad at me she made me shave off the ponytail and the Mohawk. Now I don't have any hair."

The boys jumped away from the telephone and began snickering and thrashing around the room in an effort to control their laughter. Meanwhile, George calmly continued his conversation with Jimmy.

"Well, Jimmy," he said. "It looks like I have some bad news for you, too. The other guys and I decided not to get our hair cut after all."

The phone line fell silent for several seconds. George continued to wait but heard no reply. Slightly concerned, he continued, "Hello, Jimmy, are you still there?"

A few more seconds went by and the boys huddled around the telephone once again. Finally, Jimmy responded, "Do you mean I'm the only one who cut all of my hair off?"

"Yes. I'm afraid so," said George.

Again there was a brief silence on the line. As everyone jockeyed to press their ear closer to the phone, they could hear Jimmy begin to sob.

At last the boys slowly stepped back from the receiver. They looked around at each other, and suddenly the bedroom became unusually quiet.

Sand Lot Sports

Playing sports was probably the favorite activity of most of the kids in Hurley. My friends and I used to play team sports all year long from the time I was in about third grade until we graduated from high school. We played baseball, football, or basketball during the season of that particular sport, and it was common to see kids playing team sports in the street during the warmer months of the year.

When we were in elementary school, the neighborhood kids would get together at someone's yard to play tackle football after school. We enjoyed playing on a nice lawn whenever possible, although playing in the dirt was just as fun. Some of my most memorable after school games took place in Bill Archibald's front yard and at Bryan Bartlett's house across from the old Hurley High School. We also played lots of games at the old Hurley High School football field on weekends when we had more kids and larger teams.

Some kids would wear a cheap toy helmet and/or shoulder pads they may have gotten for their birthday or Christmas, while others just played in their sneakers and jeans. Once in a while someone would get a bloody nose or a fat lip or a torn shirt, but that was about the extent of it. I never recall anyone getting seriously injured or having to leave the game with broken bones or a concussion. Everyone got dirty and skinned up but that was just part of the game.

Sometimes an older kid like Sido Bates would come and play tackle football with us. The team that had the big guy would usually win the game because it took several smaller guys to finally bring him down after being dragged down the field for 10 or 15 yards. All the kids enjoyed playing tackle football with Sido because whenever we tried to tackle him he would make noises that sounded like helmets and pads making contact, just like the big guys.

As we got a little older, we played pick-up games of touch football in the street, usually on Elguea Street in front of my house or Sido's house. My older brother was fun to play with because he was quick and shifty. Once he had the football in his hands he would dodge, juke, and fake his way around defenders while making really funny faces. He squinted his eyes, moved his eyebrows up and down, and moved his lips in all directions while he darted around. I saw him score lots of touchdowns because everyone was so weak from laughter that they couldn't run after him.

Once we were in high school we had some great games of touch football in the dirt lot across from the Chino Club. On Sunday afternoons some of my friends from Bayard would come to Hurley to play all afternoon long. We usually had full teams and we would name our team after a favorite pro team. Several of the boys who came to play were on the high school football team, which made our games more intense and competitive. When the game was over we would walk across the big ditch to the Chino Club to buy sodas, peanuts, jerky, and candy bars and rehash the game highlights. Everyone would stay until it was time to go home for Sunday dinner.

In the late fall and winter we played basketball. When we were young we played on the dirt court behind the old Hurley High School, but once we were a little older we played our games at the tennis courts/basketball court by the Chino Club. Some of our best games were on Sunday afternoon, although we would occasionally play at night as well. There were several strands of light bulbs strung above the court and all we had to do to play at night was flick a lever on a switchbox that was mounted near the corner of the courts.

Once in a while we would organize a team and play the Hispanic kids from North Hurley. They were usually pretty good basketball players but I don't remember one team ever being that much better than the other. Typically, the team that usually won had a couple of tall kids or players who played on the basketball team at school. Everyone played hard and tried to win because we were playing against new competition and didn't want to embarrass ourselves. We also wanted to have the bragging rights of being the best team in Hurley.

I first learned to roller skate at the tennis courts when I was in elementary school. If there were several skaters at the courts we would play games like "tag" or have skating races around the perimeter of the tennis courts. Sometimes we would turn on the lights at the tennis court and skate at night, but it was especially fun to skate in the dark if we had enough moonlight.

The roller skates that we used had four metal wheels with ball bearings inside. The skates had two wheels in the front and two in the rear. You could adjust the skate to the length of your shoe and then lock it into place with a skate key that you carried in your pocket. Skaters preferred shoes with leather soles because they had a lip around the edge that fit nicely into the toe clamps of the skate. By tightening the clamps with the skate key, the sole became bound to the skate. Sneakers never worked well because they frequently slipped out of the toe clamps.

In around 1965 we learned to take an old pair of roller skates and a piece of two by four and make a skateboard. First, we would separate the front half of the skates from the back half. Then, we removed the toe clamps and the heel strap. With a hammer, we would flatten the heel plate and then nail the skate halves to the ends of the two by four. Our skateboards were about two and a half feet in length.

I think we began making skateboards fairly soon after the sport of skateboarding was in its infancy. At the time none of us had ever seen a factory-made skateboard before, so our boards were crude at best. I have a hunch that someone from Hurley went to visit relatives in California in the early 1960's and saw kids skateboarding there. Then, when they came back home they shared their idea with a couple of their friends and before long a few of us made our own boards.

Baseball was the sport that influenced me the most when I was young because Hurley was a baseball community. Kennecott used to hire employees to play semiprofessional baseball on their company team. Hurley had a nice hardball stadium for adults and a little league field that was built just to the north of the stadium. The little league field doubled as a fast pitch softball field for the women's and men's leagues. On most summer nights there was baseball activity happening down at the ballparks and it wasn't uncommon for softball double headers to last until 11:00 p.m. or even later.

There were adult softball teams from Santa Rita, Bayard, Central, and Silver City that routinely came to Hurley to play. There were a few teams and individual players who I remember from the late 1950's and the early 1960's who are worth mentioning. The women's fast pitch softball team who usually won most of the time was the Copper Queens from Santa Rita. One of the best women pitchers in the league was Gwen Steyskal, who was the older sister of my friend Butch Steyskal. I remember watching her strike out a lot of ladies when I was young.

For several years, Hurley had a good men's fast pitch softball team with a pitcher named Everett Marshall. Everett was a lanky cowboy type of guy who was one of the best pitchers in the area. Another outstanding player in the league was David Lardizabal. David probably had the most potential for becoming a semi-pro ball player of anyone in the league.

Once in a while the men would need an umpire for their evening games because there was no one around to do it. If they got hard up enough they would ask one of us kids to umpire for them. I was always a little apprehensive when they asked me because, as a fourteen-year-old kid, it was intimidating to call a fast pitch softball game between two adult teams.

One time I was umpiring one of their games when a guy slid into second base and I called him "safe".

The second baseman began to hassle me about the call, so I asked him, "Well, did you tag him before he got to the base?"

He promptly replied, "Yes."

Then I said, "OK then, the runner is out."

The runner wasn't happy I changed my call, but I figured the second baseman didn't have any reason to lie to me.

After umpiring a few games I realized that if you make your calls with authority, the players were less likely to challenge you. One time there was a close play at third base when someone attempted to throw the runner out. I ran up to the base and yelled, "You are out. You are totally out. You are out, out, out!!!"

With my thumb sticking straight up and my hand flailing up and down, the players looked at me like I was crazy but they didn't challenge my call.

Little League Baseball

During the summer of 1957 or 1958 Hurley had a summer youth baseball program run by a man named Harold Stambach. He was also the wrestling coach at Cobre High School up until the mid 1960's. I tagged along with my brother every day to play baseball with the older boys and I remember all of the kids enjoyed playing for Mr. Stambach.

Practices were held at the dirt field northwest of Hurley High School. (Hurley Elementary School is currently located where the ball field was.) Since there were more kids who went out for the team than there were positions, "Stambach" as we called him, made a second team. The team with the good players was the Blue Sox and they had blue and white uniforms. My brother, who was five years older than me, made the Blue Sox.

The young and less skilled players who weren't good enough to make the Blue Sox played on the Red Sox. I played for the Red Sox and I didn't even know the rules to baseball. I was just happy to be a part of the team.

During practice, Stambach would invent a position for me if all of the positions on the field were taken. The position I remember playing the most was "center field back-up". He would have me stand behind the center fielder, and my job was to go and shag the ball in case the center fielder missed it.

When it was my turn to bat, the pitcher was instructed to slowly lob the ball so I could get a hit. Since I was so short, Stambach would always tell me to "choke-up" on the bat before each pitch. When I finally got my first hit, I was so excited that I ran to third base instead of first base. All of the kids began to yell, "You're going the wrong way. Go to first base."

By the time I changed directions and reached first base, the first baseman was standing there with his foot on the bag and the ball in his hand. That was the one and only time I ever tried to run the bases backward.

I remember the day Stambach checked out uniforms to us. It was one of the best days of my life. I couldn't wait to go home and put it on and wear it around the house and out in the yard. The pants and shirt were too big for me but I was just thrilled to have my very own uniform.

I don't remember playing in any games throughout the short season, so I must have been a batboy or bench warmer. One of my fondest memories was at the end of the season when Stambach took all of the Blue Sox and Red Sox team members on a picnic to Cherry Creek. He drove us there in the old Hurley High School bus, which was an early 1950ish Chevrolet. We had a great time at the picnic, and on the way home every kid on the bus joined in and sang "99 Bottles of Beer on the Wall". We must have driven Stambach totally crazy by the time we counted down to "0 bottles of beer on the wall".

In the spring of 1959 the Hurley Little League was formed. Coaches, parents, and kids met in the bleachers of the old Hurley baseball stadium and decided to have four teams in the league. The kids were asked to help name the teams, and we eventually came up with the Eagles, Rebels, Tigers, and Braves.

I ended up playing for the Eagles and our uniforms were red and white. Our team sponsor was the Hurley Garage. The Tigers uniforms were dark navy blue and grey and the Masonic Lodge sponsored them. The Braves were green and grey and were sponsored by A and B Grocery Store (Baca's Store in North Hurley), and the Rebels were royal blue and white and were sponsored by the American Laundry.

The duration of the Little League season was from late April until the end of June. In early July, many families from Hurley took their summer vacations because that was when Kennecott had their "vacation shut-down". During the shutdown, Kennecott did their annual maintenance on the equipment in the mill and smelter. The only people who continued working during the shutdown were the maintenance crews and the salaried employees.

During the first little league season, the Eagles won the league championship behind the pitching skills of a tall, lanky kid named Richard Marruffo. He had a pretty good fastball nobody could hit. He also hit quite a few homeruns. I was one of the youngest kids on the team that season and didn't see a lot of action. In my final season of Little League I had a good year and made the all-star team. We played the Silver City All-Stars in the post-season tournament in Bayard and lost to them by a score of 7-6.

The Little League baseball games in Hurley became a popular social event for kids and families. During the season there were usually lots of fans who filled the small bleachers behind home plate. Other families would park their cars along the chain-link fence that surrounded the ball field and watch the game from there. Once in a while some kid would hit a homer or a foul ball and smash out someone's windshield.

Photo 6-1: This is a photo of my Little League team the "Eagles" during the summer of 1960. Pictured kneeling from left to right are Bernie Marin, Jimmy Rogers, Elmo Padilla, yours truly, and George Marin. Standing from left to right are Bryan Bartlett, Gary Benavidez, Rudy Marruffo, Lee Padilla, Rudy Martinez, Arthur Padilla, Ricky Cook, Howie Miller, and Dell Herring. Coaches are Allard Bartlett on the left and Buddy Rogers on the right. Photo courtesy of Bub Bartlett.

It took several parent volunteers to make our season a success. All of the coaches and umpires were volunteers, and parents would volunteer to run the concession stand next to the bleachers. Our game announcer for several years was a man named Armand Ranyan. He had a small PA system and would sit on top of the home-team dugout when he announced each game.

The Little League players who made the All-Star team would proudly display their All-Star pin on the front of their ball cap. Kids who made the All-Star team two years in a row were considered baseball hotshots and would wear two pins on their hat. It was also fashionable among the ball players to put a special crease in their caps and round off the bill on the sides. The crease ran from the sides of the hat to the front and was a couple of inches above the bill. Players used to spend a lot of time perfecting the crease so it had that special look.

It wasn't unusual for dogs to follow the kids down to the ballpark. Occasionally a dog would wander out onto the field during a game or they would get into big fights near the concession stand. Adults would have to jump into the middle of the fight and pull the dogs apart and run them off.

During the Little League season they always scheduled double headers. The ball players from the two teams who weren't playing were usually running around the ballpark and goofing off. Sometimes the league would have some of those players go around to the parked cars and seek donations for equipment and supplies for the teams.

One night, my friend Richard Stevens and I came up with a brilliant idea while we were waiting for our game to begin. We decided to go around to every car at the ballpark and collect money to help support the "Hurley Little League Dog Fights". We went from car to car until we had worked the entire park. Most people told us things like, "Get the hell outta here," but a few people thought we were quite clever and gave us some money just for our efforts. When we were done collecting money, Richard and I went straight to the concession stand and loaded up on sodas and candy bars.

Another evening, during a double header, a man named B. J. Martin became very angry with a coach from one of the teams. I don't recall what the issue was, but he started a fistfight directly in front of the concession stand while kids and parents watched. This incident was a dark moment in the history of the newly formed Hurley Little League, and the fight was the talk of the town for several days.

Somewhere around 1960 there was a fast pitch hardball league for teenagers called the Cobre Teener League. My brother played on one of the teams and my father became the Secretary of the league. At the end of one of their baseball seasons they formed an "all-star" team made up of boys from around the mining district. The league raised money for them to travel to Hershey, PA to play in a large baseball tournament there. The boys traveled to the tournament in a bus and played teams from around the country. They also visited the Hershey chocolate factory and attended a couple of professional baseball games while they were there. When my brother returned from the trip, he had a gift box of Hershey chocolate products and a wall banner of the Pittsburgh Pirates with a team picture mounted on it.

Sido Bates was always eager and ready to play in any pick-up sandlot game of baseball, football, or basketball. Kids enjoyed playing baseball with Sido because he always made our games seem more "big league" and official for some reason. He was usually the first kid in Hurley to have the latest equipment fad in sports. For example, one summer he bought some "pop-up" sunglasses that were popular among professional baseball players at the time. Sido would play with the pop-ups in the "up" position most of the time, but when a fly ball was hit in his direction he would flip the lenses "down" before he made the catch. The glasses were supposed to reduce glare when you tracked fly balls. To me, the pop-ups were a big distraction. If I had to deal with those ridiculous glasses in addition to paying attention to the ball, I would drop the ball every time.

Sido invented a fun variation of Homerun Derby that we played regularly in his front yard during the summers. We used a wooden baseball bat, but instead of using a baseball we used a hollow yellow plastic lemon. These squeeze-bottles came with lemon juice inside and they looked like a real lemon.

Once the juice was gone, we would remove the squirt tip embedded in the end of the lemon. We discovered that when you threw the lemon without the squirt tip it would zigzag erratically and become difficult to hit with a bat. A pitcher could throw an amazing variety of tricky pitches by simply changing their grip and release. If the batter was lucky enough to hit the lemon over Sido's front fence, it was a homerun.

By the time we were in high school, there wasn't an organized fast pitch hardball summer league for the kids. Out of boredom we decided to organize our own league. Sido Bates was instrumental in helping organize our team, the games, and our schedule. When we traveled to out of town games we would pile several boys and all of our equipment into a couple of cars and head for the game.

We called kids we knew from Bayard, Santa Rita, Central, and Silver City who were interested in organizing a team for the league. That contact person would then help organize the home and away games on the schedule. For team uniforms, each player on the Hurley team saved up a little money to buy team baseball jerseys from Colby's Sporting Goods Store in Silver City.

We usually officiated our own games, although I remember playing a league championship game at the Santa Rita ballpark where a gentleman and youth sports enthusiast named Goatie Chavez volunteered to be the home plate umpire for us. Fans rarely came to watch our games and there were no adults involved in the organization of our teams, the league, the schedule, transportation, or the jerseys. As teenagers, we were quite proud of the fact that we made our summer baseball league a reality by doing it entirely on our own.

CHAPTER SEVEN: THE SOCIAL LIFE OF A HURLEY TEENAGER

"Thank goodness for penicillin."

"Dragging Main" and Cruising

The nightlife for a teenager in Hurley could be terribly boring at times, especially on the weekends. When my sister was in high school in the late 1950's, she and her friends would regularly cruise to Silver City looking for something to do. Their favorite hangout was the T & H Drive-In on Silver Heights Blvd. across from the Silver City Woman's Club. Kids from all over Grant County used to cruise by there in hopes of running into friends or meeting someone to take out on a date.

By the mid 1960's, the teenage hot spot had changed to the A & W Root Beer Drive-In located on the north side of Highway 180, just up the hill from Yucca Ford. The A & W was a great place to park and see who might be cruising around. Carloads of teenagers cruised slowly through the parking lot and proceeded back down the hill into town. From there they would follow Silver Heights Blvd./Pope Street down to Bullard Street. At the south end of Bullard St. they would "flip a U" at the Spring Street intersection before following the same route back to the A & W. Cruising this loop was referred to as "dragging main".

One of the best times to drag main was after a Silver High or Cobre High School athletic event because nearly every teenager in Grant County was cruising around after the game. On a typical Friday and Saturday night you would find carloads of teenagers driving bumper-to-bumper up and down the drag for several hours. Sometimes, when cars were stopped at a red light or there was a brief traffic jam, boys would jump out of their car and run up to a carload of girls and try to persuade them to meet somewhere off the beaten path for a private party.

Down at the very south end of Bullard Street was a dirt road that veered off to the left and continued past the old railroad station. The road then continued along San Vicente Creek past an old mill site. A short distance further down the road from the mill site was an old abandoned house that had the reputation of being haunted. The road near the haunted house was dark and isolated and was a great place to cruise at night. Sometimes we would stop and get out of the car and knock on the front door of the haunted house in hopes of summoning the ghostly residents. It was a great place to scare girls and get a good laugh.

Occasionally we would drive up to the backstreets of Brewer Hill above

Hudson Street and visit a fortuneteller named Madam Brewer. She was an older Negro lady who usually used Tarot Cards to tell your fortune. It was exciting to go see her because there was such a mystique about her. By the time our car would roll to a stop in front of her house, we were quickly overcome by an eerie feeling as we got up enough nerve to knock on her front door. She always seemed friendly to the kids and would usually invite everyone inside for the readings. After she told our fortunes it was customary to chip in and give her some money for her services.

Every once in a while a car load of high school boys would grow tired of playing the "cat and mouse" game as they chased giggling young girls up and down Bullard Street. When those situations occurred, these hungry young sex hounds would cruise over to Hudson Street and drop in to see the girls at Millie's. It was common knowledge that Millie's was the place to go if you desired to step into the underbelly of Silver City and make the ultimate connection with a goddess of infinite pleasure. Millie's was the notorious house of ill repute near downtown Silver City and provided a worthy service to the men of Grant County for many years until it was eventually closed down around 1968. Plenty of young, naïve high school boys eagerly lost their virginity in the confines of the red brick building on Hudson Street. For $5, a 15 year old boy could go from "Aw, shucks," to "Oh, baby," in under five minutes.

Cruising to Palomas or Juarez to visit the whorehouses was also a common practice for adventurous teenaged boys. Crossing the border always generated a fair amount of excitement because you never knew what you were getting into. The whorehouses were usually located in the seedy part of town and you always heard stories about people who got jumped, robbed, swindled, or arrested. Every once in a while you would hear a story about some lucky guy who brought home a rather extensive array of various and sundry laboratory specimens and would require a little shot of penicillin to mitigate the itching and oozing.

The anticipation of hooking up with a young senorita and getting drunk on your ass were the two main reasons that teenagers liked to visit these border town Mecca's. Beer was cheap and abundant and was a powerful enticement for teenagers on a tight budget or a limited allowance from their parents. Everyone also knew that Mexican bartenders would serve alcohol to anybody who was old enough to walk, stumble, or crawl through the door. And, most importantly, every girl in the bar magically transformed into a "stunningly beautiful" Mexican princess after about eight beers and a couple of shots of tequila.

Tall Tail Tales, Part I
***

"Being 15 years old and stuck in Hurley, New Mexico, can sometimes be a curse," thought Rudy, as he methodically trimmed the hedges in Mrs. Broome's yard.

"I spend most of my days wishing I had a girlfriend but there aren't any girls around here that interest me. Ted and I are going to change all of that tonight when we cruise over to Silver City. I can't wait."

Rudy then raked up the trimmings and put them into a wheelbarrow and hauled them to the garbage can in the alley. As soon as he put away his tools he hopped on his bike and headed for home. He had been working for six hours and knew there would be a nice chunk of money waiting for him when Mrs. Broome returned home later that afternoon.

It was a nice Saturday evening in October as Ted and Rudy sped toward Silver City. Ted had borrowed his parents' car to go to the late movie at the Gila Theatre at 9:30 p.m., but the boys actually had another plan in mind. Tension in the car continued to build as they got closer to town. "What do you think, Rudy?" asked Ted. "Do you still want to go through with it?"

Rudy thought about it for a minute before he responded. "Well," he said. "I guess tonight would be as good of a night as any to get our first piece of ass. I just got paid today for my yard-cleaning job and I have $12 on me. Do you think they will let us in?"

"Probably," responded Ted. "After all, it's a whore house. The worst thing they could do is turn us away at the door."

"You're probably right, Ted. They sure as hell aren't going to call our parents and tell them to come get us," joked Rudy.

Both boys laughed as they continued westward through Arenas Valley.

Instead of rolling into the parking lot in back of the Gila Theatre like they said they were going to do, the boys took a left down Hudson Street and pulled into the small, dark, dirt parking lot in front of Silver City's most famous brothel. Ted slowly maneuvered his car between three or four other parked cars until he reached the back of the parking area. He intentionally parked as far away from the street as possible in hopes that no one would recognize his father's car.

Once they were parked, the boys sat in the car for a few minutes to go over their strategy. They were both visibly nervous and had more questions about their plan than they had answers.

"What do we do if they ask for IDs?"

"If something happens and we get separated, where do we want to meet later?"

"What if the police come?"

To an outside observer it would have appeared that the two boys were having a strategy session in case something went wrong. To the contrary, what they were actually doing was getting up enough guts to go into Millie's to get laid for the first time.

Ted and Rudy had been hearing about Millie's ever since they were in eighth grade, but over the course of the last year their curiosity had been driving them crazy. At 15 years of age, neither of them had the necessary confidence to persuade young teenage girls to jump into the backseat of a car with them, so having sex with a prostitute seemed like their next best option. Their young hormones were boiling over and the sexual floodgates were about to bust wide open.

Finally, the boys took a deep breath, got out of the car, and cautiously walked up to the front door and rang the doorbell. Within a few seconds they could hear the faint sound of bedroom slippers sliding against a dirty linoleum floor. The sound got louder and louder until the main door opened and an old woman appeared in the shadows behind the screen door.

"What can I do for you boys?" she asked, in the coarse, deep voice of a chain smoker.

"We're here to see the girls," Rudy nervously replied.

Without hesitating, she opened up the screen door and told the boys to follow her down the hall. They looked at each other and followed her through a short entrance hall as if they were a couple of young puppies at feeding time. From there they turned left at the main east-west hallway where they were led to a parlor area. As they entered the parlor they gazed around and saw a few other men and three or four scantily clad women seated on the couches that were situated around the perimeter of the room.

At the south end of the room was an old, top-loading soda machine full of beer. When the girls would slide the door to the side and reach down into the cooler for a beer, they would bend over and offer the men in the room a very generous view of their firm and curvaceous posteriors. It was all part of doing business. Couches lined the walls on the east and west sides of the parlor, and on the north wall above eye level was a white, hand painted sign with black, Old English script lettering that read, "Ye Ole Whore Shop". Below the lettering was a picture of a black cat's face with pointed ears, wide eyes, and whiskers protruding from the sides of its nose.

Once the boys were seated on one of the couches, a couple of ladies came over and sat down next to them. They spoke in low, sweet, confident voices and wore nighties made of a see-through material that exposed an abundance of flesh. At first the boys were overly shy and, quite frankly, very nervous. They were obviously the youngest people in the room and they certainly didn't know how to respond to the sexual overtures from the ladies. Before long a gentleman sitting on the other side of the room began to notice that the boys appeared awkward and inexperienced and he broke out in a big smile. He pointed toward them and told the girl that was sitting on his lap, "Looky there, honey. Them boys look a little pale behind the ears."

Everyone in the room laughed and now Ted and Rudy were even more embarrassed than before.

Being new to the brothel scene, neither of the boys knew the protocol for picking a sex partner. This was becoming somewhat of an uncomfortable situation for Rudy because the lady who was getting ready to crawl into his lap wasn't the one he wanted to be with and he didn't know how to tell her so. He would have rather been with the pretty blond lady sitting next to a gentleman across the room. She caught his eye as he walked into the parlor. Ted, on the other hand, quickly became infatuated with the lady who was rubbing her hand up and down his leg and nibbling on his earlobe.

After a few more minutes of flirtation and a little bit of "touchy-rubby", the lady running her fingers through Rudy's hair disclosed that it was OK to pick any of the girls in the room. When Rudy heard her say that, he slowly perked up. At first it was, "Well, heck, this," and "Aw shucks, that," but eventually he communicated to the lady, who was now on his lap, that he wanted the blond woman on the other couch. The girl casually looked across the room at her blond co-worker and said to her in a calm tone of voice, "Tanya, why don't you come over here and visit with this gentleman," and then she graciously left to go sit with another potential suitor.

Once the boys were pleased with their selections, the ladies led them down the main hallway to the east side of the building where the bedrooms were located. Even though Rudy and Ted continued to be visibly nervous and awkward as they strode down the hallway, they knew their first encounter with a woman was only minutes away and they were beginning to experience the initial stages of sexual arousal.

Ted and his lady went into one bedroom and Tanya led Rudy into another. Once the door was closed, Tanya sat down on the edge of the bed next to Rudy and asked, "What would you like, Sweetie?"

Rudy fumbled around and thought about it for second and then nervously replied, "Well, uh, what do you mean?"

Tanya could tell by now that Rudy was an inexperienced young man and that she might as well have a little fun with the situation. She smiled as she rubbed her hand on his thigh and said, "Regular sex is $5. If you want me to do xxxx in addition to sex, that will cost a little more. If you want a second girl it will cost…"

"Oh, no, no," interrupted Rudy. "I just want regular sex."

He then pretended to be savvy and in-control as he reached into his pants pocket and pulled out a $5 bill to give to Tanya.

With his money in hand, Tanya slowly stood up and said, "I'll be right back. Go ahead and get undressed, honey."

She then left the room and closed the door behind her.

Rudy reached down and pulled off his shoes and sox and then stood up to remove the rest of his clothes. At first he felt a little vulnerable as he stood there, stark naked, in a strange room. But then, as he anticipated his inevitable meeting with Tanya, his fantasies began to run wild with excitement and lust. Suddenly he noticed a strong shift in the flow of his blood to a different part of his body, and he liked it.

A couple of minutes later he heard footsteps approaching the bedroom door. His arousal intensified. When he looked down to see what was happening between his legs, he knew Tanya would be quite impressed with what she saw as she walked through the door. He was ready to rumble.

The doorknob turned and the door began to open. As Rudy stood fully exposed next to the bed, his excitement surged. A gentle smile slowly grew across his face as he looked toward the door.

Suddenly, his state of euphoria was overcome by a surge of panic. Pearl, the elderly hostess, walked into the room beating on a cigarette and casually approached him as he stood next to the bed. Rudy's initial thought when he saw Pearl was, "Oh my God. This is a bad dream," and he quickly turned to the side in a display of modesty and total embarrassment.

"I need to check you," she said, in a business as usual tone, and pointed

Rudy's crotch.

Still not quite sure what her motive was, he slowly turned and faced her as she began to examine his fully loaded package. In her low, gravelly voice she told Rudy, "Go ahead and turn toward the light so I can get a good look at you, hon."

The long ash at the end of her cigarette fell to the floor as she talked.

As Rudy did what he was told, he thought to himself, "Oh, fuck. I think I'm gonna puke."

Pearl briefly looked him over and said, "OK," and turned around and left.

Rudy felt as though someone had just doused him with cold water.

A couple of minutes later Tanya returned to the bedroom. She sat down on the bed and smiled at Rudy as she removed her nightie. Then she slowly laid on her back and signaled for Rudy to come aboard. Suddenly Rudy regained his composure and his loins began to quiver with excitement. He nervously followed her lead as he sprawled on top of her. He raised his hips up and down a few times in an effort to make the ultimate connection, but to no avail. Tanya finally grinned as she reached down to grab his throbbing manhood and slowly slid him inside of her. It didn't take Rudy long to figure out what to do after that.

In less than two minutes Rudy was done with his business. He remained on top of Tanya for another minute until he could catch his breath before he disconnected. Once he rolled over and stood up next to the bed, Tanya gently stroked his waning member with a damp washcloth before he got dressed. By the time Rudy slipped on his jeans and began to fasten the buttons, the first thought that ran through his mind was, "Damn, that was quick."

When he finished tying his shoes, Tanya led him out of the bedroom and down the hallway to the front door. She smiled and thanked him and gave him a little peck on the cheek. "Come back and see me again sometime," she said in her low, soothing voice.

She then saw Rudy out the door and returned to the parlor.

Rudy walked out into the parking lot and back to the dark corner of the driveway where the car was parked. To his surprise, when he opened the car door he saw Ted sitting in the car waiting for him. Rudy broke into a huge grin as he climbed in and closed the door.

The first thing he asked Ted was, "How did it go?"

With a long, disappointed look on his face, Ted looked away and said, "Not too good. I think I screwed everything up. I followed her into the bedroom and paid her and, when she left the room with my money, I chickened out and left before she returned. Now I'm kicking myself in the ass for not following through with it."

Ted didn't offer up any excuses for walking away from his first sexual encounter. That's the kind of person he was. To the contrary, he vowed he was going to go back to Millie's another time and follow through with his business once and for all. Rudy had very little reason to doubt Ted's word, especially since they were a couple of horny 15-year-old kids who had recently become helpless slaves to their newly discovered libido.

A couple of weeks later the boys returned to Millie's and Ted was eager to set the record straight. Pearl led them once again down the hallway to meet the ladies and, when they entered the parlor, both boys strutted with the swagger and demeanor of seasoned whorehouse veterans. Rudy took up again with his old friend Tanya and Ted picked the same lady he was with as well. And when the boys met later that evening in the parking lot, Rudy could tell by the grin on Ted's face that he had made good on his promise.

Tall Tail Tales, Part II
***

Once Millie's became routine for Rudy and Ted, they eventually expanded their whorehouse domain to Palomas and Juarez and frequently took their friends with them on their journeys. The Mexican whorehouses made Millies in Silver City seem tame by comparison. Two advantages of going to Mexico were that the boys could drink as much as they wanted and they had a larger selection of girls to choose from. By the time they graduated from high school a couple of years later, they knew which Mexican strip clubs had the best looking whores, which clubs would rip you off for drinks, and where to go to see a good "donkey show".

In a strange sort of way these young men had a love/hate relationship with their whorehouse adventures. On the one hand, they had a great time drinking and having a pleasurable evening with the young ladies. But, every night after their business was done they would lament about how they had wasted their money and felt ashamed for having indulged in such a shallow and meaningless interaction. Their shame usually didn't last long though, because within a few weeks time they were right back at it again. While it would be difficult to speculate about the source of their shame and guilt, perhaps they were simply experiencing a temporary case of a common psychological condition known as "buyer's remorse".

One hot and humid July night, Ted, Rudy, and a couple of friends wandered down the back streets of Juarez on their way to a club called the White Lake. All of the boys agreed it was one of their favorite clubs because the club consistently had attractive young women working there. The White Lake was located several blocks from the border in the bowels of the red light district and was about a half an hour walk from the bridge on Avenida Diez y Seis de Septiembre.

It was impossible to tell beforehand whether the White Lake would be rocking or if it would be fairly quiet. If the working girls that particular night were hot and the customers there were partying hard, the boys would stick around and enjoy the evening. If things weren't jumping, Ted and Rudy knew plenty of other places to go.

Shortly after they arrived at the club they found some vacant stools at the end of the bar and summoned the bartender to order drinks. On this particular night the bar was crowded with young Fort Bliss Army recruits who were fresh out of boot camp and were obviously letting off a few weeks of pent up steam. It was easy to tell who the soldiers were because they were all about the same age and sported crew cuts from their recent induction into the Army. The room was getting more rowdy and raucous by the minute and the fledgling soldiers were drinking as if there was no tomorrow.

Most of the recruits were standing around in a large circle in the center of the bar room as they laughed, screamed, hooted, and hollered. From their barstools, Ted and the other boys were sipping their cold beers as they tried desperately to see between the soldiers and find out what was so entertaining. As the recruits shifted around on their feet it was possible to catch brief glimpses here and there of something that appeared to be happening on the floor in front of them.

After a couple of minutes it became clear what all of the excitement was about. There, in the middle of the circle, was a shirtless, drunken soldier having sex with a prostitute. His pants were down around his ankles and her legs were high in the air as they thrashed around on the floor in a ritual of drunken dissonance. The young woman was naked and would intermittently dig her heels into the bare buttocks of her lover as she arched her back and thrust her pelvis upward. The pandemonium in the room would reach a new climax every time the bumping and grinding heated up or the moans got louder.

Once the floor ordeal ended, things returned to normal. The soldiers carried their drunk, half-naked buddy out of the bar and the whores soon turned their attention elsewhere. Meanwhile, Ted and Rudy and their friends had a couple more drinks and eventually selected some women to take to the rooms in the back of the building for a little bumping and grinding of their own.

When their business was done the boys surfaced once again into the bar and ordered one last beer before heading back toward the border. It was getting late and they were faced with a long drive back to Central.

As they stepped outside of the bar and onto the street, they realized that something strange had happened while they were inside the White Lake. A torrential downpour of rain had swept through the area and the streets of Juarez were so flooded that the boys had to walk up on the sidewalks where the water only came up to their knees. The flooding was extensive and it took them much longer than usual to wade their way back to the bridge that crossed over the Rio Grande into El Paso.

Along the way they saw dozens of people scurrying to seek shelter from the continuing downpour. In certain areas of the city the water crept up and into the entrances of the businesses that lined the streets. At one point, as the boys were wading up a sidewalk a few blocks from the bridge, they glanced out into the middle of the flooded street and noticed a drunken reveler from the U.S. splashing around as the water gently drained toward the river. When they stopped to take a closer look, they realized the guy was doing the backstroke while his friends laughed hysterically from the opposite side of the street.

By the time they made it over the bridge and back to their car, everyone was sopping wet and tired from wading through the flooded streets of Juarez. Ted and Rudy took turns driving home while their two friends quietly slept in the back seat. As they listened to the radio in the mesmerizing tranquility of their late night journey back to Central, both boys knew they had just experienced a night they would never forget.

Late Night Restaurants

After a late night of carousing, drinking, and dancing, my favorite place to go at the end of the evening was the San Nicholas Café in Bayard. It was located right next to the Triangle Bar and was owned by the Flores family. The restaurant was relocated to Bayard from Santa Rita when the town site was torn down. San Nicolas Cafe catered to the late night party crowd who flocked there after the Mexican dances at the Pénjamo, Brown Derby, and the Casa Blanca bars. It was a popular place to go to eat a bowl of menudo and sober up before driving home.

The main chef was the elderly grandmother who had a reputation for her excellent menudo as well as other Mexican food dishes. My friends and I were usually the only "Gringo" customers in the restaurant at that time of night but we always felt at home when we went there. We knew some of the Flores family members from high school and many of the restaurant patrons were our schoolmates and drinking buddies.

In Silver City, there was a greasy spoon joint located at the top of the hill on Memory Lane called The Hilltop Café. They stayed open after the dances and catered mostly to the cowboy crowd, although others went there because it was the only place in Silver City that was open after midnight. It was a good place to stop for a hamburger on our way back to Hurley after a night of raising hell. The Hilltop could also be a little raucous at times because some of the patrons were boozed up and looking for a reason to fight.

The Hilltop Café Melee
***

It was Thanksgiving weekend and Tony Swanson had just returned to Hurley from his freshman year of college at New Mexico State University. He and three of his good friends from Cobre High School had been to a dance in Silver City and decided to stop at the Hilltop Cafe to get a late night meal. Tony's group had been drinking throughout the evening and had developed a voracious appetite for a burger or perhaps a chicken fried steak.

The restaurant was crowded and the only available empty booth happened to be next to a booth with four rowdy young cowboys. Tony and his friends slid into their seats, and before long a waitress brought them each a glass of water and plopped some menus onto the table. A few minutes later she returned to take everyone's order and scurried off to clip the ticket onto the rotating wheel in the order window.

The young cowboys continued with their loud and aggressive behavior and, as they waited for their meal to arrive, one of them started making provocative remarks to Tony and his friends as they quietly sat at their booth. Even though the annoying chatter was making Tony and the boys slightly concerned, they chose to ignore the cowboys in hopes that they would eventually settle down and let everyone enjoy their late night meal.

As they continued to ignore the insults, one young cowpuncher in particular wouldn't let up. He gradually became more verbose until it was obvious he wasn't going to settle for anything less than a confrontation. The last thing Tony and his friends were looking for was trouble, but once they realized the guy wasn't going to stop yapping, Tony finally turned toward him and said, "Hey, why don't you shut the fuck up."

Without wasting a second, one of the cowboys replied, "Well, you wanna step outside and make me shut up?"

Tony wasn't the kind of kid who liked to fight and he usually went out of his way to avoid confrontation, but over the course of the evening he had drained several beers and was losing his patience with the name-calling. The challenge to "step outside" somehow triggered a reaction in Tony's mind that had very little to do with "caution" and everything to do with "pissed off". Without hesitating, he turned back to the nearby booth and responded, "Damn right I do."

There were four boys in Tony's group and four cowboys. They all got up at the same time to walk outside into the parking lot in front of the Café. As the two groups approached the door to the main entrance, one of the cowboys shoved Tony from behind in an effort to provoke him even further. It worked. Now Tony couldn't wait to get his hands on this guy.

All of the boys walked out into the parking lot and formed a circle around Tony and the head jaw flapper for the bovine brigade. While the cowboy stood in the circle waiting for Tony to unzip his jacket in preparation for the slugfest, Tony quickly unleashed a sucker punch to his opponent's face. The cowboy's hat went flying off of his head and he immediately fell to the pavement. Sensing that he should quickly take advantage of the situation, Tony aggressively pounced on top of kid while he was still dazed and worked on him some more.

When Tony finally realized the other guy wasn't fighting back, he climbed off of him and stood up to see if there was going to be more of a fight. The cowboy was lying on his back and moved around slowly on the pavement. Preliminary indications were that the fighting was over. As Tony waited to see if the kid was going to get back up for another round, he noticed a cowboy hat lying on the pavement nearby. In a fit of post-fight anger and bravado, he rushed over and stomped it into the ground until it was flatter than a hot greased tortilla.

By now the other cowboys were livid. For starters, the sucker punch had violated their drunken sense of fairness and, to make matters even worse, things didn't turn out as they had planned. They also didn't like the way Tony had stomped their buddy's cowboy hat after he climbed off of him. "Why, you dirty sombitch," one of them yelled out to Tony. "That wasn't a fair fight. He wasn't even ready when you hit him."

"Fuck you," yelled Tony. "He wouldn't be lying there if he had kept his big fucking mouth shut."

While the freshly silenced loudmouth was still lying on the pavement nearby, another one of his angry friends taunted, "Come on, you chicken-shit bastard. Why don't you fight like a man? I'll whip your ass right now."

Finally, Tony's friends stepped in and reminded the cowboys that they were the ones who started the fight and should take their friend and leave before there was more trouble. Since the cowboys were now outnumbered, they reluctantly decided to tend to their incoherent partner as Tony and his friends retreated to their car and drove away. Unfortunately, Tony and the boys never got to eat the hamburgers they had ordered back at the Hilltop Café. The only thing they could find in the car to quell their appetite for the long drive back to Hurley was a leftover six-pack of Coors in bottles.

Teen Dances in the Area

Dancing to live music was a popular social activity for teens and young adults in the area. The dances were scheduled nearly every weekend at one venue or another, and sometimes there would be two or three dances happening on the same evening. Up until the mid 1960's there were only "country western bands" and "Mexican bands" that played at the dances. Local and regional rock bands didn't begin to appear in the area until the mid 1960's.

Kids from all over would show up to the dances by the carload. I can't speak for everyone else in Grant County, but the first thing my friends and I would do on our way to a dance is go somewhere to buy beer with a fake ID or get some older kid to buy it for us. Then we would cruise around on a dirt road for about an hour or so until everyone had polished off six or eight beers apiece. Then we would go to the dance. During the intermissions we would go out to the parking lot and drink even more beer with our friends. As one could imagine, there was never a shortage of drunken teenagers at some of these dances, and fights were quite common.

Our primary objective at the dances was to meet some girl who we had our eye on and take her out parking in the boondocks somewhere on the outskirts of town. If that scenario didn't work out, our fallback plan was to get drunker than hell with our buddies and act really stupid in front of everyone at the dance. As I recall, we resorted to the fallback plan most of the time.

The Hispanic community held many of their dances at the Pénjamo Night Club in North Hurley, the Casa Blanca Bar near Santa Rita, and the Brown Derby in Central. The local bands I remember seeing were The Royal Tones, Los Coronados, Zeke and the Ambassadors, The Pete Dominguez Band, and Freddy and the Starlighters. Once in a while big name bands like Sonny and the Sunliners or Little Joe and the Latinaires would come to town. I used to go to some of these dances with Sido Bates and one or two other guys when we were in high school. We were usually the only Gringos there. My fellow Gringos around town used to warn us about going to Mexican dances because, "They like to get drunk and fight a lot." We went anyway because we enjoyed the music and we always had a great time.

One night at the Pénjamo Night Club I watched a Mexican band play "Papa's Got a Brand New Bag" by James Brown, and I was amazed. The band had a horn section and the musicians were all dressed in glittery sequin sport coats. The musicians all wore their hair slicked straight back on the sides and usually wore black plastic framed sunglasses while they played. It was especially entertaining to watch the horn section sway back and forth in unison to the beat of the music. I also loved to listen to the "cumbias" and the "corridas" and studied the dance moves, just in case I got up enough nerve to ask someone to dance.

The Impacts were the first local Silver City band that played rock music in the area. Most of the kids in the band were from Silver High School and they usually played at the Murray Hotel Ballroom, the National Guard Armory on top of Brewer Hill, or sometimes at the Sheriff's Posse Arena dance hall located above the old rodeo arena east of Silver City.

The first rock band with kids from Cobre High School was called the Sons of Atlantis. They formed the band in the fall of 1965 and played rock tunes by the Rolling Stones, Jimi Hendrix, the Beatles, the Monkees, and others. They played a few gigs at the Fatima Hall in Bayard, the Bayard Lyon's Club, and in Lordsburg. They broke up in the summer of 1967 when several members of the band graduated.

In the fall of 1966 another rock band emerged onto the local music scene by the name of the Greek Five. The band originally had a couple of kids from Silver High School and four boys from Cobre High School, but the Silver High guys eventually quit the band, making it an all-Cobre High School group. They played some tunes by the Rolling Stones, the Beatles, the Yardbirds, the song "Gloria" by Them, "Mustang Sally" by Wilson Pickett, and other popular tunes of the time. I used to tag along with the band because we were all friends and I got to bang on the drums once in a while at their practices. They played several gigs at the Sheriff's Posse Arena dance hall, a gig in T or C, and a high school prom. The band folded in the summer of 1967 when most of the band graduated.

Another local band with kids from Silver City and the mining district formed in 1968. They were called the Purpl Bottl. They played tunes by popular bands like Steppenwolf, Lovin' Spoonful, and Jimi Hendrix, as well as the tune "I'm A Man" by Spencer Davis. They played all of the local venues until the band broke up in 1970. They also played several regional gigs in El Paso and Las Cruces and did a whirlwind New Mexico tour, playing small towns along the Rio Grande from T or C to Espanola.

In 1965 or 1966, rock bands from out of town would occasionally come to Grant County to play. They were treated like rock stars when they came because they were from some big city far away and had a lot of swagger. Some of the good bands I remember from out of town were the Shandells from Las Cruces and the Babies and Dearly Beloved from Tucson.

Somewhere around 1966, Silver City finally got a "big name" band to come for a show. I went to the Murray Hotel ballroom one night and saw the band Them. Their big international hit was a song called "Gloria". Van Morrison was in the band and toured with Them in the U.S. that year, but he quit the band and went back to Ireland before their U.S. tour was completed. I don't remember whether or not he was with Them when they played at the Murray Hotel.

The local country-western bands played venues like the Sherriff's Posse Arena, the Armory, and the Chino Club in Hurley. They also played in dance halls out in the country, sometimes far from Silver City. Kids would pile into cars or pickups and drive out to places like the Mimbres Round Up Lodge, the Cliff High School gymnasium, the Cliff Tavern, Glenwood, White Signal, Lake Valley near Hillsboro, and Hachita. Once in a while you would hear about a carload of drunken teenagers getting into a car wreck on the way home from one of those dances.

The Meredith Neal band was a very popular band that played country-western music in Silver City and the Southwest from the early 1950's up until 1989. Many of the musicians who played with Meredith over the years played with other country bands in the area at one time or another.

The Rhythm Wranglers were a popular local country-western band in the early 1960's until 1973 or so. They played all over Grant County, southwestern New Mexico, eastern Arizona, and even Utah. They also had a variety of local musicians play with the band over the years. I used to see them play at the Chino Club in Hurley on occasion and they always drew good crowds there.

Another country-western band I saw in the mid 1960's at the Mimbres Round Up Lodge was Forrest Delk and the Gully Jumpers. The Gully Jumpers were a family band made up mostly of Forrest Delk and his kids. In between sets, Forrest used to like to give me a "Dutch rub" when he saw me (A "Dutch rub" is when you get someone in a headlock and rub the bottom of your fist briskly on top of their head so that you mess up their hair). The Gully Jumpers dances were usually a little more "folksy" and family oriented affairs that were held out in the country, whereas the Rhythm Wranglers and Meredith Neal played more contemporary popular country-western music in Silver City and other towns nearby.

One other country band that began playing around Grant County in the later 1960's was Clay Mac and The Town and Country Playboys. The bandleader was a young man named Clay Mac and the band played all of the local venues, including the Casa Loma nightclub just east of Silver City. They were very popular and well known throughout the southwestern part of the state.

The Hachita Two-Step

One night I went all the way down to Hachita to a country-western dance with Jason Berry in his black 1952 Chevy. We left Hurley with a case of beer in the back seat of the car and managed to polish off several bottles during the long drive down to the dance. After we had been at the dance for a while, Jason drank several more beers and, for some reason, got mad at me and wanted to kick my butt. He was a few years older than me and was quite a bit bigger and stronger.

The next thing I knew, Jason was chasing me out of the dance hall and into the parking lot. I had a slight lead on him, so I ran to his car and climbed inside and locked the doors just as he started to grab the door handle. He stood outside of his car and tried to open the locked door where I was sitting, but to no avail. Jason was so drunk he didn't even notice that the windows in his car were rolled up. As he stood outside the car door screaming at me, he became furious and doubled up his fist and took a swing at me. He tried to punch me in the face, but he smashed out the window instead. As his hand went through the glass, he sustained a fairly severe cut near one of his knuckles and had to wrap a rag around his hand to control the bleeding.

When the dance was over I found a ride home with someone else because Jason was still drunk, belligerent, and unpredictable. I wasn't overly excited about being in the car with a drunk driver late at night, and I knew that he could turn on me at any moment and try to beat me up.

With no one to accompany him, Jason drove home alone in the middle of the night with the driver's side widow smashed out of the doorframe. At about 3:30 in the morning, just a few miles north of Deming, his car broke down and he had to hitchhike the rest of the way into Hurley. There wasn't much traffic on the highway at that time of night, but someone finally picked him up and gave him a ride.

By the time he walked in the front door of his parents' home, it was around 7:00 a.m. He was bloody, tired, and hung over but, unfortunately, Jason had one last chore to tend to before he went to bed. He had to get someone to take him back to Deming and help him tow his car back to Hurley. By the time he finally pulled into his back yard with his car in tow, it was mid afternoon. As it turned out, the cut on his hand required stitches but he never did go to the doctor to get it sewn up. He ended up with a fairly large scar next to his knuckle, which served as a constant reminder of our memorable trip to Hachita.

The Great Carbon Monoxide Jam Session

One evening there was an epic jam session at the Maldonado house in Bayard with the members of the Tubby and the Turd Muffins band. Juan Carlos' parents had just left town for a couple of days, so he and Eloy decided it would be the perfect time to have a party in their living room. I rode my motorcycle to the session from Hurley and was looking forward to hearing some of the new tunes the Turd Muffins had worked up for the evening.

Band members and friends from around the county converged on the Maldonado's place and everyone was ready to party. In addition to the live music, there was also quite a bit of beer floating around throughout the evening. To no one's surprise, by midway through the jam session everyone was starting to get a little drunk, and I was no exception.

As the evening wore on and we drank more beer, the music got louder and everyone got wilder and wilder. For some unknown reason, I decided to take it upon myself to elevate the party to another level and get a few laughs while I was at it. With a beer in hand, I wandered out to the street and started my motorcycle and put it into first gear. I then slowly crept up to the front door of the house and began to rev my motor. It wasn't long before the door cracked open and a head poked out to see where all of the commotion was coming from. Once they saw me sitting there on my motorcycle with a beer in my hand and a grin with mischief written all over it, they held the door wide open and stepped out of the way so I could make my grand entrance into the house.

Several drunken teenagers cheered on as I sat in the middle of the living room and revved the motor. Meanwhile, Tubby smiled and plucked away on one of his dramatic guitar solos to keep the pandemonium at a high level. By all accounts, we officially had a wild-ass party in session and the beer was now flowing freely.

As crazy as things were getting at that point in the evening, I actually would have preferred to drive my motorcycle around to the other rooms in the house, but there were too many people scattered about and the doorways were fairly narrow. Instead, I decided to take the motorcycle back outside because the room was beginning to fill with exhaust fumes. I signaled to Eloy and he opened the door for me.

With kids cheering me on, I slowly turned my Honda Super 90 around and headed for the front door. I carefully inched it through the doorway until my front wheel was outside and my rear tire was still inside the doorframe. As the rear tire rolled up to the threshold, I made a dramatic exit from the living room by revving the motor and "peeling out" through the door. Unfortunately, my tire tore out a patch of linoleum from the floor and left a fairly large black skid mark in its place.

At the end of the evening, Juan Carlos assessed the damage and decided to put a floor mat over the skid mark to cover it up. It was an easy fix and hopefully his parents wouldn't notice anything unusual or out of place when they returned home the following day.

Well, doggone it! As luck would have it, it wasn't long before Juan Carlos' and Eloy's parents discovered the torn linoleum, and I don't think they were too happy about it. I will never know what story the boys told their parents about that night, but it must have been a good one because I never heard anything more about it. Isn't it interesting how little problems of this nature always seem to happen while parents of teenaged kids are gone for the weekend.

Movie Theaters

When we were kids our parents used to drive us from Hurley to one of the movie theaters in the area. I went to many movies at the Bayard Theater before I was in high school, but as we got older we usually went to the Gila Theater and the Silco Theater on Bullard Street in Silver City.

I remember going to the movies on several occasions with my brother and cousin James. James and I would always buy Pom Poms or peanuts so we could throw them at the back of people's heads as they watched the movie. If the movie happened to be boring, we would get up and walk across the stage in front of the screen and then run out the exit door on the side of the stage. We always managed to keep the ushers busy, and on rare occasions we would get thrown out of the theater for yelling and raising hell during the movie.

One evening at the Silco Theater I went to see Alfred Hitchcock's movie "Psycho". It was a cold night, and I was wearing a pair of gloves that had fake rabbit fur lining the inside of the gloves. When I inverted a glove and slipped it onto my hand, it looked like I had a big, furry monster hand. During the scariest scene in the movie, when Norman Bates approached the woman in the shower with a butcher knife in his hand, I reached around with my glove and scared the girl sitting in front of me. Her head snapped back and she let out a blood-curdling scream, but she never reported me to the usher.

There were two drive-in movie theaters in Grant County and they were especially popular in the summers. The Sundowner Drive-In, which was previously known as the Copper Drive-In, was located in Arenas Valley, and the Silver Sky-Vue drive-in was located on the outskirts of Silver City near what is now Albertson's grocery store. We enjoyed taking dates to the drive-in movies because we spent more time making-out than we did watching the movie. We also took beer or liquor with us because we could get drunk in the car without getting hassled by the employees or the police. Of course, the next morning the theater maintenance crew had to bring in a dump truck to haul away all of the empty beer cans and bottles that were scattered around our car.

When we were in high school, it was a common practice to sneak friends into the drive-in theaters if we didn't have enough money to pay admission for everyone in the car. We would stop up the road and stuff kids into the trunk of the car before we approached the pay booth at the main entrance.

One night I went to the Copper Drive-In with Sido Bates and another kid who was broke. He wanted to sneak into the movie so Sido stopped to open the trunk and stuff him inside. After the kid climbed in, Sido shut the lid and we drove away.

As we approached the admission booth of the drive-in we decided to play a prank on the kid. Once we paid our admission fees, Sido put his finger to his mouth and whispered, "Shhhhh." Then he handed the car keys to the man and pointed to his trunk and whispered, "Go take a look."

The ticket guy grinned, took the keys, and walked around to the trunk. As soon as he popped it open, the kid instantly sprang out of the trunk and ran away because he figured he had just been busted. The ticket-taker got such a good laugh from our prank he let the kid into the movie for free.

When I was in high school I took my parents' 1953 Chevy to the Sky-Vue drive-in and met some friends near the theater entrance. Since I was too broke to pay admission, I parked my car in front of the theater and walked over to the dirt road on the eastern border of the theater property to sneak in. I had to bushwhack my way across an arroyo and slip through a barbed wire fence that surrounded the theater property. Once I was inside, I sat with my friends in their car and watched the movie.

When the movie was over, we drove out of the exit where my car had been parked, but to my surprise, my car was gone. Someone had stolen it. I didn't know what to do at first, but after a few minutes I decided to call the police and tell them what had happened. About 10 minutes later an officer showed up and filled out a police report. When he was done, he offered to take me cruising around with him to look for my car. Since it was a Saturday night, we knew that lots of kids would be dragging main in downtown Silver. If we were going to find it, that would be the best place to start our search.

We didn't have much luck at first, but as we were cruising down Bullard Street I noticed my car up ahead as it approached a stop light at the corner of Bullard and Broadway. The officer quickly put on his red lights and siren and we pulled the car thieves over near the Buffalo Bar.

As the officer approached the car on foot, the doors on the driver and passenger sides opened up simultaneously and two smiling girls climbed out of the car. Once they were out in the open and I could get a good look at them, I immediately recognized them. We were all good friends, and I knew instantly they had just pulled a joke on me.

I walked over to the cop and explained to him that the girls and I knew each other and I didn't want to press charges against them. He wasn't particularly amused about the situation, so he ran a background check on the girls anyway. Once he discovered that neither of them had a criminal record or any traffic citations, he released them and I gave them a ride back to their car. As we drove away, the girls disclosed to me that they simply couldn't resist getting even with me for all of the pranks I had pulled on everyone else over the years.

Romantic Parking Places

For a little one-horse town out in the middle of nowhere, the Hurley area had quite a few places to go if you happened to be in the mood for a little romance. For those young lovers who wanted to stay close to town, you could drive down to the baseball park at the south end of town and park behind the old baseball stadium. Another great spot to explore the joys of Mother Nature was down on the pigpen road, where lovebirds could drive a couple of miles south of town and park behind one of the many horse corrals along the way.

The B Ranch area was another popular place to go parking. Situated between Little Geronimo Mountain and the base of a mountainous slag dump near the smelter, a small slag train would come out onto the dump every hour or two and pour red-hot, molten slag down the side of the dump. The slag would illuminate the entire valley with an orange hue and made the bluffs at the top of Little Geronimo look daunting. About a quarter of a mile away along Whitewater Creek was a roping arena that also was a great place to park.

Photo 7-1: Shown here is a nighttime photo of molten slag as it is being poured onto the slag dump. The slag illuminated the sky, which made for a magnificent nighttime view of Whitewater Creek and Little Geronimo Mountain. Photo courtesy of New Mexico State University Library, Archives and Special Collections.

If you wanted to drive a little farther out of town to seek a greater degree of privacy, you could always head out to the cottonwood grove in Cameron Creek. The grove was popular for lovers as well as partiers and there were lots of little private spots to hide along the creek.

Sometimes we would take our dates up onto the top of the tailings where you could see for miles to the south and west. It was a perfect place to look at the stars and ponder your role as a citizen of the vast universe that unfolded before you. Before long, as the windows to your car began to fog up, the answers to all of your metaphysical musings would gradually unveil themselves in the form of pure ecstasy. Interestingly, the mysteries of the universe weren't the only thing that became unveiled.

There were also lots of places to park on the side roads and in the ravines along the Ridge Road and Whitewater Road. Some people would even drive all the way around to the east side of the tailings to the Bolton Wells pumping station. Over the years, there was a lot of pumping going on at Bolton Wells.

One of the funniest stories I heard on the subject of young lovers came from one of the Hurley cops as he and I drove around town one night in the patrol car. (The cops took me with them occasionally because they could keep an eye on me and control the level of vandalism in Hurley.) Anyway, he told me that he had cruised down a dirt road north of the Catholic Cemetery one night and stumbled upon a couple of high school kids as they were "makin' bacon". When he walked up to the parked car to shine his flashlight inside, he saw two people frantically scrambling around in search of clothing articles. He tapped on the window with his flashlight and after a brief delay it slowly began to open. There before him sat a young couple who were partially dressed and totally embarrassed. The situation became even more awkward when he realized he knew the kids as well as their parents. I got a good laugh from the story, especially because I also knew everyone involved. Getting caught with your pants down, so to speak, is just another example of the perils of growing up in a small town.

Car Troubles on the Pig Pen Road

Not long after I had graduated from high school I took a girl from Silver City named Lana Perkins on a date in a green 1967 Mercury Comet that I borrowed from Gene Valles. I had been on several dates and outings with her over the previous couple of years and I liked her a lot. I don't remember exactly where we went on our date, but at the end of the evening we decided to go for a drive in the Hurley area.

With my libido in full gear, I wheeled Gene's Comet onto the pigpen road south of Hurley. On the west side of the dirt road was a huge pipeline that ran parallel to the road and transported water from the Apache Tejo wells south of town into Hurley. On the opposite side of the pipeline, about every half mile or so, there were private corrals where Hurley residents kept their horses and livestock. There were dirt ramps located at each corral location so horse owners could drive up and over the pipe to get to their animals. It was oftentimes difficult to see a parked car at one of the corrals because the pipeline blocked your view as you drove by.

We cruised down Pig Pen Road until we came upon a well-hidden corral and slowly inched our way over the dirt ramp to the other side of the pipeline. I turned off the engine, turned on the radio, and within a matter of seconds my date and I began to talk, kiss, and giggle the night away. It was a beautiful, warm night and Lana and I had a wonderful time together.

The night seemed to go on forever but, before we knew it, the sky was starting to get light in the east. We embraced and kissed one more time as we reluctantly faced the inevitable realization that it was time to bid farewell to our little love nest and drive Lana back to her parents' house in Silver City. Lana was beginning to feel a slight sense of urgency because she knew her parents would probably be upset with her if she came dragging in at dawn.

I looked into the rearview mirror and combed my hair, checked for lipstick marks on my face, and straightened up my shirt before I finally turned the ignition key to start the car. Click, click, click… nothing happened. I tried again several more times and still, nothing happened. I got out of the car and opened the hood to check the battery cables. They were both attached securely. I knew that pushing the car to get it started wasn't an option because it was situated in a small space between the pipeline and the corral. For the next 10 minutes we tried everything possible to start the Comet but in the end there was only one miserable and embarrassing option left. We had to walk a couple of miles back to Hurley to borrow my dad's car and return with jumper cables to jump-start Gene's car.

When we arrived at my parents' house, it was 6:30 a.m. My mother was cooking breakfast and my dad was in the bathroom shaving. I don't know which of my parents had the biggest look of shock on their face as we sheepishly strolled through the front door. Embarrassed and totally exposed, I had to draw on my creative verbal skills to explain to them how Lana and I happened to be stuck in a car with a dead battery at a corral on the pigpen road at 5:30 in the morning.

As it turned out, I think having Lana with me that morning actually helped my situation somewhat. For reasons I will never know, my dad gave me the keys to his car and some jumper cables without subjecting me to his customary bout of whining and moaning. Maybe my parents didn't want to appear upset with me or make a scene in front of someone they didn't know.

Lana and I went back to the corral and jump-started Gene's car and returned my father's car. Then, I drove her back to Silver City and dropped her off at her parents' house at around 7:30 a.m. As we approached her house, Lana informed me that it would be best if I didn't accompany her inside to explain things to her parents. She said her father was overly protective and probably wouldn't be quite as civil as my parents were. We kissed once more and I watched her walk up to her porch and disappear through the front door. That was the last time I ever saw her.

CHAPTER EIGHT: DRINKING STORIES

"The best beer I ever had was the next one."...Famous quote, by Johnny Barfield.

How It All Started

The first time I ever got drunk was in eighth grade with Roy Hill and Pete Huerta. A couple of days before our drinking adventure, Roy liberated a bottle of vodka from his parents' bar in Bayard and we mixed it with some sodas we had bought at the Chino Club. The general consensus among our older teenaged friends who were self-proclaimed "veterans of the drinking wars" was that you couldn't smell vodka on your breath, which made it easy to disguise the fact you had been drinking. We believed this was true because it said right on the bottle that it "leaves you breathless".

We started spiking our sodas around 8:00 p.m. and walked around the streets of Hurley as we slugged them down. After a few drinks I remember laughing a lot and not being able to walk very well. Finally, Roy and Pete grabbed me by each arm and helped me find my way home.

Apparently my drinking buddies were in a sporting mood that night. When the three of us reached my house, they walked me up to my front porch and knocked on the front door. Then they took off running up the street and left me standing there alone. When my mother came to the door, she looked out onto the porch and saw me standing there, giggling and acting extremely stupid.

That was the first of many times over the next few years that I would come home in that condition. High school was the perfect environment for kids to party and have good times and, by the time I entered the halls of Cobre High School, I was hitting on all cylinders and running in full stride.

A Few Drinking Adventures (Viva La Peda)

Early one Sunday evening I was hanging out at the Chino Club with Tubby Porkman, John Dempsey and Eddie Bowman. It was July and the monsoon thunderclouds were building to the north. Out of boredom, we decided to drive to Santa Rita to buy some beer at the Chula Grande Bar. The Chula Grande was one of the few bars that sold package liquor on Sunday, even though it was against the law at the time. And it was common knowledge that, as long as they were illegally selling package liquor on Sunday, they might as well sell it to minors while they were at it.

We climbed into John's old 1953 Plymouth and set out for Santa Rita. John was driving, Eddie was in the passenger seat, and Tubby and I were in the back seat. The sky was getting darker as we headed north out of Bayard, and by the time we got to the Hanover intersection next to the railroad tracks, we encountered a torrential downpour of rain.

From the stop sign we turned right and accelerated up the long hill toward Santa Rita. Within a few seconds our vision through the windshield became blurry, even with the wipers flapping away at full speed. We were cruising along about 25 M.P.H. when, all of a sudden, I felt a jolt and heard a loud smashing sound. John quickly pulled the car off the road and got out to see what had happened. As the rain poured down, he walked to the front of the car and realized we had just hit a cow that had been standing in the middle of the road.

The impact from the accident smashed in the driver's side front quarter panel of the car. The fender was rubbing against the front tire and the car was unable to turn to the left. After several attempts, the four of us were eventually able to pry the quarter panel away from the tire just enough so we could steer the car and continue our journey.

By the time we jumped back into the car, everyone was sopping wet. Nevertheless, we failed to become discouraged by our stroke of bad luck and continued our Sunday evening beer run. By the time we pulled up to the package window at the Chula Grande, it had stopped raining and the night skies were clearing. John was initially upset about the damage to his parents' car, but after a few beers he mellowed out and we enjoyed our return trip to Hurley.

Another time I went out drinking with a fellow teammate on the Cobre High School tennis team named Charlie Reynolds. Charlie drove from Bayard to Hurley to pick me up in his parents' 1956 Chevy and we immediately headed toward Silver City for the evening. Along the way we got someone to buy us a bottle of cherry flavored vodka.

It was a school night and Charlie and I didn't want to stay out too late. We decided it would be best if we cruised around Silver while we drank the vodka and when we were done we would work our way back toward Bayard and Hurley.

By the time we finished the bottle, Charlie became so drunk he couldn't drive anymore. He finally pulled over and climbed into the back seat of the car to lie down while I took over the driving duties. By this time I was pretty drunk as well, but I was determined to make it back to Hurley without getting arrested.

I was driving somewhere between Arenas Valley and Central when it suddenly began to rain so hard that the windshield wipers were ineffective against the deluge of water covering the windshield. I had to roll down the driver's side window and stick my head out as we cruised down the highway in order to see where I was going. I immediately slowed down because the raindrops were pelting me so hard that my entire face was stinging.

I miraculously made it home to Hurley with Charlie still passed out in the back seat of his own car. Once the car was parked, I woke him up to tell him he had to drive back home to Bayard. When he finally climbed out of the car he was so disoriented and drunk that he didn't know where we were. The last thing I remember that night was when I stood next to his car and pointed up Elguea

Street to the west and said, "Charlie, go that way to get back to Bayard."

When I saw him at school the next day he looked pretty rough, but I was glad to see he miraculously navigated his way back to Bayard without crashing his car.

Fortunately, as I was growing up I acquired a knack for using humor to keep from getting in serious trouble or getting my skinny little butt kicked. With all of the drinking and running around we did, it was a miracle I graduated from high school without ever getting into a fight.

One night I was out drinking beer with some of my drinking buddies when I accidentally spilled about half of my beer in the back seat of Jack Hammerman's car. We were cruising through the A and W Root Beer Drive-In in Silver City at the time when I announced, "Oh, shit. I just spilled some of my beer on your car seat, Jack."

Jack quickly glanced into the rear view mirror before he pulled his car over and said, "Well, find something to wipe it up with."

(Now, it is important to know a little background history between Jack and me before you read on. He and I went through every grade since first grade together and he was one of the most good-natured guys I have ever known. He was also the star fullback on the football team and the fastest sprinter at Cobre High School. Furthermore, he weighed about 185 lbs. and was solid muscle.)

OK. Now back to the story. I looked around to find something to wipe up the puddle of beer next to me, but the only thing I could find was a brand new, white, Cobre High School letterman's sweater with lots of track and football medals pinned onto the large red letter "C" that was sewn onto the front of it. In desperate need of an absorbent material, I quickly grabbed the sweater and began using it to sop up the beer. After a minute or so, Jack peered again into the rear view mirror and asked, "Did you find anything to wipe up the beer with?"

Confident that I had done the right thing, I held up the sopping wet, beer stained letterman's sweater, and replied, "Just this sweater."

The next thing I knew, Jack jerked his head around and said, "You son-of-a-bitch. That's my brand new letterman's sweater. I'm gonna kick your fucking ass."

In a state of fury and rage, Jack jumped out and ran around the front of the car to get to my door. As soon as I realized I was going to die unless I reacted quickly, I hopped out and ran around the car to keep away from him. The last thing I wanted to do was get into a foot race with him, so staying by the car was my only chance of survival. My strategy paid off because I was able to keep the car between us as he chased me around it several times.

After a few minutes of playing "cat and mouse" I decided that my only chance of avoiding a genuine ass kicking was to start cracking jokes in hopes I could make Jack laugh. Somehow my strategy worked and it wasn't long before Jack's rage soon turned to deep laughter. Once I felt like Jack had calmed down enough, we eventually got back into his car and continued our beer drinking adventure as if nothing had ever happened. I think I may have paid a few bucks to get his sweater dry-cleaned, but that was sure a lot better than getting beat half to death.

The Amphibian Dump Truck
***

The boys were at it again. It was a Friday night and they were "cruising and boozing" on dirt roads southwest of Hurley. Duane had his parents' car and his friends Sammy, Brit, and Felix were along for the ride. Duane had just turned onto a remote secondary dirt road when the boys noticed something off in the distance.

"What's that weird shaped thing on the side of the road up ahead?" asked Brit.

"I don't know," replied Duane, as he tossed another empty beer can out the window. "It looks like some kind of tower with a conveyor belt. Let's go check it out."

Duane continued along the bumpy road until they approached what appeared to be some sort of construction site.

"Look. There's a bulldozer, a loader, and a couple of dump trucks behind that big metal tank," said Sammy.

Duane pointed to a big pile of gravel nearby and said, "Hey, It looks like one of those plants where they make asphalt for paving roads. That looks like a rock crusher over there."

Felix agreed as he flipped his empty beer can out the window. "Let's stop and check this place out."

The boys got out of the car and walked around the work area. It was late at night and they were the only ones there. After a few minutes of snooping around the plant in the dark, the boys heard Brit yell out, "Hey, there is a huge pond over here. Come take a look."

The other three boys walked over and noticed a large pond about 40 or 50 yards in diameter that apparently provided water for use in the operation of the plant. Sammy chucked his empty beer can out into the pond as he approached it and declared, "Shit. This pond can't be that deep. I'll bet you could drive all the way across it without getting stuck."

"No way," exclaimed Brit. "It's probably a lot deeper than you think."

Sammy looked at Brit and told him, "Bullshit. I bet I could easily drive one of those dump trucks across the pond with no problem."

When the other boys heard Sammy say that, Duane quickly responded with a sly grin on his face, "How much you want to bet?"

Sammy had just enough beer in him to dig in his heels and be as stubborn as a mule. After thinking about Duane's challenge for a few seconds, he looked at the other three boys and blurted out, "If you guys give me five bucks, I'll do it."

The other boys knew Sammy was getting a little drunk and didn't want to be proven wrong. They also knew that if they egged Sammy on, he would do just about anything for a laugh. Finally, Felix replied on behalf of all of the other boys, "You're on."

That was all Sammy needed to hear. He stumbled his way over to the nearest dump truck and climbed up onto the running board and reached up to grab the door handle. The truck was unlocked and the door flew open. The other boys began to laugh as they stood nearby and watched while Sammy climbed into the cab.

Once Sammy was sitting behind the large steering wheel, he immediately started fooling around with several buttons on the dashboard. Suddenly, the boys heard rrr, rrr, rrr, rrr, rrr, vaaarrrrrooooommmm, and the motor in the dump truck roared to life.

Everyone's attention was now on Sammy. He slammed the door shut and looked down at his friends. They were nearly hysterical with laughter. None of the other boys could believe Sammy had actually started the dump truck.

With a huge grin on his face, Sammy ground the shift lever into first gear. He pumped the accelerator pedal a couple of times, slowly let out the clutch, and the dump truck lunged forward.

At first Sammy found the truck hard to steer, but as it began to roll he was able to turn it around and slowly guide it toward the pond. With the shoreline in sight, he built up some speed and ground the transmission into second gear. He knew he would have to be moving along at a pretty good clip in order to make it across the pond.

Sammy began to bounce around in the driver's seat as he accelerated across the bumpy desert terrain. With his left elbow sticking out of the driver's side window and a gleeful look in his eyes, he glanced over one last time to see his friends laughing uncontrollably at the edge of the pond.

All of a sudden there was a big splash and Sammy felt the front of the truck enter the pond. He continued to look forward and kept his right foot pressed down hard onto the gas pedal. Tension mounted as he and the truck muscled their way into the ever-deepening water. All of the boys were aware that if the truck slowed down too much, Sammy probably wouldn't make it across to the other side.

The diesel motor was now revving at a high pitch as they splashed their way toward the center of the pond. It didn't take long before the water level quickly rose up over the running boards. Sammy suddenly noticed the rear tires were not getting as much traction as they were before and the truck was gradually beginning to lose forward momentum. As the RPM's of the diesel motor revved up even higher, Sammy continued onward with his foot clamped down on the gas pedal.

The truck quickly slowed down and finally came to a complete stop in the middle of the pond. Sammy frantically pushed in the clutch, downshifted into first gear, and let out the clutch. The truck only sank deeper into the mud. He then put the truck into reverse and tried to back out of the pond, but it only sank deeper until the rear axle finally bottomed-out in the soft mud below. As a last resort, Sammy tried to rock the truck back and forth by quickly shifting from first gear to reverse and back to first gear, but to no avail. Sammy and the dump truck were now stranded.

The other three boys stood near the edge of the pond, doubled over from laughter. Just when they thought they couldn't laugh any harder, Sammy opened the door to the cab and stepped down into the crotch-deep muddy water and began to wade his way to the shore.

"You dumb ass, Sammy," yelled Brit as he tried to catch his breath. "You owe us five bucks."

The boys could hear Sammy mumbling a string of cuss words as he waded towards them in the silted waters near the shore.

Partying with Silver High Kids

On a cold February night some friends and I were cruising around Silver City looking for something to do. David Combs was driving his parents' car and Toby Parker, Tod Smith, and I were his passengers. Somewhere in the downtown area of town we happened to run into one of our friends from Silver High School who told us about some Silver High kids who were having a party west of town on the Cliff highway.

Going to a party seemed like more fun than cruising around all evening, so we headed out of town for a few miles and turned north on a dirt road until we came upon a group of cars parked near a bonfire. We parked our car on the side of the road and walked up to the bonfire to make sure we were at the right place. Just as we had hoped, there were some Silver High boys, along with a few girls, standing around the fire drinking beer and visiting. As we approached the fire we encountered a couple of guys we knew and exchanged greetings with them. Everyone seemed friendly, but it didn't take us long to figure out that the Silver High boys were more interested in being alone with the girls than visiting with us.

For the next several minutes my friends and I stood around the campfire and talked among ourselves until we finished the beers we were drinking. Then, when we went back to David's car to get ourselves another beer we suddenly realized our beer supply was almost gone. We each reached into the front seat of the car and grabbed one last beer and returned to the bonfire. As we walked past a large tree on our way back to the fire we noticed that the SHS kids had stashed a few six packs of beer beneath the low hanging branches.

We huddled around the fire once again and slowly finished our last beers, while the Silver High boys continued to flirt with the girls and ignore us. Once we polished off our last beers, we walked back to David's car to discuss whether we should stay at the party or go back to town and buy more beer. We knew if we stayed at the party for a while longer we would have to bum our next beer from the Silver High kids. Based on our lukewarm reception, we figured that bumming beer from them was probably not a good idea. We also decided that if we left the party to go buy beer in town, we probably wouldn't return to the party because we weren't having that much fun anyway.

Finally, we concluded that the Silver High kids didn't want us at their party and were being a little snooty toward us. Therefore, it would be best if we left. And, as long as we were leaving, we might as well take some of their beer with us. Of course, if we were going to steal their beer right out from under their noses, we needed to figure out how to load it into our car and leave the party without getting caught or creating a scene.

Here was our plan. Tod and I agreed to serve as decoys. Our job was to distract the Silver High kids while David and Toby snatched their beer. So, Tod and I went back to our car, removed our pants, and threw them into the back seat of David's car. Then, we walked back over to the bonfire where the boys were getting cuddly and cozy with the girls.

Once the Silver High kids saw Tod and I approach the fire wearing only our jackets, underwear, and shoes, everyone began to laugh. We then paraded around the fire and started cracking jokes and intentionally acting goofy to preoccupy the Silver High kids. Meanwhile, David and Toby snuck over behind the tree where their beer was stashed, grabbed a few six-packs, and quickly threw the beer into the back seat of our car. When they were done, they gave us the signal indicating that the beer was loaded and it was time to leave.

As the four of us piled into David's car to make our escape, one of the Silver High guys noticed that most of their beer was gone. Once he saw us scrambling into our car, he quickly sensed something was fishy and walked over toward us to investigate.

Toby was sitting shotgun and rolled down the window as the boy approached. When he got to the car he placed his hands on the passenger side door of the car and leaned forward to talk to us through the open window. He made a simple plea. "Hey, c'mon guys, give us our beer back."

Toby quickly reached down to the floorboard near his feet and grabbed a fairly heavy stick that he had picked up near the bonfire. As the kid pleaded with us to return the beer, Toby began hitting the top of the door panel with the stick, forcing the kid to continually move his hands around to avoid getting his fingers rapped. Whap...Whap...Whap...Whap... and the kid eventually stood up and took his hands away from the car door. As soon as he stepped away from the car to protect his fingers, David punched the accelerator and off we went with their stash of beer.

When we got back to town we went to a second story apartment on the corner of Broadway and Texas Street that belonged to Toby's older brother. For the remainder of the evening we had our own party in the warmth of his cozy little abode. And best of all, the beer was compliments of our good friends from Silver High School.

Teddy's Beam

About 9:00 p.m. one evening during our senior year in high school, Tod and Greg returned to Tod's house after they had been out drinking a few beers. When they walked into the living room they noticed Tod's younger brother Teddy, who was about 5 years old at the time, lying on the couch watching TV in his "tidy-whitey" underwear. As usual, Teddy had his thumb in his mouth with his index finger curled around the bridge of his nose and was oblivious to everything except the TV in front of him. Teddy was a fun kid and the older boys used to always joke around with him because he made them laugh.

Shortly after they sat down to join Teddy in the TV room, Greg realized he had a miniature bottle of Jim Beam whiskey in his pocket that was left over from their night of carousing. He playfully pulled the little bottle out of his pocket and asked Teddy if he wanted to take a drink. To his surprise Teddy took the bottle and gulped it down in a couple of sips.

It wasn't long before the booze kicked in and young Teddy became quite entertaining to watch. For the remainder of the evening he stumbled around the house, laughing at everything and acting extremely silly. In hindsight, it was a lucky thing his parents weren't home because they probably wouldn't have found much humor in seeing their underwear-clad five-year-old running all over the house acting like a wild animal.

Ridge Road Theatre

One night some friends and I were cruising on the Ridge Road south of Hurley with an ice chest full of beer. It was common practice in our drinking circle to stop every few miles and get out of the car and drink beer, throw a Frisbee or a football around, and simply horse around.

As the evening progressed, we decided to turn onto a less traveled side road and continue driving until we found a suitable place to get out of the car to drink. We poked along on the bumpy stock tank road until we finally found a place that was remote and private. At the end of the road, we pulled over and took the ice chest out of the back seat and placed it near the front bumper of the car, and the party was on.

Everyone grabbed a cold beer out of the ice chest and leaned against the hood of the car to begin another one of our coveted "Ridge Road bullshit sessions". It was one of those rare nights where the beers were going down nicely and everyone was in a good mood. Guys were telling jokes and laughing, and it wasn't long before everyone began to get fairly drunk and animated.

Toby Parker was with us that night and, if there was one thing he loved to do when he drank, it was crack jokes and make the rest of us laugh. This particular night Toby was on a roll. Over the course of the evening he kept getting funnier and funnier and the beer continued to taste better and better. Finally, while we were still gathered around the hood of the car, Toby reached inside the window on the driver's side door and turned on the headlights. Then, he walked back around to the front of the car and, before we knew it, he was putting on an impromptu one-man skit with the headlights illuminating his outdoor stage.

Toby's skit had two characters in it and he was both of them. He would stand on one side of the headlight beams and pretend he was a cowboy. Then he would jump over to the other side and pretend he was a Mexican. He improvised a short dialogue between the two angry characters until finally the cowboy, in a deep Texas drawl, said to the Mexican, "By God, I'm gonna have to whup yer sorry "Meskin" ass."

Then he jumped over to the other side and became the Mexican. Speaking in broken English, he said something like, "Chinga tu madre, you pinche Gringo salado. I could keek your ass a la chingada."

He then jumped back to the cowboy's side and said, "Well put up your dukes, you sombitch."

Suddenly the Mexican started flailing and kicking at the cowboy while the cowboy tried to box the Mexican. Toby jumped back and forth several times as he was kicking and swinging, and the fight was on. Eventually, he wrapped his arms around himself and threw himself down onto the ground and rolled and thrashed around while his fists and feet were flying in every direction. Two guys couldn't get into a better fight than Toby got into with himself. Every couple of seconds a fist would come flying up out of the cloud of dust and the cuss words, in both English and Spanish, were flowing freely.

Finally, after a couple of minutes of intense fighting, Toby jumped up from the ground and ran toward a three-strand barbed wire fence that was nearby. When he got to the fence he dove head first over the top strand of wire. When he landed on the other side he did a perfect summersault to break his fall and then stood up to face the headlights of the car. He then threw his hands up in the air and took a bow before his captivated audience.

Just when we thought the skit was over, Toby turned and ran toward a yucca standing a few yards away and tackled it headfirst, as if he was a linebacker on the football team. By the time he was done we were laughing so hard we were crying. Of all the things I had ever witnessed during my numerous nights of drinking, this may have been the funniest and most incredible of them all.

Hard Luck Stories

One night during my senior year in high school I was out drinking with my friends Toby Parker, Willy Martin, and Roy Hill. We were cruising in Roy's white Ford pick-up that had a camper mounted on the bed. We had just bought a case of beer and were headed into Central (Santa Clara) when we decided the cab was too crowded for four people. We pulled over just outside of town and Roy and Toby walked to the back of the truck and climbed into the camper while Willy and I remained in the cab. Willy assumed the driving duties and I rode on the passenger side.

As we drove through Central, Willy and I sipped on our beers and began a rather serious discussion about our plans after graduation from high school and how we wanted to go to college and be successful in life. Willy made very good grades in school and we both agreed that he had a great chance to be successful at whatever career he pursued. I, on the other hand, knew I would have to acquire some self-discipline if I were to graduate from college.

By the time Willy finished his beer, I had popped open another one and handed it to him as we continued to talk. In the middle of our discussion Willy happened to glance into the rear view mirror and noticed a car behind us. As the car got closer, we kept our beers down and made it a point to drive very carefully in case it was a cop who was following us. Willy placed both hands on the steering wheel and kept an eye on the speedometer to make sure he wasn't speeding.

Before we had a chance to turn off on a side street, the cop behind us turned on his red lights and pulled up close behind us. Everything happened so fast we didn't have a chance to slug down the beers we had in our hand and there was nowhere to stash the three six packs lying on the floorboard near my feet. We slowly pulled off to the side of the street and waited to see why the cop pulled us over.

The cop walked up to the driver's side door and asked Willy for his driver's license. Once Willy handed him the license, he told us that the reason he pulled us over was because we had crossed the centerline of the road a ways back. Willy and I both knew that if we did indeed cross the centerline of the street, it was hardly noticeable. We had been driving slowly and paying attention to all of the road signs. It soon became clear that the cop was looking for an excuse to pull us over because he was on the lookout for under-aged drinkers, and we fit the profile perfectly.

When the cop shined his flashlight into the cab of the truck, the first thing he noticed was the beer on the floorboard. Unfortunately for us, that was all he needed to see before he made us get out of the truck. He then took my driver's license, asked us a few questions, and told us to get into the back of the patrol car. After he was done snooping around the cab in search of more beer, he returned to the patrol car and made a call on the radio to request a toe truck. Finally, he put the patrol car in gear and took Willy and me on a scenic, one-way cruise through the charming streets of Central. Our destination was the police station, and we were going to jail.

Once we arrived at police headquarters, the cop told us we had to get a parent to come pick us up and take us home. Willy explained that his parents were gone for a couple of months and he was living temporarily with the Foy family in Bayard. He told the police that his guardian was Tommy Foy Sr.

Willy gave an officer Mr. Foy's phone number so he could call him from the dispatcher's desk as we stood nearby. It took a few minutes to apprise Mr. Foy of the situation and they asked him to come to the police station to pick us up and take us home. When the officer was done talking, he hung up the phone and told us Mr. Foy was on his way.

As time slowly ticked away, Willy and I were beginning to dread the thought of seeing Tommy Foy Sr. walk into the police station at 11:00 p.m. to bail us out of jail. We figured we were most certainly going to get our asses chewed out, and when we were done with that, we were going to have to deal with the juvenile courts. To make matters even worse, Willy was especially embarrassed about creating problems for Mr. Foy while he was living with his family.

About a half an hour later Mr. Foy pulled up in front of the police station, which was strategically located across the street from the Brown Derby Night Club. He got out of his car and entered the dispatcher's area of the police station where we were being held. As he walked through the door, Willy and I had to do a double-take to make sure we weren't seeing things. Into the police station strolled Mr. Foy wearing his bedroom slippers and a bathrobe. Apparently he had been asleep in bed when the Central police called him.

Mr. Foy was an attorney in Silver City and everybody at the station knew him well. Once he was briefed about our situation, he informed the officer that he would act as Willy's guardian and take care of whatever needed to be done.

He then read the police report and talked for a few more minutes with the officer. When he was done talking and the matter was settled, we followed him out to the car and drove away.

At first it was difficult to tell whether Mr. Foy was upset for having to deal with our little problem, but to our surprise, he handled the situation with respect and dignity. He asked us a few questions but didn't lecture us or give us a hard time about what had happened. The good news was he was able to schmoose the police officer into dropping our charges. The bad news was, Willy and I were taken straight home and were done for the night.

Meanwhile, the tow truck came to pick up Roy's truck from the side of the road. The driver attached a chain to the front bumper, hoisted the front end off of the ground, and towed the truck away. Miraculously, neither the police officer nor the tow truck driver ever checked the camper to see if anyone was inside. Willy and I found out the next day that Toby and Roy had locked themselves inside the camper just as the police pulled us over and remained perfectly still throughout the entire ordeal.

The truck was towed to Bayard and locked in a shop at the Porter Oil facility in the downtown area. As soon as the tow truck driver locked the shop door and slammed it shut, he drove away. Toby and Roy continued to lie quietly in the camper for a few minutes to make sure the coast was clear. Then, they quickly climbed out of the camper and headed for the door. After they exited the shop they carefully relocked the door and set out on foot to make their final escape.

As Toby and Roy began walking across the Porter Oil property they quickly figured out where they were. They couldn't have had better luck. Toby's house happened to be located right next to the Porter Oil yard, about 50 yards away. Realizing their good fortune, they simply walked over to Toby's place and hopped into his parents' little yellow Datsun sedan and drove away. Three minutes later they were sitting at the nearest package liquor window ordering more beer and gearing up for a second round of drinking.

The two boys continued partying into the early morning hours to celebrate their escape from the Central police. They figured Willy and I were probably still in jail as they cruised around and pounded more beers. As far as I was concerned, I was happy the police didn't arrest them, but I was pissed off because Willy and I didn't get to go out again and raise more hell.

During our last couple of years of high school, things got pretty wild. It seemed like every time we turned around there was another party somewhere in the county. Unfortunately, our revved-up social lives vastly increased our chances of becoming involved in skirmishes with local law enforcement agencies and, for many of us, our grades in school weren't what they could have been.

Around 9:00 p.m. one Saturday evening, Jack Hammerman, David Combs, and I were cruising around Silver City with Cleto Ramirez in his parents' car. We had just bought an ice-cold case of Coors in bottles and were driving through the parking lot of the A and W Root Beer Drive-In to see if we could run into some girls.

I don't know what Cleto did wrong as he was driving, but a cop followed us into the parking lot and turned on his red lights to pull us over. The untouched case of beer was in the back seat and we were unable to hide it before the cop came to the car and shined his flashlight inside. To make a long story short, we were arrested and taken to the Grant County jail, located on the second floor of the Grant County Courthouse.

Once we were booked and thrown into jail cells, we were told we weren't going to get out of jail until our parents came to pick us up. We all gave the cops our home phone numbers but the only person the police made contact with was David's father, Buford Combs. Apparently, Mr. Combs agreed to come get all of us and give us a ride home.

About an hour after the calls were made, Mr. Combs showed up at the jail and bailed us out. Cleto got into trouble with his parents because his car was impounded and they had to pay money for its release. Jack and I got off the hook because our parents never found out we were in jail. I always felt it was a crying shame we never even got to open one bottle of beer out of our ice-cold case of Coors before we were arrested. I'm sure the police officers who were involved in our arrest acted ethically and disposed of the beer according to standard procedure.

As long as I'm on the subject of getting thrown in jail, I might as well tell you one more story that represents the pinnacle of our high school drinking careers. It would be impossible to recount the vast majority of parties and wild times we had, but this particular story should give you a pretty good idea of what it was like to be a graduating senior at Cobre High School in 1968.

Finally, after 12 long years of confinement in the state sponsored youth slave labor camp commonly known as the public schools, the door to the Cobre High birdcage was about to open. After all those years, it was our turn to fly freely, off into the wild, to make our mark in life. It was May of 1968, and many of the "soon to be" graduates were friends whom had attended classes with me since first grade. There was an aura of festivity and excitement in the school during the last few days of class, and the seniors were released a week before the underclassmen in celebration of "Senior Week".

I'd be a liar if I told you we didn't party like crazy during Senior Week. My friends and I knew there was something going on every night and we made it a point to cruise around until we found it. We would drink until all hours of the night and then go out and do it again the following night. By the time graduation day rolled around, everyone was wound up and ready to make our graduation experience one for the record books.

A group of my fellow seniors and I decided that the best way to kick off graduation day would be to spend the day in Palomas at the Paquimé Night Club. When we were done there we would return for graduation ceremonies "lookin' out of one eye", as Troy Wakefield used to say. After the ceremony we would finally have one last big party somewhere out in the boondocks until the sun came up.

Our plan was executed on schedule. When David Combs came to Hurley to pick up Roy Hill and me at 9:30 a.m., he had our good friends Toby and Willy in the car with him. Roy and I were icing down a case of beer under a shade tree in his front yard when the other boys pulled up in front of the house. Roy always liked to take a garden hose and squirt a little water over the iced down beer because it made the beer get cold quickly. (Roy's parents owned a bar in Bayard and if there was anyone who knew how to enhance the flavor and drinkability of booze, it was Roy). When we were done we loaded the ice chest into David's car and headed for Palomas. By the time we got to Deming most of the beer was gone.

It was a hot, sunny day in Palomas as we pulled into the parking lot on the U.S. side of the border. We parked the car and walked through the Mexican customs checkpoint and continued down the main dirt street into Palomas. We went about a half a block from the border and headed straight to the Paquimé Nightclub, where we immediately bellied up to the bar and ordered a round of beers.

The Paquimé was a fairly large building with a bar in front and a dance hall and restaurant in the back. As you walked into the Paquimé through the front entrance, the bar stretched from left to right and the customers sat at bar stools with their backs to the front door. It always took a minute for your eyes to adjust to the dark barroom, especially if it was hot, dry, and sunny outside. If you had been drinking, it took even longer for your eyes to adjust.

The floors were made of concrete and the urinal in the men's restroom was a long trough made of Mexican tile. The trough usually had a few cigarette butts floating around in it and on a good day you could find puke splattered near the drain in the center. Fortunately, the swamp coolers kept the building nice and cool and tended to spread the bathroom stench over a larger area so that the smell wasn't too bad at any seat in the bar.

There were doorways at either end of the bar that led you into the dance hall area. The dance hall had a stage and a large dance floor, with tables situated around the perimeter of it. On Sundays people would drive to the Paquimé to enjoy a Mexican dance band and eat a cheap steak while they got drunk and partied with their friends. The joint was usually crawling with waiters and the service was excellent. It was a great place for both old and young Americans to get a taste of the good times in lawless Mexico.

Our first beer at the Paquimé was ice cold and went down very quickly, so we ordered another one, and then another one. After a while, now that we were drunk and had become close friends with the bartender, he recommended a drink called a "Zombie", which consisted of a splash of just about every liquor on the shelf. As one could imagine, the Zombie was a fairly stiff drink. After about two or three Zombies we quickly moved up a few notches on the "universal borracho scale".

All in all, we were in the Paquimé for about three hours. We were certainly drunk by then, but we hadn't lost track of time. By mid afternoon we decided to go walking around town to sober up a little before we made the long drive home for graduation ceremonies that evening.

We left the bar with our drinks in hand, and along the way Toby and I wandered into the little store next to the Paquimé called Tillie's. As we strolled up and down the aisles of the store, we casually sipped our Zombies through a straw. The shelves were full of things like brightly colored toy snakes made out of short sections of wood (the sections would pivot back and forth to make the snake wiggle like a real snake), guiros (a musical instrument that looks like a fish and is played by scraping a stick along the corrugated ripples of the fish's back), wooden claves and maracas, and of course, baleros (the wooden toy with a hollowed out cup on the end of a handle, with a wooden ball on the end of a string. The object of the toy game was to try to make the ball swing around and land inside of the cup). There were also Mexican rugs, cheap leather goods, clothes, shoes, sombreros, shot glasses, and tons of other things too numerous to mention.

On a shelf in the back of the store, Toby and I noticed a woman's wig mounted on a white Styrofoam display head. I looked over to Toby to get his attention as we walked down the aisle toward the wig. I wanted to make Toby laugh, so I drew some of my drink up into the straw and blew it out the other end. Suddenly, a small wad of my Zombie hurled through the air and landed on the wig. Toby smiled and tried to control his laughter.

I must have been drunker than I thought because the owner of the store had apparently been watching every move I made. Her name was Tillie and she immediately came back and started yelling at me and kicked both of us out of the store. Toby and I sheepishly walked back out into the street as Tillie followed us, hands flailing and yelling at us every step of the way. By now we had created quite a scene on the main street of Palomas, so we decided to walk toward a side street to get away from her. Tillie eventually relented and turned around to walk back to her store, but it was now apparent that Toby and I had just about worn out our welcome for the day in Palomas.

We quickly doubled back toward the border crossing by heading up another side street. We figured it would be wise to get out of town immediately in case Tillie decided to catch up to us and raise more hell. Unfortunately, Palomas was Tillie's town and she was one step ahead of us. As we approached the guard station at the border crossing, Tillie was already standing there among the guards and telling them "¡Estos!", as she pointed towards us.

Immediately one of the guards approached us and said in a firm voice, "Ven conmigo."

As we turned to follow the guard, Toby and I were starting to get a little more concerned about our situation. It seemed like our graduation day was suddenly unraveling and things were beginning to take a turn for the worse. Up until now, things had been pretty damn funny.

The guard led us down a dirt side street, around a corner, and down another street until we arrived at a makeshift police headquarters. As soon as we arrived, a Mexican police officer confiscated our wallets and led us into a large enclosed outdoor courtyard that was surrounded by tall adobe walls lined with broken glass along the top. As we stood in the hot sun looking up at the jagged edges of the broken glass, we suddenly realized we were officially in a Mexican jail.

It was starting to get a little late in the afternoon when it dawned on us we might miss our high school graduation. We knew that if we didn't come up with a plan to get out of jail pronto, our friends would have to leave us there for the night. After some frantic deliberation, we approached one of the guards and asked him, "What do we need to do to get out of here?"

He told us we needed to pay a fine before he would release us. That was a problem for us because neither Toby nor I had any money in our confiscated wallets. The only way we could come up with any money for the fine was to talk the jailer into letting one of us out of jail to go find our friends.

At first the guard didn't want to let either one of us out, but after a few minutes of haggling he finally relented and agreed to let Toby leave. I remained in the courtyard. Within a few minutes Toby and the other boys returned and we eventually bargained the guard down to a fine of $7 to let us out of jail. We didn't waste a minute as we quickly left the jail and crossed the border to return to our car.

By the time we got back on the road toward Deming we were definitely pressed for time. We knew we had an hour and a half drive ahead of us and we needed time to shower and get dressed in our caps and gowns before graduation. David did a good job of driving and kept the car moving along as fast as possible without catching the attention of the highway patrol.

Everyone was still fairly drunk as we cruised through Columbus and, for some reason, an argument developed between Willy and Roy as we headed out of town toward Deming. Within minutes they were screaming at each other and ordered David to stop the car so they could get out and fight. Finally, after a few miles of screaming and pleading, David pulled over onto the side of the road. Everyone climbed out of the car and Roy and Willy began to beat the hell out of each other.

The fight ended with both boys getting dirty, bloody and exhausted. Things quickly calmed down a bit and we got back into the car and continued on our way. We weren't even five miles down the road before Roy and Willie were at each other's throats again and demanded that David stop the car for another round of fighting.

Again David pulled over and another slugfest ensued. Both boys were now showing quite an assortment of cuts, lumps and bruises on their faces and bodies. When Roy and Willy were done with their second fight, we got back into the car and David again continued down the road. At last, we thought their problems were finally resolved and the fighting was over for the day.

We soon realized we were wrong. Within a matter of minutes they were screaming at each other again and demanding to fight a third time. By now, David was starting to get really mad at Willy and Roy. Not only was he fed up with all of the screaming and drama in the car, he knew we were all going to be late for graduation if we continued to pull over and allow the drunken brawls to continue.

Roy and Willy wouldn't let things rest. They continued to dog each other until David finally got fed up with both of them and stopped the car. This time it was he and Roy who were going to fight. Fortunately, their fight turned out to be the last one of the afternoon. Roy was now totally exhausted from his three fights and the remainder of the drive home was fairly quiet and uneventful. We somehow made it home with just enough time to get ready for the graduation ceremony.

My most memorable moment during the ceremony was watching Willy go to the podium and receive his Navy R.O.T.C. scholarship to U.N.M. He was an honor student and scored very high on his college entrance exams. As he accepted his awards at the podium, I could clearly see his black eye, fat lip, and numerous marks and lumps all over his face from the fights with Roy. I've often wondered what the principal was thinking as he handed Willy his diploma that night.

Word leaked out at the ceremony about the huge graduation party that was about to take place under the cottonwood trees at Cameron Creek, just west of Hurley. Even though my friends and I were feeling tired and hung-over from the day's activities in Palomas, we somehow found our second wind and looked forward to staying up all night long. As soon as we left Cobre High School for the last time, we bought more beer and cruised out to the party spot to celebrate our newly acquired status as high school graduates.

By the time we arrived, the party was in full swing. Cars were parked everywhere and people were standing around visiting and having fun. This was the one party we had been looking forward to because it was our last opportunity to spend time with our classmates. Everyone had lots of beer and some of the kids were already getting wound up.

Toby and I hadn't been at the party for an hour when, all of a sudden, we looked up and noticed a group of cop cars descending down the hill toward the party. Panic spread like wildfire. The kids who drove cars to the party were trapped and had nowhere to go, but many of us who didn't have cars decided to scatter in several directions to avoid getting caught.

Making a split second decision, Toby and I ran across Cameron Creek and onto the hillside west of the party. From our vantage point we could see the cops pull up and begin shining their flashlights everywhere, confiscating beer, and sending kids home from the party. Before long there was a steady line of cars heading back up the hill and the party began to dwindle.

The fact that the cops ruined our graduation party pissed Toby and me off. We had been waiting years for this moment and suddenly felt the need to let the cops know we didn't approve of their actions. From the hillside where we stood, we began to yell, "Fuck you, pigs," as the cops continued to break up the party. The officers repeatedly shined their flashlights toward us as we yelled, but they were smart enough to know they would never be able to catch us.

Toby and I looked on in dismay as the cops escorted the last car up the hill and out of sight. The canyon grew eerily quiet and we were now alone and on our own. It was now time to walk several miles back to Hurley in the dark, and we would have to stay away from the roads to avoid being picked up by the police.

After more than two hours of bushwhacking across the prairie in the dark of night, Toby and I finally made it back to the highway near North Hurley. We were both exhausted from the long and eventful day and neither of us relished the idea of hitchhiking or walking home at 3:30 in the morning. As a last resort, we walked to Wanda Hinson's house nearby and woke her up to ask her for a ride home. We explained our predicament to her and, without hesitation she got dressed and gave us a ride home. It was after 4:00 a.m. when she dropped me off, and I fell asleep as soon as my head hit the pillow. Wanda was one of our best friends and she certainly didn't let us down that night.

Water Skiing Stories

As you may have been able to tell from my previous stories, one of my best drinking buddies in high school was a kid named David Combs. I had known David since we were four or five years old and we did a lot of fun things together throughout our school days. His parents enjoyed having kids around and they were always friendly and generous to me when I was at their home.

David's parents had a ski boat they kept in a storage unit near Elephant Butte Lake, and during the summers they would invite me to go water skiing on the weekends. Some of my fondest high school memories are from the many trips we took to the lake. We would always set up our camp at Lion's Beach and take water skiing excursions all over the lake from there. When David and I weren't skiing, we would play Frisbee on the beach or walk along the shore and look for girls at the neighboring campsites.

Water skiing was a very fun activity but, if you weren't careful, there were many ways in which danger could suddenly sneak up on you. For example, one morning David and I were skiing tandem and we signaled for the driver to take us close to the beach to drop us off at our campsite. With the boat at full throttle (over 30 mph.) the driver circled toward the shallow water so David and I could swing wide and pick up some speed to help us catapult toward the beach. If our timing was right, we could let go of the towrope and coast right up to the water's edge without having to swim ashore.

For some reason I wasn't paying attention and, before I knew it, my skis slid up onto the beach. Now, the laws of physics dictate that whenever a situation like this occurs, the skis stop abruptly but the individual who was wearing them continues to travel forward and becomes temporarily airborne. With the forces of gravity, velocity and friction controlling my forward momentum in this situation, I predictably blasted my way through our campsite and smashed through a tent as I helplessly tumbled end-over-end across the beach.

When I finally came to a stop, my back, knees, and shoulders were bleeding from sand abrasion. For all practical purposes, the accident put an end to my skiing for the weekend because I didn't want to go into the water again with so many open wounds. Sometimes it takes me a while to learn certain things, but this was one mistake I never made again.

The perils of water skiing have been known to manifest themselves in a variety of strange ways. If you are willing to take certain risks in order to partake in such a seemingly harmless activity, then you should not be surprised if the hand of terror or even death reaches out to brush against you. I know it may sound confusing to hear me say this in the context of a story about something as mundane as water skiing, but after a couple of unnerving experiences, I can tell you with relative confidence that sometimes it is better to stay out of the water. Yes, sometimes it is better to stay out of the water.

The following summer David's parents went to the lake one Friday afternoon. David and I planned to join them later that night, but we told his parents we wanted to hang out in Silver for the evening before we drove to the lake in his parents' car.

The real reason we didn't go to the lake earlier in the evening was because we wanted to attempt a feat we had discussed many times before but had never been able to accomplish. We wanted to drink a case of beer apiece. David and I considered ourselves to be accomplished party animals and felt that drinking 24 beers apiece was within our reach. We took a great deal of pride in the fact that, as seniors in high school, we could pound a shit-load of beers without getting too drunk or sick.

By the time we left Silver City at around midnight we were already blistering drunk and a little bit sleepy. We drove late into the night and continued our drinking binge as we cruised over the Black Range toward Hillsboro. By the time we got to Emory Pass we had drunk 20 beers apiece and fatigue was becoming more of an issue by the minute. The sharp curves and steep cliffs on the side of the mountainous road didn't intimidate us that night because we had driven over the Black Range many times before and were very familiar with the road.

As we descended down the east side of the Black Range, David told me he was starting to nod off behind the wheel and asked me to take over for him. I agreed, so we pulled over and changed seats and continued down the road. I miraculously made it to Kingston and beyond Hillsboro as David dozed away in the passenger seat.

Once we got to the straight stretch of road between Hillsboro and Caballo Lake, my eyelids were starting to feel like lead and I was fighting to stay awake. At one point I was cruising about 60 m.p.h. when, all of a sudden, I heard gravel hitting the bottom of the car. When I finally opened my eyes, my initial reaction was to slam on the brakes and nudge the steering wheel enough to get back onto the pavement. Before I knew it, the car was out of control and began to spin in a circle as we went down the road. I kept my foot on the brakes as the car continued to spin in hopes we would slow down more quickly.

Somehow we ended up in the middle of the road, surrounded by a cloud of dust and the smell of burnt rubber. I looked over to David and said, "I think you better take over for me. I'm too drunk to drive."

Once the dust settled, we got out of the car to switch drivers again. Even though we were somewhat alarmed at what had just happened, we were too drunk and tired to care. With David now driving and me dozing against the passenger door, we eventually made it through downtown T or C and turned east at the intersection by the Sierra County Courthouse. This was the final stretch of road heading toward the lake and we were only about 20 minutes from Lyon's

Beach.

By the time we got past the courthouse, David woke me up to pop open our 22nd beer. The party was still alive, but we were overcome with fatigue once again just a few miles down the road. It wasn't long before David was having trouble driving. Just as we approached the bridge that crossed the Rio Grande River, David nodded off one final time and I was too drunk to notice. The last thing I remember was watching the car gradually leave the road and slide sideways toward the bridge ahead. Then, I heard a loud noise and we suddenly came to a stop at the riverbank next to the bridge. Luckily, next to the bridge was a utility pole that was directly in our path. The rear of the car had spun around and slammed into it.

Once we came to our senses, we got out of the car and staggered around to check for damage. The first thing we noticed was the large dent in the rear quarter panel where the utility pole had caved it in. The lid to the trunk also had a large dent and it wouldn't stay shut, no matter how hard we slammed it down. The other thing we noticed was, the utility pole was the only thing that kept us from going into the water.

David and I climbed back into the car one final time and drove out to the lake with the trunk bobbing up and down every time we hit a bump. We finally rolled into the campsite at about 3:30 a.m. and got our bedrolls out of the trunk and went to sleep. We were as drunk as we could possibly be without getting sick and we were still at 22 beers apiece.

We were fast asleep at about 7:30 a.m. when, all of a sudden, we heard a loud slamming noise nearby and then someone yelled, "God damn it."

David and I slowly rolled over in our bedrolls and lifted our throbbing heads to find out where all the commotion was coming from. As we slowly made the transition from a deep sleep to semi-consciousness, we were viciously greeted with a dreadful case of nausea, dehydration, and a splitting headache. I remember peering through my blood shot, squinting eyes and seeing David's father standing next to the rear of the car. He tried to slam the trunk lid shut once more, but it just bounced back up in his face.

All hell broke loose at that point. Mr. Combs abruptly walked over to us and saw to it that we got our asses out of bed to answer a few friendly questions. David and I could tell by his tone of voice that our party was officially over for the weekend.

By 10:00 a.m., Mr. Combs had both of us standing in the lobby of the T or C police station to report the accident. David told the cops he had fallen asleep while he was driving to the lake. As I recall, we didn't mention anything about being so drunk at the time of the accident we couldn't see straight. The police also failed to notice the shadows being cast onto the sidewalk from the evaporation of alcohol fumes emanating from the tops of our heads as we stood before them in the bright sun and sweltering heat.

To cap off the morning's activities, David was issued a traffic citation for careless driving. By the time we returned to the lake we were in a state of absolute physical misery and spent the remainder of the weekend licking our hangover wounds and feeling shameful for wrecking his family's car. We also felt a tad foolish for nearly driving into the river and killing ourselves.

As I thought about our accident at the bridge on the Rio Grande River over the next few weeks, I came to realize that the only thing determining whether we lived or died that night was the path of the car as it spun out of control. A few inches one way or the other and the outcome of our reckless misadventure could have turned out tragically different. On several occasions, as I would fall into a deep slumber at night, a very dark and disturbing image would continually reoccur that left me with a feeling of tension and uneasiness. Then, without warning, I would suddenly awaken to a soft voice calling from some unknown place in time that gently whispered so only I could hear, "Sometimes it is better to stay out of the water".

CHAPTER NINE: LIFE AFTER HIGH SCHOOL

"I bet the cops were glad to see you leave town."

Summer Jobs

The summer after high school graduation was busy and action packed for most kids in my class. Some kids joined the military and were soon shipped to Viet Nam while others found permanent jobs or prepared to enter college. Many of the college bound kids looked for temporary summer jobs to help pay for their freshman college expenses.

A few of the boys in my class signed up to be stand-by fire fighters for the Forest Service. I was on the stand-by list and I made it a point to stay close to home during the hot month of June in case the Forest Service called. The pay could be very good if the spring and summer were dry and there were lots of fires. The fire season typically ended by the middle of July when the monsoon rains saturated the forest and reduced the threat of wildfire.

It wasn't long before a fire bust occurred and several of us were called to report to the Forest Service headquarters on Hudson Street in Silver City. We were each issued a hard hat, a fire pack, and some tools. The fire pack was a backpack made of canvas and some sort of plywood frame with shoulder straps. The packs contained a few boxes of C-rations, which were military food rations consisting of canned goods. Each box had several cans containing a main course, fruit, bread, a dessert, and a small can opener about the shape and size of a paper clip. Also included in the fire pack was a disposable paper bedroll and one or two round canteens that were orange in color and held a half a gallon of water each. The tools we received were a shovel and a Pulaski, which was a combination of an axe and a hoe. We also were issued a McCloud, which was sort of a rake/fire-line digging tool, but most fire fighters rarely used them. We were instructed to bury our empty food cans and paper bedroll when we finished putting out the fire so we wouldn't have to carry the extra weight in our packs as we hiked out to the nearest road.

From Silver City we were driven out to Meown Firebase, located on the North Star Mesa road to Wall Lake. The base consisted of a helicopter landing-pad, an office, living quarters for fire fighters, and a workstation. Firefighters would spend the day working around the firebase until we were dispatched to fires via helicopter.

Fire fighters would frequently stop by the helitack foreman's office during the course of the day to keep informed of new fires in the forest. Eusavio Serna was the foreman, and the trailer that served as his office was equipped with a forest service radio, a desk, and a large Gila National Forest map mounted on the wall. There were pins with colored heads stuck in the map that indicated the location of fires. Eusavio had everyone's name on a waiting list for fires and, whenever a new fire was reported, the people at the top of the list would fly out to man the fire. Whenever your name was called you would stack your fire pack and tools in the cargo baskets that were mounted on the helicopter's skid bars. Once the pilot ran through their pre-flight checklist, you would board the ship and take off to the fire.

The helicopter they used at the time was a Bell 47 helicopter that had a large Plexiglas bubble for a cockpit. This was a fun helicopter because the bubble curved around and came almost to where you placed your feet on the floorboard. The pilot and passengers could see clearly in all directions, including directly below your feet. I remember flying to a fire once when we ran across a large herd of elk running through the forest below. The pilot descended to about 50 feet above the trees and fell in behind the herd as they were on the run. We followed them for about half a mile before we pulled up and continued on our journey to the fire.

The work around the firebase could get boring at times. We woke up in the mornings and started our daily routine by going to a trailer to cook our breakfast before being assigned jobs for the day. Typical jobs for the crew were building fence, doing basic carpentry, or painting things around the compound. The work we did wasn't very meaningful and was designed to keep the crew busy while we waited to be dispatched to a fire. When the fire danger subsided due to the July rains, most of the crew was sent home.

There were a couple of funny stories I remember from my fire fighting job that summer. One story occurred as we were preparing biscuits for breakfast one morning. We had been having trouble lighting the pilot light in the gas range that was in a trailer used by the fire crew. A large young man named Albert Santos was squatting down in front of the oven as he held a lit match inside near the very back. The gas had been turned on for 15 or 20 seconds when, suddenly, there was a loud "Caboooom". A large flash of light shot out from inside the oven and knocked Albert against the wall on the opposite side of the trailer. He abruptly came to rest on the floor with his back against the wall. Fortunately, only the hair on his eyebrows and arms had been significantly singed. We certainly got a good laugh when we saw the surprised look on Albert's face as the smoke rose from his smoldering eyebrows.

A few days later, I was dispatched to a fire with a friend named John Bauer and a guy named Jesse. John and Jesse were good friends and John called Jesse "The Duke" because he was a funny guy who loved to joke around.

After fighting our fire for two days, we radioed the Forest Service Dispatcher to inform them the fire was out and we needed to be picked up. The next morning we hiked for several miles to a trailhead where we eventually connected with our ride. The driver was in an old International Harvester crew cab Forest Service truck and was instructed to shuttle us back to the Meown firebase.

Like all firefighters, we were hot, tired and dirty from working on the fire and hiking out of the woods with a heavy pack. We had also been drinking warm water for three days and were craving something cold to drink. On the way back to Meown our driver was kind enough to stop at Doc Campbell's Store near the Gila Cliff Dwellings so we could get some cold sodas and snacks for the remainder of our ride.

The three of us paid for our goodies and returned to the truck that was parked in front of the store. As soon as we were situated in the back seat of the crew cab, John tilted his full soda up and started glugging it down. Jesse and I looked on with amazement as John killed off his drink.

When he was done, he belched and then looked over to Jesse and said, "Hey Jesse, give me a drink of your soda. I'm still thirsty."

Surprised by John's request, Jesse replied, "hell no. You already drank yours. I bought this soda for me."

John and Jesse bantered back and forth for a bit until Jesse reluctantly agreed to let him take a swig. In a sly and sarcastic tone of voice, Jesse said, "OK, you can have a drink of my soda."

Then, just before he handed the bottle to John, Jesse put it up to his mouth and spat into it. Then he said to John, "Here you go," and offered John the bottle.

John called Jesse's bluff by quickly grabbing his soda and taking a big swig out of it, spit and all. Then, before he gave the soda back to Jesse, he snarled and inhaled through his nose and hacked up a huge, slimy wad of greenish/yellow mucus. He spat his snot into the bottle and handed it back to Jesse. Smiling, he looked over and said, "Here's your soda back."

Jesse was so repulsed from seeing John spit into his soda that he refused to take it back. "Fuck you, dude," he said to John. "I'm not going to drink that shit. It's yours."

John broke out in laughter as he drank the remainder of Jesse's soda, slimy snot and all. He was delighted that he had just gotten the better end of a deal with "The Duke".

College students in the Grant County area were very fortunate that Kennecott Copper Corp. generously provided good paying summer jobs to help put them through school. Although most of the jobs were offered to kids whose parents worked for the company, there were a few student employees with parents who worked elsewhere. I worked for three summers at Kennecott and probably would not have been able to continue my education without these employment opportunities.

During the summers of 1969 and 1970 I was given a job working in the "Machine Accounting" section of the comptroller's office. This was an office job working with computer equipment. Kennecott started using computers in around 1966 after a few of their employees received specialized training to operate the new equipment. A nice man named Frank Heslin was the department supervisor and Walter Toy was his right-hand man. We used to call him "Shakey Frank" because his hands would shake as he worked with the various machines.

The Machine Accounting Department was located in the basement of the

Comptroller's Office on Anza Street in Hurley. On one side of a large room were six or seven women who sat at keypunch machines and typed data onto keypunch cards. The keypunch cards were made of a tag-board like material and were about three inches wide and seven inches long. By typing on a regular typewriter keyboard, the keypunch machines would punch small rectangular holes into the cards. The position of these holes represented numbers and letters.

Once the data was encoded in the cards, the machine accounting crew would organize the cards and get them ready for various reports. The three main machines we used in this process were a collator, interpreter, and sorter. We would load the keypunch cards into the hopper of these machines so they could be shuffled into a desired order based on a particular category, alphabetical order, or numerical order.

Photo caption 9-1: A keypunch operator sits at her keypunch machine. Photo courtesy of New Mexico State University Library, Archives and Special Collections.

To program the machines for various jobs, we had to remove a rectangular circuit board panel located in the bottom of the machines and change their wiring configuration. Each panel had hundreds of holes and we would pull wires from certain holes and stick them into others.

Once we had organized our stack of cards for a desired report, we would feed them into the hopper of the IBM System 360 computer. The 360 computer was a large, heavy box about twice the size of a refrigerator lying on its side. Connected to the computer was a huge dot matrix, tractor-feed printer which probably weighed about 150 lbs. The computer would run the cards through a card reader and print out our report.

Some of the reports we typically ran were ore haulage reports, attendance reports, payroll data, and inventory reports. We also printed payroll checks for the entire Chino Mines operation. Before we printed the paychecks we had to insert the blank checks into the tractor-feed mechanism on the printer. We then had to call Kennecott headquarters in Salt Lake City on a telephone hotline to tell them we were ready to print the checks. They would release the payroll data to our computer via the hotline and all we had to do was stand around and make sure the checks were feeding into the printer properly and keep it from jamming. If the printer jammed it could take up to 30 minutes to get things back on-line and running again. It typically took several hours to print paychecks for 1,300 employees.

This turned out to be a great job for me. I worked a shift from noon until 8:00 p.m. For a young college man, that meant I could stay out late every night and party with my friends. Then, I could sleep until 11:00 a.m. every morning and still make it to work, well rested and hangover free.

Photo caption 9-2: The IBM 360 computer, located behind the employees, was a huge machine. Note the large, tractor-fed printer on the left with paper hanging from it. Courtesy of New Mexico State University Library, Archives and Special Collections.

Final Tales of Mischief

Making the transition from adolescence to adulthood can be a slow and arduous process. American cultural norms frequently attempt to portray high school graduation as a threshold where adolescents step forward into the early stages of adulthood and leave their childhood behind. While this can be a fairly easy process for some teenagers, others are caught in a state of "limbo", where adolescent behavior becomes more sophisticated rather than abandoned. The hope is, of course, for everyone to eventually outgrow this silliness and become responsible citizens. In the scheme of things, it just takes some folks a little longer than others to accept the plight of adulthood. Perhaps this is the way it should be.

The Twilight Fire Bugs
***

Sometime in 1969 several teenaged friends converged on the Pacheco home in North Hurley for a small private party. Nano Pacheco was a sophomore at WNMU that year and he had invited a nice mix of new friends from college and old high school friends to come help him celebrate. Nano was excited about drinking a few beers one last time with everyone because in two weeks he was leaving to serve Uncle Sam in the U.S. Army. Since Nano's parents were out of town for the evening, their home on B Street was the perfect gathering place for an all-night drinking fest. In the Pacheco party tradition, Nano and his friends stayed up nearly all night drinking beer, laughing, and listening to music.

It was about an hour before sunrise when Brent and Vance decided it was time to head home from the party. They had been partying all night long and were getting sleepy and downright drunk. Realizing that both boys were in no condition to drive, Nano tried to convince them to walk home to Brent's house instead of attempting to drive.

"Look, it's not that far to Pattie Street on the south side," said Nano. "Just leave your car here and walk home. You can come get it tomorrow. If you walk, you'll be home in less than a half an hour."

"Yeah, but when do I get my car back, cabron?" slurred Vance.

Brent finished chugging his last beer and then chirped in. "TOMORROW, pendejo. He just said you could get it TOMORROW."

"Just leave me your keys and I'll bring your car to you at noon," added Nano. "You won't even have to walk back over here to get it."

Finally Vance relented and gave Nano his car keys. "Bueno. Here are my llaves. And, don't forget. Tomorrow at noon."

Vance then drained the last of his beer and tossed his can in Nano's garbage can next to the kitchen sink. As the boys departed through the kitchen door and wandered into Nano's back yard, Nano followed them out to the back porch with a nearly empty bottle of Jose Quervo Gold tequila in his right hand.

Before the boys got out of the yard, Nano raised the bottle of tequila into the air above his head and playfully mumbled, "Hey, putos. Don't do anything I wouldn't do, and if you do, name it after me."

Everyone got one last laugh before Brent and Vance disappeared behind the garage and began their tenuous journey across town to Brent's house.

Brent had grown up in Hurley and knew the easiest route to his house. Once he and Vance emerged from the alley off of B Street they staggered down a side street and eventually cut across an open dirt lot toward the railroad tracks. From there, they stumbled their way to the north entrance of the underpass, which went under the railroad tracks and surfaced in South Hurley between the two Hurley Store buildings. The underpass was the only pedestrian passage to South Hurley.

Holding on to the metal handrail, they passed through the concrete underground tunnel and surfaced a couple of minutes later in South Hurley. Their tongues were heavy and lethargic from the alcohol but they still managed to carry on a light-hearted conversation as they forged their way into the night.

From the underpass, Brent led Vance southward across Cortez Avenue to the sidewalk in front of a large two-story building which housed several businesses in downtown Hurley. The building was one of the oldest structures in Hurley. On the ground floor was the Hurley Post Office, a barbershop on the east of the building, and the Chino Sweet Shop on the west side. The Sweet Shop had a soda fountain and restaurant and was the social hub of downtown Hurley. On the second floor was a large, open room that for many years was the home of the secretive Hurley Masonic Lodge.

As the boys slowly weaved their way down the sidewalk in front of the Post Office, they happened to notice a couple of large bundles of El Paso Times newspapers that were sitting near the edge of the sidewalk. Sometime before 4:30 a.m. every morning a delivery truck from El Paso would make its rounds to all of the towns in the area to drop off the newspaper bundles at a designated location in each town. For the town of Hurley, the post office was that location.

At around 5:30 a.m. a paperboy would show up to stuff the papers in his large canvass bag and deliver them around town.

In a slapstick stupor, the boys bumped into each other as they stopped to gander at the bundles. Neither of them had ever imagined that a stack of newspapers for the entire town of Hurley could be so large. It was Sunday morning and the two bundles were much larger than usual, mostly due to comic strips, advertisement inserts, and the Parade Magazine.

Out of curiosity, Brent reached over to pick up one of the bundles and mumbled, "Damn. That thing sure is heavy."

Vance burped and quickly replied, "Who gives a shit how heavy it is. Let's get the hell outta here."

Brent stood up and put his hand on his chin in deep contemplation. Then he looked over to Vance with a strange gleam in his eye and asked, "I don't suppose you have any matches on you by chance, do you?"

At first, Vance looked back at Brent with a puzzled expression. "What the hell does this dumb shit want with matches?" he asked himself. Then, a large grin slowly spread across Vance's face as he fished around in the bottom of his pants pocket for a cigarette lighter. By the time his hand finally reappeared, both boys knew that a little mischief in downtown Hurley was about to happen.

Each boy grabbed one of the heavy bundles and began dragging them down the sidewalk to the west side of the building. They continued past the Sweet Shop and turned left at the corner and eventually stopped at a spot near the entrance to the Masonic Lodge. Then, they slid the bundles close to each other and stepped back to assess the situation.

One flick of the lighter, a few seconds of flame here and there, and before long the boys had a nice little fire going. Vance put his lighter back into his pocket and both boys looked around to make sure they weren't being watched by anyone. The eastern sky was starting to get light at the horizon so the boys knew they couldn't stick around too much longer. If they were still around by daybreak, they risked getting caught red-handed.

As Brent stood nearby and watched the intensity of the fire slowly increase, it suddenly dawned on him that a paperboy could show up at any moment. He knew the newspapers had to be delivered by 6:30 a.m. so customers could to read it over breakfast before they left for work. That didn't give them much time to make their escape from the crime scene.

"Hey man, I think we should get the hell out of here before somebody comes," exclaimed Brent.

The boys stood around a bit longer to make sure the fire would continue burning on its own. Once the size of the fire met their rather nebulous and arbitrary expectations, they would work their way along the big ditch toward Pattie Street where they would be safe.

To their surprise, the flames began to grow and spread much more quickly than they had anticipated. In fact, the flames became so tall and hot that the boys had to take a couple of steps away from the bundles to avoid being burned. The bundles were also just a few feet from the Masonic Lodge entrance and the building was beginning to heat up as well. As a last ditch effort to avert disaster,

Brent lunged forward to kick one of the bundles away from the building toward the street. That turned out to be a futile move. The heat was getting too intense.

"Oh shit," exclaimed Brent, as he quickly jumped back away from the growing orange flames. "We've got to get these bundles away from the building."

Vance then darted around to the other side of the bundles and attempted to kick them away from the building, but also to no avail. At last, Brent looked over to Vance with an expression of panic on his face and yelled, "Let's get the hell out of here before the building catches on fire. Follow me."

It was absolutely amazing how these young men made the transition from being a couple of slow walking, slobbering, aimless drunks to highly trained, Olympic caliber, world-class sprinters, all in a matter of seconds. They took off running so fast that a pack of greyhounds would have had trouble keeping up with them. After running at full speed for about a block, they turned back and saw that the flames were now burning directly underneath the second story roof that extended outward from the Masonic Lodge. Realizing the building was on the verge of igniting, Vance frantically exclaimed, "Holy fuck. The building is going to burn down. We're in deep shit now."

Then he turned back around and continued running stride-for-stride with Brent as they headed for Pattie Street.

They ran down alleys, darted across streets, and flew through people's yards as they navigated their way back to Brent's house. Ten minutes later and totally exhausted from the long run, Vance and Brent quickly disappeared through the front door and went straight to his bedroom. Brent's parents quietly snoozed away and never heard a thing.

The following day a front-page article appeared in the Silver City Daily Press about the newspaper fire in downtown Hurley. It explained to the readers that the reason no one received their El Paso Times newspaper the previous morning was because they were senselessly set ablaze by some no-count hooligans in the area. It also went on to say that, by a stroke of good fortune, there was no damage to the old historic building in downtown Hurley. But it was the last paragraph of the article that really got their attention. It stated that there was an investigation underway and the Hurley police had a couple of suspects in the case.

"A couple of suspects in the case?" pondered Vance. "How can that be? We got out of there before anyone saw us."

For several days, our favorite young arsonists laid low and were constantly looking over their shoulders in anticipation of trouble from local law enforcement authorities. They made a vow to never tell a soul about their misdeed and they constantly kept their ears open for new developments in the investigation. For now, the boys were suspended in a temporary state of paranoia because they didn't know how much information the cops had or who "the suspects" were.

A few days later the Daily Press finally printed a follow-up article. It stated that there was a breakthrough in the case and the Hurley Police had apprehended two juveniles who admitted to the crime.

When Brent and Vance read the latest article, their first reaction was it had to be some sort of trap. Being the cautious vandals they were, they continued to lay low for another couple of weeks until more information surfaced. In the meantime, they figured either the cops were lying and didn't have a clue who committed the crime, or they must have scared and pressured a couple of younger kids into confessing to something they didn't do.

Neither Brent nor Vance were new to skirmishes with the law while growing up in Grant County. They were well acquainted with the tactics of authority figures such as policemen and school administrators as they attempted to pry confessions out of kids. They also knew the best thing they could do for the moment was keep their mouths shut and go on about their business as if nothing had ever happened.

Over the years the two small town troublemakers remained good beer drinking buddies and, every once in a while, would reminisce about their teenage arson adventure. Brent knew he could always make Vance laugh whenever he dramatically reenacted his impression of a mean-faced policeman looking down at some scared Hurley kid while wagging an accusatory finger in his face. "We know it was you who burned those newspapers, you little punk. Just admit it and we will go a little easier on you."

In the fall of 1968 I left Grant County to attend college and didn't spend much time in Grant County for the next few years. It was always fun to come home and visit with many of my good friends who were either living in the area or who had returned home from college or the military service. During my stay, I would be on the phone several times a day to chat with friends, and at night there was usually a party or a get-together somewhere, especially during the holidays.

While I was home for Christmas break a few years after I graduated from high school I went to Central to visit with Steven Price and his family. Steve was also home from college and I always looked forward to spending some time with him and his brothers and sisters. There were five kids in the family and there was always something fun happening at their home.

Steve's younger sister Janie was the Student Body President at Cobre High School at the time and enjoyed being involved in the many social events at school. One afternoon, as we were sitting around the living room visiting, Janie happened to mention that the Cobre High School student council was planning an all-school Christmas program in the high school auditorium in a couple of days. The itinerary was to have a few short skits and a performance by the school choir, but the student council was looking for someone to put together one last short skit to round out the program. The skit had to have a Christmas theme.

I don't remember whose suggestion it was, but somehow Steve and I got roped into creating the skit for Janie's program. Even though we were Cobre alumni and had been out of high school for some time, Janie welcomed the idea of having us participate in the program.

The truth of the matter was Steve and I embraced the idea of performing on stage in front of nearly 600 people. In fact, after only a few minutes of brainstorming we came up with a great idea for a simple skit involving two characters. Our goal was to do a funny skit that required simple costumes and props and would be socially and politically relevant. Steve would play Santa Claus and I would be Mrs. Santa Claus and, to make things easy, our dialog would allow for lots of improvisation.

On the afternoon of the program Steve and I pulled up to the back of Cobre High School in his parents' car. We wanted to avoid running into some of our old teachers so we entered through the back stage door and went directly into the dressing room to put on our costumes. A few minutes before the program began, we took a peek from behind the curtains and were thrilled to see an auditorium packed with students and teachers.

Janie took the stage to greet the large audience while serving as the MC for the program. Her introduction was brief and before long the program was under way. Steve and I knew from our copy of the itinerary there were a few performances before ours. To kill time, we remained behind the stage and in the dressing room until we were called to do our skit.

Finally, about midway through the program, someone came back stage and informed us we were up next and we needed to come stand off to the side of the stage near the exit. Then, once the curtains closed at the conclusion of the previous act, Steve and I were instructed to quickly walk out to the center of the stage and await the beginning of our skit.

As the curtains slowly opened, a large yellow spotlight beam slid across the floor and focused on the center of the stage where we stood. A few chuckles from the audience could be heard as they easily identified one of the characters standing before them. Santa was dressed in a traditional red Santa Claus costume and had a big, chubby belly but, to the surprise of the audience, the color of his skin was black. Steve had used black make-up on his face and hands to become a Negro Santa.

Standing next to Santa was a pregnant Caucasian Mrs. Santa Claus. My costume consisted of a wig, a long dress, and a large, inflated balloon stuffed under my dress in front of my stomach. I also had one of Janie's dolls hidden under my dress that was to be part of a stunt at the end of our skit.

"Oh, Santa," I said, as I looked adoringly into Santa's eyes. "I'm so excited about our new baby. I wonder if it will be a boy or a girl."

"I don't know, my love, but I'm so excited I just want to dance."

As music began to play, Santa grabbed Mrs. Claus and began to playfully dance around the stage in an indubitable state of utter bliss. Hidden in one of his hands, and unbeknown to the audience, was a long, sharp pin that would soon be used to pop the balloon.

When we got to the front of the stage, Santa Claus twirled me around so my back was temporarily to the audience. At just the right moment he quickly reached out and stuck the pin into my large stomach. When I heard the balloon pop, I twirled around toward the audience and released the baby doll from under my dress. Our stunt worked flawlessly.

By the time we both faced the audience, the doll was lying on the floor in front of me and was in plain sight of everyone in the auditorium. Laughter quickly broke out at the sight of the naked newborn baby at my feet. I bent over to gently pick it up and proudly held it up to show the audience. People began to clap as Santa danced around and jumped for joy.

As I held the doll up into the spotlight near the front edge of the stage, it soon became clear the doll was of mixed racial decent. It had been painted black from the waist up but was left unpainted from the waist down. Once the audience got a good look at our precious newborn child, I cradled it in my arms and turned lovingly towards Santa Claus. I looked him and said, "Oh, how cute. It's a baby girl."

Laughter, whistling, and applause filled the room. That was the end of the skit and, as the curtains closed in front of us, Steve and I retreated to the back of the stage and wasted no time running for the exit door where the car was parked. We knew we had to get the hell out of that auditorium before school officials could catch up and have a few words with us.

Our escape from the building went according to plan. We ran out the back door and jumped into his car, started the engine, and made our break for his parents' house. As we changed out of our costumes in Steve's living room we were laughing so hard we could barely stand up. The skit had come off perfectly, with no botched scenes or malfunctions during our stunt. The students loved it. For a few moments we were "stars" in our own minds.

Well, for a few moments, that is. Janie arrived home shortly after we finished changing and had a look of disbelief on her face. As soon as she walked in the door she began filling us in on the various reactions to our skit. She said that most of the students enjoyed it and thought it was very funny, but the faculty members weren't too pleased with it. In fact, she said it was probably a good thing we got out of the building as quickly as we did.

It was more than a decade before I ever returned to the halls of Cobre High School, but when I finally did, I was a teacher.

"You became a WHAT?"

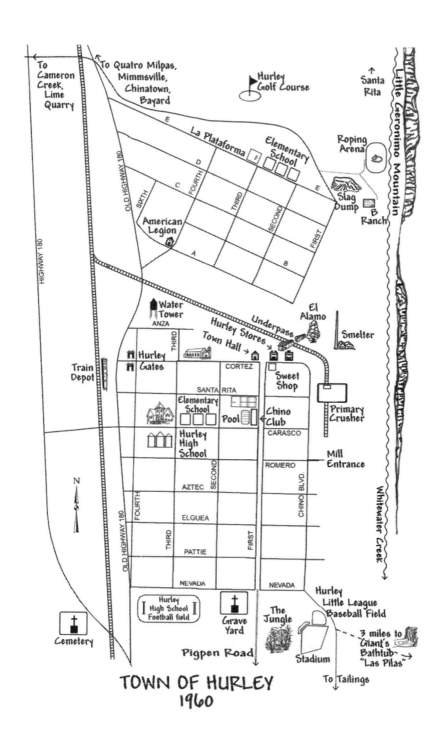

TOWN OF HURLEY
1960

ABOUT THE AUTHOR

Jerry Boswell was born in Santa Rita, New Mexico, and grew up in Hurley, New Mexico, in the 1950's and 1960's. He graduated from Cobre High School in 1968. As a boy, Jerry had a Silver City Daily Press paper route for seven years and an El Paso Times route for two summers. Being a paper boy allowed him to become intimately familiar with nearly every family, house, street, and alley in town. He also had an older brother and sister who provided a window into the social lives of many older kids in the community. These connections and experiences helped to form his perspectives and attitudes as he worked his way through the local schools and on to college.

As a young man Jerry enjoyed racing and touring on motorcycles. He also loved to play various Frisbee disc games and became a co-director for the first New Mexico State Frisbee Championships in 1977. He later worked for the U.S. Forest Service in the Gila National Forest and lived at No Cattle Company on the Mimbres River for several years. Jerry eventually became a teacher and school administrator, and retired from public education as the first principal of the Aldo Leopold High School charter school in Silver City, New Mexico.

Jerry currently performs as a drummer and percussionist in the Silver City area and spends much of his time hiking the trails throughout the southwest. He also loves to travel and enjoys spending as much time as possible on the beaches of Mexico.

ACKNOWLEDGMENTS

I would like to thank the following people and institutions for providing me with valuable historical information, photos, technical advice, and services. Without their generous offerings of information and support, this book would have been much less informative and its design and formatting would have been much more simple.

Howie and Kathy Miller, historical information, photos
Bernie Marin, historical information
George Marin, historical information
Sammy Cabrera, historical information'
Bill Archibald, historical information
Ronnie Hickman, historical information
Richard Marruffo, historical information
Tom McCoy, proof reading and editing
Judy Wuthrich, proof reading and editing, photographs
Town Hall in Hurley, New Mexico, access to photo and history files
Silver City Museum, access to photo and history files
WNMU Museum, access to photo and history files
WNMU Library, access to newspaper archives
NMSU Library, access to Archives and Special Collections photos
Don and Marty Trammell, historical information
Don and Mary Clifton, historical information
Guy and Frances Ozment, historical information
David Lawrence, cartographer for the Town of Silver City
Southwest Council of Governments, population and demographic data
Grant County Clerk's Office, newspaper archives
Johnny Menard, historical information
Terry Humble, photos and historical information
Unicorn Press, Cover design
Patricia Taber, cover design and formatting, map artwork
Billy Faust, historical information
Joseph Wade, photos
Grant Moser, legal advice, proof reading
Robert Perea, historical information
Brandon Beard, technical information
Oop Ford, Historical information
Rudy Martinez, historical information
Bridget O'Leary, Photoshop expertise
Byron Trammell, proof reading
Marilyn York, historical information

Emilia Valles, historical information
Velia Miranda, photo identification
Rob Hawkins, historical information
Victor Nanez, historical information
Joe Vencill, historical information
Bub Bartlett, photos and historical information
Richard Mahler, book formatting and design
Woody Schmidt, photos and historical information
Hurley, New Mexico, Historical Data from 1910-1960: 50 Years of Recorded
Memories by Claude Dannelley
Susan Berry, editing and formatting, back cover paragraph
Edward Encinas, back cover paragraph
CreateSpace for book publication
Jeff Ray, editing and distribution

54175029R00135

Made in the USA
San Bernardino, CA
09 October 2017